| DATE DUE | | |
|---|---|---|
| AUG 1 3 1992 | | |
| AUG 1 9 1992 | | |
| OCT 1 0 1992 | | |
| NOV 1 2 1992 | | |
| SEP 2 9 1997 | | |
| MAR 3 0 1999 | | |
| | | |
| | | |
| | | |

COPY 98

920.073   Dickerson, Robert B          1955-
D              Final placement : a guide to deaths,
          funerals, and burials of famous Ameri-
          cans / by Robert B. Dickerson, Jr. Al-
          gonac, MI : Reference Publications,
          Inc., 1982.
              250 p. : ill.

              ISBN 0-917256-18-2 : $19.95

          1.United States--Biography. 2.Funeral
          rites and ceremonies--United States.
          3.Cemeteries--United States.

                                            12474 D82
                                            81-52598
MILFORD   DEMCO CARD CORPORATION OF AMERICA®   JAN. 2 5 1983   CIP MARC   58

# Final Placement

The glories of our blood and state
  Are shadows, not substantial things;
There is no armour against fate;
  Death lays his icy hand on kings.

Sceptre and crown must tumble down
And in the dust be equal made
With the poor crooked scythe and spade.

Only the actions of the just
  Smell sweet and blossom in the dust.


James Shirley
(1596-1666)

# Final Placement

*A Guide to the Deaths, Funerals,*
*and Burials of Notable Americans*

**Robert B. Dickerson, Jr.**

REFERENCE PUBLICATIONS, INC.

Published 1982

Printed in the United States of America

**Library of Congress Cataloging in Publication Data**

Dickerson, Robert B., 1955-
  Final placement

  Includes index
  1. United States—Biography. 2. Funeral rites and
ceremonies—United States. 3. Cemeteries—United
States. I Title.


CT215.D46 920'.073 (B) 81-52598
ISBN 0-917256-18-2 AACR2

*Library of Congress Catalog Card Number: 81-52598*
*International Standard Book Number: 0-917256-18-2*

Reference Publications, Inc.
218 St. Clair River Drive, Box 344
Algonac, Michigan 48001

*To My Parents:*
*Robert B. Dickerson*
*1927—1979*
*and*
*Anna J. (Marlow) Dickerson*

# Acknowledgments

There were many people who were helpful during the three years it took to research and write *Final Placement*. I have more gratitude than I could possibly express for my friends and others who constituted the support group which grew up around the project.

My editor Keith Irvine, who suggested the project, gave me constant help and encouragement throughout what has proved to be a long, arduous, and fascinating task. Sam Baker traveled to Boston and Philadelphia to take some of the pictures in this book. He also made himself available as a very close friend. Barbara A. Black gave me much personal support and facilitated the re-writing during the page-proof stages. Tom and Mary Christensen read proofs and came up with many last-minute suggestions. Sanford Davis was not only generous with his time, but also put at my disposal his extensive knowledge of American history which is reflected in the final product. Brian J. Nienhaus provided suggestions from the earliest to the last stages of the project, was an avid proofreader, and made available his Ann Arbor home while I was undertaking research in that city. Gerald M. Zamborowski offered the full use of his law office, and made the services of his legal secretary, Laurie Bischoff-Glied, available.

I am also deeply appreciative of the help, encouragement and suggestions I have received from the following friends: Sunny Davis; Charles Duprey; my sister, Robbie Ann Dickerson; Aline Irvine; David Irvine; David Kirchinger; Marion Dianne Leonardi; Clifford L. Nienhaus; Tom Nienhaus, Kandise Maynard-Schnoor; Cynthia Santoro; and Marge and Rhonda Welchko. I also wish to thank Leona Schunck for technical help during the production phase.

While the help provided by the entire staff of the Macomb County Library is acknowledged individually below, I should like to give special thanks to William Luft and CoraEllen DeVinney and their staff, especially Linda Champion, Elizabeth Erlich, Pat Kosuth, Stan Lisica, and Sherry Schmidli, who went beyond the call of duty in providing vital support. Most authors owe a special debt to one particular library and its staff. Mine is to the Macomb County Library.

A number of libraries, special collections, institutes, scholars, and authors contributed unselfishly to the project—many times going to great lengths to answer questions. I offer my most heartfelt thanks to the following, and can only beg the forgiveness of any whose names may have been omitted.

# ACKNOWLEDGMENTS

G. Donald Adams, Greenfield Village & Henry Ford Museum; Carol Andrews, Illinois Department of Conservation; V.E. Angerole, Ferncliff Cemetery Association; Gary J. Arnold, the Ohio Historical Society, Inc.; Linda L. Ayres, National Gallery of Art.

James Babcock; Shirley Baig, The *New York Times*; Douglas Bakken, Greenfield Village & Henry Ford Museum; Susan Bang, National Audubon Society; Phyllis Barr, Parish Archives Trinity Church, New York City; Wendy Bassett, Thornwood, N.Y.; Dan Bast, Dan Bast Photography; Frederick R. Bell, United States Department of the Interior; J.E. Bennett, Department of the Navy; *Belton Raymore Star Herald*; Patti Bilo, Galesburg Chamber of Commerce; Samuel S. Blane of Petersburg, Illinois; Joseph Blotner of Ann Arbor; Carolyn Bossard, Steele Memorial Library System; Joyce M. Botelho, The Rhode Island Historical Society; Homer A. Boynton, Jr., The Historical Society of Pennsylvania; Mrs. M. Brown, Poughkeepsie Area Chamber of Commerce; Vernon Brown, *Des Moines Register and Tribune*; Dr. Samuel Engle Burr, Jr. The Aaron Burr Association; Patricia T. Burt, Maryland-Municipal Reference Rockville Library.

Det. Richard J. Cann, Township of Hillside New Jersey; Margaret S. Cheney, Mark Twain Memorial; Christine Chow, City of Los Angeles Public Library; Stephen Catlett, American Philosophical Society Library; Eugene Coe for fraternal orders' terminology; Daniel Coffey, Rockville, Maryland; Karen Cole for information on Gar Wood's death and funeral; Reba Collins, Will Rogers Memorial; Evelyn Converse, Evergreen Memorial Cemetery; Anthony J. Costello, *Courier-Journal*, Rochester, New York; Edwin N. Cotter, Jr., John Brown Farm; Carol Coverly, Morse Institute; Stewart Cowan, Greenwood Union Cemetery, Rye, New York; Ruth O. Cowell, The Association for Gravestone Studies; Joseph Mason Andrew Cox; Bronx, New York; Sonia Cramer, Southhold Restorations, Inc.; Chuck Creesy, *Princeton Alumni Weekly*; David R. Crippen, Greenfield Village & Henry Ford Museum; Patrick D. Crosland, United States Department of the Interior; Nancy E. Crowell, Scarborough Public Library; George H. Curtis, National Archives Harry S. Truman Library; William Cushing, Oliver H. Bair Funeral Home in Philadelphia.

John P. Danglade, American Cemetery Association, Columbus, Ohio; Benjamin M. Davis; Department of the Army; Vera A. Dederich, Bossard Memorial Library; Charlotte DeFilippo, Township of Hillside, Union County, New Jersey; Steven D. Derene, Wisconsin Department of Justice; Maier Deshell, the Jewish Publication Society of America; Greg J. Derr, Mariner Newspapers, Marshfield, Massachusetts; Eunice Gillman DiBella, Connecticut State Library; Guy C. Dobson, Irvington, New York; Fred Dromke, Sterling Heights, Michigan; Jack R. Dyson, Kit Carson Memorial Foundation, Inc..

Jerry, C. Ellenwood, Day Funeral Home, Bloomington, Indiana; Robert L. Engols, Pierce Brothers, Beverly Hills, California.

Ruth-Marie Fahr, Poughkeepsie Newspapers Inc.; Miriam Favorite, Camden County Historical Society, New Jersey; Thomas Featherstone, Wayne State University; Mrs. Ellen Fiedler; Dick Fisher, Office of Community Affairs, Forest Lawn, Glendale; Chad J. Flake, Brigham Young University; John C. Flexner; the Harwood Foundation of the University of New Mexico; Lambert Florin, Photo Histories Western America, Portland, Oregon; Guy Franks, West Branch, Iowa; Alan D. Frazer, the New Jersey Historical Society; Nancy R. Frazier, the University of North Carolina; Marianne B. Frisch, the Museum of Modern Art, New York City; David W. Fuchs Dewitt Clinton High School, Bronx, New York.

Mrs. Elsie Gilbert; Orlena Gilmore, Belton Branch, Cass County Library, Belton, Missouri; Louis Gioffre, Greenwood Cemetery, Brooklyn; Mrs. Marge Gleason, Christ Church Episcopal Church Rye, New York; Judith Kremsdorf Golden, Colorado Historical Society; Jessica Goldzweig, Congregational Library, Boston; Jayne Gordon, Orchard House, Concord, Massachusetts; Tom Gratopp, PDQ Press; Mrs. Ruth Gross, Florida Collection, Miami Public Library; Charles E. Greene, Princeton University Library; Marion Gribetz, Paul Revere House, Boston; Solmon Guggenheim Foundation Library; Ellen Guillemette, Wright State University;

T. Guines, District of Columbia Public Schools; Jack Gurner, *Memphis Press-Scimitar*; Jo Hall, the *Mobridge Tribune*, Mobridge, South Dakota.

Lyman H. Hammond, Jr., City of Norfolk Virginia; Marie F. Harper, the Rhode Island Historical Society; Patricia Harpole, Minnesota Historical Society; Betty Lou Harris, Monroe County Chamber of Commerce, Madisonville and Sweetwater, Tennessee; Wilhelmina S. Harris, United States Department of the Interior; Mike Hayden, Veterans Administration Medical Center, Louisville, Kentucky; Walter Hayes, Vice-President for Public Affairs, the Ford Motor Company; Venable Herndon; Betty E. Heurich, American Cemetery Association, Columbus, Ohio; Cheryl Higgins, Quincy, Massachusetts; Lloyd H. Hill, Quincy Public Schools, Quincy, Massachuetts; Maureen Hill, the Herbert Hoover Presidential Library; Calvin Hite, United States Department of the Interior; Milo B. Howard, Jr., State of Alabama Department of Archives and History; J. L. Howze, Texas Department of Health; Nancy Jones Howse, Jackson, Tennessee; Frederick M. Huchel, Brigham City Museum Gallery; Louis S. Hudgins, City of Norfolk, Virginia; Doris G. Huntington, United States of America General Services Administration.

Jill Irvine; Bloomington Public Library, Bloomington, Illinois; Peter Jacobsohn; Robert Jerome, Mark Twain Society; John M. Jordan, Allen County-Fort Wayne Historical Society; Diane A. Jung, United States Department of the Interior.

Beatrice Kaya, Hawaii Newspaper Agency Library, Honolulu, Hawaii; R.S. Keefe, Washington and Lee University; Terri Keefe, League of Women Voters of the United States, Washington, D.C.; Margaret M. Keenan, *Princeton Alumni Weekly*; Diane J. Kelly, National Wildlife Federation; Chauncey Kenney, Reflector Yearbook, Galesburg, Illinois; Jay Kenney; Martin Luther King Center for Social Change, Atlanta, Georgia; Russ Kingman, the World of Jack London Museum and Bookstore, Glen Ellen, California; A. Roberts Koenig, Greenwood Cemetery, Brooklyn, New York; Richard C. Kogelschatz, Christie Memorial Chapel; Shirley Kondogan; Pat Kosuth; James R. Kulavic, Oakridge Cemetery, Springfield, Illinois.

Roberta LaChiusa, Susan B. Anthony Memorial, Inc.; Dorothy Laird, Bayside High School, Bayside, New York; Carolyn Lalas, Chamber of Commerce, Frankfort, Michigan; John Langan, Concord Public Schools, Concord, Massachusetts; Kay Lange, Harlan-Lincoln House, Mt. Pleasant, Iowa; Anne M. Lariviere, Marshfield, Massachusetts; Hugh A. Lawing, United States Department of the Interior; L. Don LeFevre, The Church of Jesus Christ of Latter-Day Saints, Salt Lake City, Utah; Jolene Lively, Bend, Texas; Jean M. Leyman, Wheaton Public Library, Wheaton, Illinois; Robert F. Loffer, the Cemetery Supply Association, Columbus, Ohio; Marc Loonan, Adlai E. Stevenson H.S. Bronx, N.Y.; Robert F. Looney, City of Philadelphia, Pennsylvania.

Edith H. McCauley, Portland Public Library, Portland, Maine; John W. McDowell, Community Unit, District No. 5, Mt. Olive, Illinois; Father Richard McGuire, Mepkin Abbey, Moncks Corner, South Carolina; Frank H. Mackaman, the Dirksen Center, Pekin, Illinois; Lars Mahinske, Encyclopaedia Britannica; Elsie Mann, Chamber of Commerce, Atlanta, Georgia; Vicki Manos; John Francis Marion, Philadelphia, Pennsylvania; Rev. Joseph P. Marshall, Saint Denis Rectory, Yonkers, New York; Rodney Martin, Oliver H. Bair Funeral Home, Philadelphia, Pennsylvania; Janice G. Marugg, Chamber of Commerce, Monrovia, California; Julie Ann Maserjian, Poughkeepsie, New York; Lt. Col. Ron Mayhew, U.S. Army; Christine Meadows, Mount Vernon Ladies' Association Of The Union, Mount Vernon, Virginia; Bob Mervine, Walt Disney World; James A. Michener, Pipersville, Pennsylvania; Irene Miles, B. Dalton Bookseller; Marcia Muth Miller, Museum of New Mexico, Santa Fe, New Mexico; Margo C. Miller, Chamber of Commerce, Inc., Louisville, Kentucky; Emilie W. Mills, the University of North Carolina; Alwena Mistal, St. Petersburg Area Chamber of Commerce, St. Petersburg, Florida; John S. Mohlhenrich, United States Department of the Interior; A.S. Mollica, the Gar Wood Society, Syracuse, New York; Nancy Montez; Helen Morganti, Lead-Deadwood School District No. 40-1, Lead, South Dakota; William A. Morrison, Mobridge Chamber of Commerce, Mobridge, South Dakota; Loyle Mueller, Greater Davenport

# ACKNOWLEDGMENTS

Chamber of Commerce, Davenport, Iowa; Kenneth K. Muir, Montgomery County Public Schools, Rockville, Maryland; Nancy Mullen, Ventress Memorial Library, Marshfield, Massachusetts; James R. Mulvaney, National Catholic Cemetery Conference, Des Plaines, Illinois.

Roy Nerg, Frankfort, Michigan;

Don O'Dette, Bix Beiderbecke Memorial Society, Davenport, Iowa.

Paul R. Palmer, Columbia University, New York City; Robert L. Parkinson, Circus World Museum, Baraboo, Wisconsin; Thomas L. Parsons, Pine Bluff Commercial, Pine Bluff, Arkansas; Sue McCauley Patterson, City of Rockville, Maryland; Claudia Peirce, The People's Almanac, Los Angeles, California; Helen S. Perry, Department of the Army, Arlington National Cemetery; Ferdinand J. Peters, Cold Spring Granite Company, Cold Spring, Minnesota; A. W. Phinney, The First Church of Christ, Scientist, Boston, Massachusetts; Elaine Pisani, United States Department of the Interior; C. Ben Pitcher, Association of Commerce and Industry of McLean County, Bloomington, Illinois; Dr. Kumud Prasanna, Hillside Public Library, Hillisde, New Jersey; Dr. Arnold Prater, Arnold Prater Ministries, Inc., Joplin, Missouri; Peter C. Prochaska, United States Chess Federation, New Windsor, New York.

Joyce A. Rahn, Ludington Area Chamber of Commerce, Ludington, Michigan; Margaret M. Reno, Sharon Hill Library, Sharon Hill, Pennsylvania; John H. Rhodehamel, Mount Vernon Ladies' Association of The Union, Mount Vernon, Virginia; Patricia Rissberger, Gannett Rochester Newspapers, Rochester, New York; Helen Roberts, Sleepy Hollow Chamber of Commerce, Inc., Tarrytown, New York; Linda S. Rogers, Harper & Row, Publishers, Inc.; Jaanus Roht, Marshfield Historical Society, Marshfield Massachusetts; Elizabeth R. Rychling, Coventry, Connecticut; William E. Ryan, Jr., the American Battle Monuments Commission.

Susan Sadenburg, Research Library, Museum of American Folk Art, New York City; George J. Sadowski, Sadowski Funeral Home, Chicago, Illinois; Lee D. Saegesser, National Aeronautics and Space Administration, Washington, D.C.; Srta. Santiago, Chamber of Commerce of Puerto Rico, San Juan, Puerto Rico; Jennifer Saville, National Gallery of Art, Washington, D.C.; Kandise Maynard Schnoor; Jean Scribner, the Crematonist of North America, Sherman Oaks, California; Larry Sebold, Gendernalik & Sebold Funeral Home, Inc.; Joyce H. Seifert, Walt Disney Productions; Margaret P. Sevier, South Bend Public Library, South Bend, Indiana; Marian Shepherd, CEL Regional Library, Savannah, Georgia; Arthur D. Shy, Solidarity House, Detroit, Michigan; Patricia Shymanski, Historic Pullman Foundation, Chicago, Illinois; Liston Leyendecker, Fort Collins, Colorado; John Philip Sousa III, New York, New York; Glen Spencer, W.L. Philbrick Funeral Home, Coral Gables, Florida; Susan P. Starkey, Franklin Public Library, Franklin, New Hampshire; Mike Steen, Westwood Village Mortuary; Martha R. Stewart, State of Utah, Department of Development Services; George H. Straub, Mamaroneck Chamber of Commerce, Inc. Mamaroneck, New York; Nancy Sullivan, Quincy High School, Quincy, Massachusetts; Marjorie Sweeney, the Greater Golden Area Chamber of Commerce, Golden, Colorado; Henry Sweets, Mark Twain Home & Museum, Hannibal, Missouri; Pat Sylvester, Santa Rosa Chamber of Commerce, Santa Rosa California.

Nancy Temple, Altoona Area Public Library, Altoona, Pennsylvania; John K. Bolger, Supervisor; John C. Bolger, Inc. Funeral Home, Martinsburg, Pennsylvania; Thomas T. Thalken, Herbert Hoover Presidential Library, West Branch, Iowa; Dorothy L. Thomas, The Community Library Association, Inc., Ketchum, Idaho; J.D. Thomson, Uncle Tom's Cabin Museum, Dresden, Ontario, Canada; Carol Thorpe, B. Dalton Bookseller; Ruth Tiley, Cherry Hill Free Public Library, New Jersey; Robert W. Tissing, Jr., the Lyndon Baines Johnson Library, Austin, Texas; Terrence S. Todish, Mason County Historical Society Inc., Ludington, Michigan; Mary Jane Trout, State of Michigan Department of Education, Lansing, Michigan; Harold Tuckett, University of Michigan Undergraduate Library; Patrick Tuft, Chiswick Vicarage.

Charles A. Wagner, Peru Public Library, Peru, Indiana; Frank A. Ward, II, Galesburg, Illinois; Patricia A. Ward, Winslow Township, Camden County, Braddock, New Jersey; Allan M. Watnik, New York State Industrial Arts Association, Elmira Free Academy, Elmira, New York; Edward Weber, Curator of the Labadie Collection of the Harlan Hatcher Graduate Library at the University of Michigan; Emily Weingarth, Boston Pops Orchestra, Boston, Massachusetts; Renee Weisenberg, Palisades Branch Library, Pacific Palisades, California; Linda Wheatley, Chamber of Commerce, Inc., Hyde Park, New York; Edward Wheeler, Erie County Historical Society, Erie, Pennsylvania; Robert L. Wheeler, Forest Lawn Memorial-Parks and Mortuaries, Glendale, California; Hilary White, Schocken Books Inc. New York, New York; Tom Wilhite, Walt Disney Productions; Corinne Wilson, County Music Foundation Library and Media Center, Nashville, Tennessee; Walter W. Wood, Grosse Pointe, Michigan; Mrs. Carol Woodger, Port Chester Public Library; Marjorie Wyler, the Jewish Theological Seminary of America, New York, New York.

Martin I. Yoelson, United States Department of the Interior.

I would also like to thank the following libraries, collections, and organizations:

The *Advertiser-Journal*, Montgomery, Alabama; Circus World Museum Library and Research Center, Baraboo, Wisconsin; the Burton Historical Collection at the Detroit Public Library; Camden County Historical Society, Camden, New Jersey; Frank E. Campbell's, Madison Avenue, New York City; the Library Chicago Historical Society; the Clement's Library at the University of Michigan; Connecticut State Library, Hartford, Connecticut; Enoch Pratt Free Library, Baltimore, Maryland; the staff of the Harlan Hatcher Graduate Library at the University of Michigan; Institute for Advanced Studies, Princeton, New Jersey; Lilly Library, University of Indiana; Maryland Historical Society Library, Baltimore; Massachusetts Historical Society Library, Boston; State of Michigan Department of Natural Resources, Mackinac Island State Park Commission; New England Historic Genealogical Society Library, Boston; the New York Public Library, New York, New York; Norfolk Chamber of Commerce, Norfolk, Virginia; Patton Museum of Cavalry & Armor, Fort Knox, Kentucky; Peru Area Chamber of Commerce, Peru, Indiana; The Greater Philadelphia Chamber of Commerce, Philadelphia, Pennsylvania; Pilgrim Hall Library, the Pilgrim Society, Plymouth, Massachusetts; Plymouth Public Library, Massachusetts; The Rhode Island Historical Society, Providence, Rhode Island; St. Ignace Area Chamber of Commerce, St. Ignace, Michigan; Sam Rayburn House, Bonham, Texas; *Savannah Morning News*, Savannah, Georgia; Sinclair Lewis Foundation, Inc., Sauk Centre, Minnesota; Sonoma Valley Chamber of Commerce, Sonoma, California; the Tokyo Chamber of Commerce and Industry, Tokyo, Japan; US Army Field Artillery and Fort Sill Museum, Fort Sill, Oklahoma; John G. White Collection, Cleveland Public Library, Cleveland, Ohio; Walt Whitman Association, Camden, New Jersey.

My special thanks to the staff at the Macomb County Library including:

Janet Awdey; Barbara Bondy; Barbara Brown; Barbara Buckingham; Gertrude Burchard; Diane Burgeson; Linda Champion; CoraEllen DeVinney; Patty Decorte; Sandra Cottrell; Carolyn Deis; Virginia Delbridge; Lora Dinnell; Kelly Dolland; Mary Belle Doucette; Elizabeth Erlich; George Gemmer; Hank Hachey; Denise Hartig; Linda Kennedy; Kay Kirchhoff; Mary Ling; Stan Lisica; William Luft; Sheila Moore; Karen Murmyluk; Louise Pohly; Johanna Poupard; Florence Rayos; Sherry Schmidli; Tim Schutt; Kim Shearer; Douglas Watson; Elizabeth Williams; Carol Windorf; Marilyn Zawadzki.

Several people have gone out of their way through the years to give me special help or encouragement. These include:

Jared Baker; Karen Booth; Dr. David Bricker; Charlotte and Sheldon Colman; Jay and Bessie Criscillis; Edna M. Foss; Robert P. Griffin; Lucy Guinan; Carol Harney; Harry Hurd; Mike and Marilyn Klipper; Michael Kozicki; Mike Martin; Joseph Z. Nederlander; Chris Reggio; Dick Szumanski; Dr. and Mrs. Al F. Tews; Carl and Dawn Ventimeglia; Laura Van Tiem-Pypkawski; John G. Way.

# Introduction

The concept of this book first took shape when it was reported in the American press that an English guidebook to the gravesites of historic figures in the Greater London area had just been published. Why should there not be a comparable work covering the United States? Why not a work that, in comprehensive and accessible form, would ennumerate the basic facts about the last resting places of notable Americans?

Robert B. Dickerson, Jr. became interested in this concept, and was invited to research and write the book—a task that he undertook with willingness and enthusiasm. The result is his *Final Placement*, a unique work that ranges over thousands of miles and down recent centuries to make a totally new contribution to the field of Americana.

The geographic scope of the work alone, of course, precludes the guidebook approach that inspired the English original. The burial sites of most famous Americans cannot be reached on any single subway system comparable to the London Underground. They lie throughout the Union—and beyond—in city cemeteries, in fields, on hills, by riverbanks, and in quiet village churchyards. This circumstance alone made necessary a different approach.

The often strange and unexpected circumstances surrounding the deaths and burials of the subjects of this book do much to throw a light on changing American social history and culture. Furthermore, the appearance of this book at this juncture would also seem to signal another cultural change—the turning away from the youthful dream of a culture in which death had no place, and the emergence, in its stead, of a new maturity, in which death too forms a part of the total human experience. Allied to this is the fact that this book has a fascination of its own, taking us, as it does, to the very limit of "that bourne from which no traveler returns."

The necessary limitations of such a work ensure that, while the author has performed a prodigious feat of research, each of us may well find some favorite name missing from the list of 312 selected for inclusion. How could it be otherwise, when each reader has slightly differing interests and preferences? There are, for example, 34 women included—a ratio of about nine men to one woman. The responsibility for this inequity, however, evidently lies with the historic record, and not with the author.

The distribution of names by state of burial reflects the patterns of American history, with by far the greater number lying east of the Mississippi. New York, with 60 names is the leading state. Massachusetts and California, with about 30 each, come next—the former with a plethora of Founding Fathers, the latter with a preponderance of movie stars or producers. Not all movie names, however, were finally placed in California. D.W. Griffith, for example, is somewhat surprisingly buried in Kentucky.

Some burial spots remain unidentified. The last resting places of, among others, Davy Crockett and Pontiac appear to have become obscured by time. Woody Guthrie, William James, Janis Joplin, and Robert Oppenheimer are among those who have had their ashes scattered, by land or by sea. In other instances, ashes have been given into the keeping of the immediate family, who have sometimes kept the facts of their disposition private. Among the more unusual circumstances recorded in this book are the widespread distribution of Joe Hill's ashes through the mails, and the burial of "Mad" Anthony Wayne's remains in two places—in Erie and Radnor, both in Pennsylvania.

The great majority of those listed are buried in the continental United States. Exceptions include Alexander Graham Bell, and Tecumseh, both of whom are buried in Canada. Apart from these, and General Patton, who lies in a United States Army cemetery in Luxembourg, no others who are buried abroad are included—not even the celebrated John Reed, author of *Ten Days Which Shook the World*, who is buried in Moscow's Kremlin Wall. Also included are some distinguished foreigners who are buried in the United States—such as Béla Bartók, D.H. Lawrence, Sergei Rachmaninoff, and Pierre Teilhard de Chardin.

Of the many cemeteries cited, Arlington National Cemetery—the burial place of 13 notables listed, including two presidents, William Taft and John F. Kennedy is especially significant. Hollywood Cemetery in Richmond, Virginia, is the leading historic Southern cemetery, and is also the burial place of two presidents, James Monroe and John Tyler—as well as of the leader of the Confederacy, Jefferson Davis.

It is above all by their deeds that all these men and women are remembered. Some have left us their thought in the form of the printed word. Others have left us sound recordings of their voices, or records of their likenesses, movements, and characteristics on film. But the burial place of each, when this is identifiable, remains the last signal that each has left for posterity. Our thanks are due to the author for having painstakingly researched and mapped this vital data.

KEITH IRVINE
President
Reference Publications

# Contents

# CONTENTS

# CONTENTS

# Adams, John

John Adams, born in Braintree, (now Quincy), Massachusetts, on October 30, (October 19, old style), 1735, was second president of the United States, serving from 1797-1801. Earlier, he had helped the 13 American colonies obtain peace with, and independence from, Great Britain, and had been elected first vice-president under the new constitution in 1788.

After a carriage ride on July 1, 1826, Adams felt weak and stayed in bed for two days. On the morning of July 4, he asked to be dressed and placed in front of his window. His last words, spoken near noon, were: "Thomas Jefferson survives." Unknown to him, however, Jefferson *(q.v.)* had died some hours earlier. Having spoken, Adams fell into unconsciousness. When his grandson, George, entered his bedroom, he regained consciousness, and tried to speak, but could not.

The fact that both Adams and Jefferson had died on the same day, and that that day should be July 4, and the 50th anniversary of the Declaration of Independence, created a sensation, as the news slowly spread across the nation. Instead of being struck dumb, however, Americans expressed their wonder and awe aloud, in outpourings that were expressed in a great variety of ways. Some felt that the remarkable event signified America's coming of age.

Adams is buried in a crypt, beside his wife, Abigail, in the Stone Temple at the First Unitarian Church in Quincy, approximately halfway between his birthplace, and the Adams Mansion where he later lived.

His epitaph is: "On the Fourth of July 1776, he pledged his life, fortune and sacred honour to the independence of his country. On the third of September 1783, he affixed his seal to the definitive treaty with Great Britain which acknowledges that independence, and consumated the redemption of his pledge. On the Fourth of July 1826 he was summoned to the independence of immortality and the judgement of his God."

Hancock Cemetery, Hancock Street at Quincy Center, Quincy, Massachusetts 02169.

# Adams, John Quincy

John Quincy Adams, born in Braintree, (now Quincy), Massachusetts, on July 11, 1767, was the eldest son of John Adams *(q.v.)*, second president of the United States. He himself became sixth president, serving from 1825-29. Later in his life, he gained a second reputation in the U.S. House of Representatives for his epic struggle in favor of the right of petition. His victory on this issue enabled the question of slavery to be debated openly in Congress, which would not otherwise have been possible.

On February 21, 1848, Adams rode to the U.S. Capitol. While a resolution was being debated, concerning the presentation of swords to officers who had fought in the Mexican-American War, a vote was called. Adams considered the war unrighteous, and his loud "No" was heard above the "Ayes." He then became flushed, moved his lips in a desperate attempt to speak, clutched the left corner of his desk, and fell unconscious to the floor. He was placed on a sofa, and carried to the Speaker's chamber. There his friends, and four doctors who were members of the House, stayed with him. A few minutes later he said: "This is the last of earth. I am content." He fell into a coma and died two days later, on February 23, 1848.

His remains were placed in a silver mounted coffin on a catafalque in front of the Speaker's platform in the House of Representatives. Daniel Webster wrote the inscription engraved on it. His funeral service was attended by most of the nation's leading dignitaries, as well as members of Congress and the diplomatic corps. James Polk (q.v.) called his funeral procession "a splendid pageant."

The body was taken to the Congressional Cemetery in Washington, D.C. to await shipment to Quincy. The journey to Quincy was made by train, and the casket was accompanied by an entourage consisting of one representative from each state and territory of the United States. In Quincy, along the entire route to the family tomb, flags were flown at half-mast, businesses were closed, and onlookers grieved, paying their last respects with bowed heads.

Hancock Cemetery, Hancock Street at Quincy Center, Quincy, Massachusetts 02169.

# *Aiken, Conrad*

Conrad Potter Aiken, born in Savannah, Georgia, on August 5, 1889, was a poet, novelist, and critic. At the age of 11, he was taken to live with relatives in Massachusetts after his father, having murdered his wife, committed suicide.

In the course of his distinguished career, Aiken received the Pulitzer Prize for poetry in 1929, and the National Medal for Literature in 1969.

Aiken spent his last birthday in the hospital, in a state of debilitation caused by recurring illnesses, and by a concussion brought on by a fall in his Savannah home. He died on August 17, 1973, at Savannah, Georgia, at about 6:30 p.m., following a heart attack. Sources close to the family said that he and his wife had just returned from a walk when he collapsed, and that he had died in a nursing home. His last days had been clouded by illness, including a disease of his inner-ear, which had impaired his sense of balance, thereby contributing to his fall.

About his own death Aiken had said: "I'm running out of time, all things come to an end."

He was survived by his wife, Mary Augusta Hoover Aiken, a painter, as well as by two daughters, one of them a writer, and by a son, also a writer. Graveside services were held at 5:00 p.m. on August 20, 1971 at Bonaventure Cemetery, in Savannah. The family requested that, instead of flowers, memorials be sent to Goodwill Industries.

Bonaventure Cemetery, Bonaventure Road, Savannah, Georgia 31404.

# Alcott, Louisa May

Louisa May Alcott was born in Germantown, Pennsylvania, on November 29, 1832. Educated by her father, she was also tutored by a neighbor, Henry David Thoreau *(q.v.)*, and also by the historian Theodore Parker. After serving as a nurse in the Civil War, she won renown with her two volumes of *Little Women* (1868 and 1869) and other works.

She died in Boston, Massachusetts, on March 6, 1888—the day of her father's funeral. It was said that she had been ill for some time, suffering from nervous prostration, brought on by her constant nursing of her father. While visiting her father some days earlier she had also caught a cold, which was said to have resulted in spinal meningitis.

*The Alcott Plot:*
*Sleepy Hollow*
*Cemetery, Concord,*
*Massachusetts.*

Photo: Clive E. Driver

Her casket was adorned with wreaths of ivy, and with violets and wild roses. It rested, together with her father's, in the Alcott mansion. Her funeral service was simple. The body was then taken by train to Concord, Massachusetts, where it was buried in the family plot. Sleepy Hollow Cemetery, Bedford Street, Concord, Massachusetts 01742.

# Alger, Horatio

Horatio Alger, born in Revere, Massachusetts, on January 13, 1834, was one of the most widely read American writers in the last 30 years of the 19th century. His stories told of boys who rose from rags to riches by exhibiting the virtues of honesty, industry, perseverance, and good humor. In all, he wrote more than 100 books. The first of these, *Ragged Dick: or Street Life in New York*, was published in 1867. The phrase "A Horatio Alger hero" became a byword for those who rose from poverty to fortune by their own efforts. Alger's work influenced a generation at a time when the incoming wave of immigration to the United States was at its height, and helped place a mark upon the emergent national character.

On July 18, 1899, in Natick, Massachusetts, where Alger lived with his sister, he suffered a severe asthmatic attack. Although his breathing improved, a nurse was brought from Boston to be by his side. He grew steadily weaker. A letter from his mistress, for which he had been waiting, arrived, and he struggled to open it, but was too weak to do so. His niece read him a few lines, and he dozed off. A moment later he gasped for air, and whispered: "She comes home the 28th. I must be there to meet her. I'll be better then, won't I?" His nurse nodded in affirmation. "Good," he said. "Please prepare my things. I am going to New York. I'm sleepy now. I shall have a nap. Later I can pack and leave on the evening train. But I'm tired. Let me rest." He closed his eyes, never to awaken.

The funeral service at the Eliot Unitarian Church in South Natick was attended by his first publisher, A.K. Loring of Boston. Four young men of Natick, whom Alger had known when they were boys, were his pallbearers. He was cremated at Forest Hills, and the ashes were then buried at Glenwood Cemetery, South Natick, Massachusetts 01760.

# *Anthony, Susan B.*

Susan B. Anthony, born in Adams, Massachusetts, on February 15, 1820, was a Quaker abolitionist, and a pioneer in the women's suffrage movement. From 1868-70, she co-published a radical New York weekly, the *Revolution*. She is best remembered, however, for leading a group of women to the polls in the November 1872 election, to test their right to vote. She was brought to trial and convicted, but refused to pay the fine that was imposed. As a lecturer and writer on women's rights, she became known throughout the United States and Europe.

On February 18, 1906, she had an attack of "neuralgia." Two days later, on February 20, she fell ill on her way home from the National Suffrage Convention, held in Baltimore, Maryland, in honor of her 86th birthday. Pneumonia developed after her arrival in Rochester, New York. By March 5, both lungs were affected. Early in her illness she told friends that she expected to live to be as old as her father, who was more than 90 when he died.

Two hours before she became unconscious, on March 11, she told her sister, Ann Shaw: "To think that I have had more than sixty years of hard struggle for a little liberty, and then to die without it seems so cruel." She remained unconscious for more than 24 hours, and then the end came peacefully, on March 13. Her doctor attributed her death to heart disease, and pneumonia of both lungs.

Her funeral service was held at 2:00 p.m. on March 15, in the Central Presbyterian Church in Rochester, New York. Throughout the day, flags on Rochester's public buildings, and at the University of Rochester, were flown at half-mast. Many private buildings were draped in black. Three clergymen officiated at the funeral service. Placed in front of the church were a row of palms, a sheaf of wheat, and a bouquet of white roses. A bunch of violets covered the middle of the casket, and an American flag was draped over the lower section. A group of young women, chosen from the Political Equality Club, and from the Anthony League, and dressed in white gowns, formed the honor guard at the casket.

Despite a severe snow storm, some 8,000 to 10,000 people waited in the street around the church during the funeral service, to have a last look at her coffin. After a two hour wait, the church doors were opened, and the public was allowed to file past the open coffin.

The service at the grave was private and extremely simple. As the coffin was being lowered into the ground, her sister stepped forward and said: "Dear Friend: thou hast tarried with us long; thou hast now gone to thy well earned rest. We beseech the Infinite Spirit who has upheld us to make us worthy to follow in thy steps and carry on thy work. Farewell." Burial was at Mt. Hope Cemetery, 791 Mt. Hope Avenue, Rochester, New York 14620.

# *Armstrong, Louis*

Louis Daniel Armstrong, the most outstanding trumpet player in jazz history, was born on July 4, 1900, in New Orleans, Louisiana. At 13 he was sent to the Colored Waif's Home, a New Orleans reform school, for 18 months for having fired a blank revolver shot at a New Year's Day parade. At the reform school he learned to play the trumpet. Later he played with King Oliver's Creole Jazz Band in Chicago (1922-24), and in Fletcher Henderson's Orchestra in New York (1924-25). In the later 1920s he was billed as "The Greatest Trumpet Player in the World," and thereafter led his own orchestra. By the 1930s he had become the dominant figure in the history of jazz, a distinction he retained for the rest of his life and, indeed, thereafter.

In March 1971 he fell ill, and was placed in intensive care in a New York hospital. On May 7, he returned to his home in Queens, New York. On July 6, two days after celebrating his seventy-first birthday, he died in his sleep, of an apparent heart attack. President Richard Nixon released a statement which said: "Mrs. Nixon and I share the sorrow of millions of Americans at the death of Louis Armstrong." Tributes also came from jazz musicians, including Duke Ellington (q.v.), Gene Krupa (q.v.), Benny Goodman, Al Hirt, and Eddie Condon. Ellington said: "He is what I call an American standard, an original." Mrs. Armstrong, his second wife, asked that instead of flowers, donations be sent to the Kidney Research Foundation, and to the Sickle Cell Anemia Foundation.

Armstrong lay in state at the Seventh Regiment Armory at Park Avenue and 66th Street in New York City. He was dressed in a navy-blue suit, a pink shirt, and a pink and silver tie. The opened gray steel coffin was lined with white velvet and placed under the armory's ornate winding wooden staircase. Above the coffin a simple gold plaque said: "Louis Satchmo Armstrong." ("Satchmo," short for "Satchelmouth," was a nickname of his, derived from his singing style.) An honor guard, composed of young black children, members of an anti-poverty group, and of the Cadet Corps of Central Harlem, stood at attention as 25,000 persons passed the coffin. The crowd at the armory was mostly composed of ordinary people who had come to pay their last respects. One mourner, Tommy Benford, a jazz drummer who had played with Jelly Roll Morton (q.v.), said: "He was a lovely beautiful person, and I just had to bid him goodbye."

His family requested that no music be played as he lay in state, but one man tried to, and got into an argument with a policeman, saying: "But Pops is inside." After questioning, the man was allowed to play three renditions of taps. He said: "I wanted to play my heart out for this great hero."

His funeral was held on July 9, 1971, at 1:00 p.m., at the Corona Congregational Church at 34th Avenue and 102-18 Street in Queens. There were no funeral bands. His manager, Ira Mangel, stated: "He wanted a simple church, simple everything—no music, no sadness. He said that if he had one band he would have all of them." In fact, many bands did offer to play. Before his death Armstrong had given an interview at which he said: "In New Orleans I played as many funerals as I could get, and cats died like flies, so I got a lot of nice little gigs out of that. They're going to enjoy blowing over me, ain't they? Cats will be coming from California and everywhere else just to play." In his autobiography, Satchmo, he recalled traditional jazz funerals, writing: "After the brother was six feet under the ground, the bands would strike up one of those good old tunes like "Didn't He Ramble," and all the people would leave their worries behind."

Peggy Lee, the singer, came from California to sing "The Lord's Prayer" at the service. Her voice was so soft that at one point it was drowned out by a jet leaving from nearby La Guardia Airport. After her song, there was a brief eulogy for Armstrong. At the conclusion of the service, Al Hibbler sang "When The Saints Go Marchin' In." It was then that a Ghanaian musician, Little Joe Ayesu, stood up, walked over to the pulpit, and began to imitate Armstrong's style of playing on a kazoo. An usher immediately stopped the impromptu performance.

Honorary pallbearers included Governor Nelson Rockefeller (q.v.), Mayor John Lindsay, Bing Crosby (q.v.), Ella Fitzgerald, Duke Ellington (q.v.), Pearl Bailey, Guy Lombardo, Dizzie Gillespie, Count Basie, and Harry James, as well as such television personalities as Ed Sullivan (q.v.), Frank Sinatra, Johnny Carson, Merv Griffin, David Frost, and Dick Cavett.

En route to Flushing Cemetery, crowds gathered along the way, while at Parsons and Northern Boulevard a sign was raised that said: "We All Loved You Louis." The burial service was disrupted by souvenir hunters trying to get pieces of the floral wreaths. A bronze cover is over his vault, inscribed "Louis Armstrong," and "Satchmo."

Flushing Cemetery, 3901 Main Street, Flushing, Queens, New York 11354.

# Arthur, Chester A.

Chester Alan Arthur, born in Fairfield, Vermont on October 5, 1829, became the 21st president of the United States, holding office from 1881 to 1885.

The son of an Irish immigrant, he became a lawyer. He was elected vice-president under President James A. Garfield *(q.v.)*, and became president upon the assassination of Garfield on September 19, 1881.

*Chester Arthur's grave, in Albany Rural Cemetery.*

(Photo: John Spellos)

After leaving the presidency, he lived in New York City. Here, on Wednesday, November 17, 1886, at 8:00 a.m., his maid entered his room to prepare him for breakfast. When, after speaking to him several times, she received no reply, the family doctor was summoned. Both the doctor and his immediate family remained at his bedside throughout the day. It was realized that he was conscious by his recognition of those close to him. After midnight the doctor left. Arthur's breathing then became rapid and intermittent. As death approached, he retained enough consciousness to notice the ticking of the clock in his room. His family claimed that, while he breathed with difficulty, he did so in rhythm with the clock. At 5:10 a.m., he turned his head on his pillow, and his irregular breathing stopped. An assistant doctor was at his side, together with Arthur's two sisters and his son. The cause of death was said to be cerebral apoplexy, due to the rupture of a small artery in the brain.

Sympathizing friends arrived at the house early in the morning, but the family remained in seclusion. No one was permitted to see the body, which lay upstairs in the bedroom in which he had died. The family doctor said that although he had lost much flesh in the past six months, "his face would look quite natural in the coffin."

As people lined Lexington Avenue, near his home, many notables, including President Grover Cleveland *(q.v.)*, arrived. After expressing his regrets to the family, he viewed the body of his predecessor in office. The pallbearers, including Robert Todd Lincoln, the son of Abraham Lincoln *(q.v.)*, wore large white bands pinned at the shoulder and the waist. The funeral service was held at the Church of the Heavenly Rest, at Fifth Avenue near 45th Street. As the coffin was placed at the altar, a cross of white roses covered the head, while a cross of violets was placed at the foot. Between them were ferns, palms, and laurel.

The coffin was then put on a train bound for Albany, New York, where it arrived at 1:22 p.m., having covered the distance of 141 miles in three hours. Few were at the station to greet it, as it had arrived much sooner than expected. The train then switched tracks from the New York Central to the Delaware-Hudson railroad for the trip to Albany Rural Cemetery. By the time the train arrived at the plot, its sides had been covered with palms and ferns. During the service at the Protestant-Episcopal Church, at which a bishop officiated, Arthur's son could hardly keep from crying, while his sister wept continuously. At the end of the service, the bishop picked up a bunch of roses that lay near the grave's edge, and placed them on the coffin. The gravediggers then cast so many other floral tributes after it, that the oaken casket was hidden from sight. When the cemetery was cleared of visitors, the mound was covered with a single piece of turf.

Albany Rural Cemetery, Cemetery Avenue, Albany, New York 12204.

# *Audubon, John James*

John James Audubon, the naturalist, was born in San Domingo (now Haiti), on April 26, 1785. The illegitimate son of a French naval officer, he spent some of his boyhood in France, before being sent to the United States at the age of 18. His interest in drawing birds, and his keen powers of observation of the wildlife he saw in the eastern seaboard and Midwestern states, eventually led to the publication of his 4-volume collection of magnificent illustrations, *The Birds of America* (1827-38), and other works.

In his last years he lived on his 30 or 40-acre estate, Minnie's Land, on the banks of the Hudson River, in what is now New York City, west of Amsterdam Avenue, and between 155th and 158th Streets.

He declined both physically and mentally in his last years, and rarely spoke. Upon receiving an unexpected visit from an in-law, however, he broke into speech, saying: "Yes, yes, Billy! You go down that side of Long Pond, and I'll go this side, and we'll get the ducks." These were his last words. Shortly after, in January 1851, he had a slight stroke, as a result of which he became partially paralyzed, and was in much pain.

On January 22, his condition began to deteriorate. His wife and two sons were with him when he died, on the evening of January 27. One of his sons, Victor, said that before he died he turned his head to give his loved ones a farewell glance, which was wistful and clear. His wife, Lucy, closed his eyes at 10:15 p.m. The following morning his son John made a sketch of his head, after which both sons took a death mask.

The *Evening Post*, in announcing his death, gave his name as "Anderson," instead of "Audubon." This may have led to a smaller number of mourning friends gathering in the parlor of his house on January 29 than would otherwise have been the case. The day was a gusty one as the funeral procession made its way to nearby Trinity Churchyard, a place Audubon had chosen for his burial. The cemetery was later moved when Broadway was widened. Later in the century, a Celtic cross was erected on Audubon's grave, erroneously giving his birthdate as May 4, 1780. The cross still marks his grave, at Trinity Chapel of the Intercession, Broadway at 155th Street, New York City, New York 10032.

# Barnum, Phineas Taylor

Phineas Taylor Barnum, the famous showman, was born in Bethel, Connecticut, on July 5, 1810. In partnership with James A. Bailey, he won renown as the world's most successful circus entrepreneur, presenting such acts as Jenny Lind (the soprano

Photographs: Bill Cole,

*Barnum's grave, at Bridgeport, Connecticut*

*A monument to Barnum, at Seaside Park, Bridgeport.*

singer known as the "Swedish nightingale"), "General Tom Thumb" [*q.v.*] (an English dwarf), and Jumbo the elephant.

Barnum fell ill on November 6, 1890 at Marina, his residence in Bridgeport, Connecticut. During his illness he left his sickroom only twice. He had requested that when his end was apparent, sedatives be administered "to make the passage to the next world more peaceful." Just after midnight on April 7, 1891, the doctors at his side noted that his pulse weakened, his heart action diminished, and his body temperature became lower. He seemed to pass the night in much pain, and his wife was constantly at his bedside. When asked if he wanted a drink of water, he replied, "Yes," and this was his last word. He then sank into a semi-conscious state. The doctors began to administer sedatives around 10:00 a.m., and at frequent intervals thereafter. The end, which was peaceful and apparently without pain, came at 6:22 p.m. on April 7. The immediate cause of death was said to be degeneration of the heart muscles. The news of his death reached his partner at 6:30 p.m., along with a message from Barnum that the show must go on as usual, and that the circus was to close only on the day of the funeral.

Funeral services were held at 1:30 p.m. on April 10, 1891, in the parlor of his Bridgeport mansion. Only a small number of Barnum's most intimate friends and relatives were present, and the pastor of the Church of the Redeemer officiated. The casket was then closed for the last time, and Mrs. Barnum placed a bouquet of lilies-of-the-valley and pansies on top. The coffin was taken to the South Church in Bridgeport for a second service, but it was not opened, as it had been Barnum's wish that no one should see his body during the funeral. Two hymns were sung—Whittier's "I Long For Household Voices," and "O Lord Divine," both of which Barnum had requested for this occasion only a few days earlier.

All businesses and schools in Bridgeport were closed in tribute to the great showman. He was buried opposite a column that had been erected to the memory of Charles S. Stratton (General Tom Thumb), whose act had enabled Barnum to regain his fortune after the burning of his New York Museum in 1868.

Mountain Grove Cemetery, 2675 North Avenue, Bridgeport, Connecticut 06604.

# *Bartók, Béla*

Béla Bartók, the composer and musicologist, was born on March 25, 1881 in Nagyszentmiklos, Austria-Hungary, in what is now Romania.

After studying at the Royal Academy of Music in Budapest, he compiled a collection of Hungarian folk music, which influenced the compositions he eventually wrote. After World War I, he established an international reputation as a pianist. In 1940 he emigrated to the United States, where he continued his work as a pianist and composer.

Bartók, who had had tuberculosis as a child, had never had much physical stamina. In 1941 he often complained of rheumatic pains, later commenting: "For a while I could not raise my right arm at all, to say nothing of being able to play the piano." In the fall of that year, his condition improved, but he then began to run fevers. By February 1942 his strength had deteriorated, and he collapsed while giving a lecture at Harvard University. By this time his weight had dropped to 87 lbs. Harvard offered to pay all immediate hospital expenses, and the American Society of Composers, Authors, and Publishers (ASCAP) offered to pay for further treatment, even though Bartók was not a member of the organization.

In December, 1943, Bartók went to Asheville, North Carolina, to escape from New York City's winter weather. He wrote: "At present I feel quite well. I have no temperature, my strength has returned, and I am able to take nice walks in the mountain forests—Yes, I climb mountains (only very cautiously of course)." He also reported that his weight had risen to 105 lbs.

After returning to New York from Asheville, his spleen became infected and he underwent x-ray treatment. In March 1945 he had an attack of acute pneumonia, which was cured by the then newly-discovered antibiotic, penicillin. By September his condition had become very bad. His temperature rose each evening. He was treated at home, while continuing to work on the score of *Concerto No. 3 for Piano.*

On September 21, his temperature dropped suddenly. The Hungarian doctor who was treating him considered this to be a bad sign, and arranged for him to be taken to New York City's West Side Hospital. There he was given blood transfusions, infusions of dextrose, and oxygen, which kept him alive for a few days. During one transfusion he asked for the needle to be taken away. Seeming to know that he could not be helped, he said: "In my last moment they cannot leave me in peace." He died on September 26, 1945. It was said that, as he died, his eyes slowly became like ice.

His funeral service, attended by only a few friends, was at the University Chapel, Lexington Avenue at 52nd Street, New York City, on September 28, 1945. Burial was at Ferncliff Cemetery, Hartsdale, New York 10530.

# *Beecher, Henry Ward*

Henry Ward Beecher, a leading 19th-century liberal Protestant spokesman, was born in Litchfield, Connecticut, on June 24, 1813. He had a forceful style of oratory which won him a large following. He was unconventional in dress, which added to his charisma. In 1847 he became pastor of the Plymouth Congregational Church in Brooklyn, New York. From this pulpit he spoke out on national political issues, including abolition. He was an eloquent supporter of the Northern cause during the Civil War. In 1874 he was sued for adultery, but the charge was not proven. Despite the scandal, he returned to his pulpit.

In the early part of 1887, Beecher, being anxious to finish his *Life of Christ*, confined himself to his Brooklyn home for a month, going out only to take an evening walk. On March 5, 1887 he took his usual walk, but that night experienced a severe headache and nausea, which he attributed to "some bilious trouble." He was restless for most of the night, and fell asleep in the early morning hours. The following afternoon the family sent for a doctor, who ruled out paralysis but was unable to make a diagnosis. The following night Beecher's breathing became heavy, and he had difficulty answering questions. A second doctor was called, who examined the patient and found that his left side was completely paralyzed, and that he was in a coma. The doctors then placed an announcement on Beecher's front door, which read:

> March 5, 3:00 p.m. Mr. Beecher has had an attack of apoplexy—he is very ill, but suffering no pain. A bulletin will be issued each morning, noon, and night.

There was a constant stream of visitors through the Beecher home during the next few days. Beecher himself remained in a coma most of the time. On the morning of March 8, surrounded by his family and with a doctor bending over his bed, Beecher's breathing became choked, and he experienced body contortions. By 9:00 a.m. his pulse slowed and his breathing had become shallow. By 9:30 a.m. no vital life signs could be detected. Another bulletin was then posted, which announced: "9:30 a.m. Mr. Beecher has just breathed his last." At 10:00 a.m. another bulletin was posted, which said in part:

> He breathed his last breath quietly. His remains are in the care of his faithful and excellent nurses until the arrival of Mr. Hopper the undertaker...J. Quincy Ward, the sculptor, is expected to take a cast of his face for the statue long provided for by his staunch and old friend, Mr. Henry Sage of Ithaca.

Beecher's remains were placed at the altar of Plymouth Congregational Church for some hours, during which time it was estimated that 30,000 people passed the coffin. As it was guessed Beecher would have wished, much of Brooklyn was adorned not with black crepe, as was the custom, but with flowers and wreaths instead. During the day and the evening, Mrs. Beecher stayed at home, surrounded by her late husband's personal effects and letters. Services were held at most churches across the city, and he was eulogized by rich and poor alike.

At 9:00 a.m. on March 13, 1887, Mrs. Beecher took a last look at her husband's mortal remains. The coffin was sealed permanently, and taken to a receiving vault at Green-Wood Cemetery to await burial.

The Green-Wood Cemetery, 17 Battery Place, 5th and 25th Street, Brooklyn, New York 11232.

## *Beiderbecke, Bix*

"Bix" Beiderbecke, the famous jazz cornetist, was born Leon Bismark Beiderbecke on March 10, 1903, in Davenport, Iowa. Renowned for his pure tone and melodic invention, he has become the subject of a cult, the influence of which was augmented by the publication in 1938 of a novel based on his life, *Young Man With a Horn*, by Dorothy Baker. Beiderbecke was one of the first white jazz artists to receive recognition from his black contemporaries, including Louis Armstrong (*q.v.*). While it has been said that Bix's greatest solos were never recorded, his renderings of "Singing the Blues," and other tunes, are revered jazz classics.

The final years of his short life were marked by bouts of depression, alcoholism, and failing health. Most of his friends, including many of the great names in the world of jazz music, sought to help him, although it was generally conceded that he was difficult to help.

A few weeks before his death he began to drink less after meeting with a girl called Alice O'Connell, (some say her name was Helen Weiss), who sought to "straighten him out." It was rumored that they intended to get married. The two had dinner together at the apartment of Hoagy Carmichael, the jazz pianist and composer, on 57th Street in New York City. Carmichael, an old friend, was struck by Bix's improved appearance. After this, available data as to what happened is sparse. Researchers have been hindered in their quest by their inability to contact Alice O'Connell.

At 9:30 p.m. on August 6, 1931, Bix, who had welts on his arms, called in the superintendent of his apartment in Queens, New York. He was screaming that there were two Mexicans under his bed, who wanted to kill him. He then collapsed. A doctor was called, examined his body, and pronounced him dead. The cause of death was officially listed as lobar pneumonia, with edema of the brain, but the effects of alcohol seem to have played a major role. The opinion has been advanced that at the time of his death he was suffering from delirium tremens, combined with a fever.

Bix's mother, Agatha, and his sister, Burnette, had already been summoned from Davenport to New York by friends. They arrived too late. Meanwhile, in Davenport, his father, Bismark, had received a telegram informing him of the death. Bix's

23, 1859, was one of the West's most infamous desperadoes.

He spent most of his earlier life gambling and drinking in some of the seedier establishments of Colorado, New Mexico, and Arizona. He was wrongly said to have committed his first murder at the age of 12—it was in fact in 1877 when he was 18. When he was 21 he boasted that he had killed a man for every year of his life: the total is, however, believed to have been nine. He was noted for killing Sheriff Jim Brady in Lincoln, New Mexico, in 1878. In 1880 Sheriff Pat F. Garrett captured Billy, but on April 28, 1881 he escaped, killing two guards.

Garrett lay low in the weeks following the escape, probably trying to convey the impression that Billy was not being hunted. On July 15, 1881, Garrett found him at the home of some of his Mexican friends, at Fort Sumner, New Mexico. The Kid entered the room and cried out in Spanish: "Quíen es? Quíen es?" ("Who's there? Who's there?"). Garrett pulled his revolver and shot him twice. The Kid gasped loudly, trying to catch his last breath, and then fell to the floor. It was Garrett's opinion that "the ball struck him just above the heart and cut through the ventricles." A coroner's jury found that the homicide was justifiable, and "was inflicted by the said Garrett in the discharge of his official duty as sheriff."

Bonney's mortal remains were dressed and buried in the Fort Sumner Military Cemetery on July 15, 1881. After the burial, many showmen and swindlers claimed to have stolen his remains, and charged admission to view the body at traveling shows. Sheriff Garrett said bluntly, however: "I say that the Kid's body lies undisturbed in the grave—and I speak of what I know."

His epitaph, written in telegraphic style, reads: "Truth and History. 21 men. The Boy Bandit King—He Died As He Lived." Fort Sumner Military Cemetery, Fort Sumner, New Mexico 88119.

# Black Hawk

Black Hawk was a Sauk Indian leader, who gave his name to the Black Hawk War of 1832, fought between Indians and whites over possession of the lands at the confluence of the Rock and Mississippi rivers in Illinois.

He was born in 1767, near present day Rock Island, Illinois, and was named Makataimeshekiakiak ("Black Sparrow Hawk"). After the defeat of Black Hawk and his Indian followers by federal troops and state militia in the War of 1832, he was captured. He was imprisoned for a month in Fortress Monroe, Virginia, after which he was taken on tour through the main cities of the eastern United States, where his appearance aroused great interest. In 1834 he was handed over to the custody of a rival chief, Keokuk, west of the Mississippi River. He later settled in Davis County, on the Des Moines River, near Iowaville, Iowa. Here he fell ill, in September, 1838, with what was described as "a violent bilious attack." He asked for the help of a white doctor, but none could be found, and he died on October 3.

His body was not buried, but was placed on the surface of the ground dressed in the military uniform presented to him by President Andrew Jackson (q.v.), and accompanied by a sword and medal presented to him by Jackson, a cane given him by Henry Clay, and medals given him by John Quincy Adams (q.v.), and the city of

*The statue of Black Hawk at Lowden State Park, Oregon, Illinois, overlooking the Rock River. Built in 1925 by the sculptor Lorado Taft, it was intended to represent a prototypical Indian, but it quickly became known locally as "Black Hawk." A life mask of Black Hawk is preserved nearby at Black Hawk State Park, Rock Island, Illinois.*
*Illustration by Vicki Manos.*

of Boston. The body and all these objects were stolen in July 1839, and were taken to St. Louis, Missouri. Here the body was cleaned, and the bones sent to Quincy, Illinois, to be articulated. The Governor of Iowa protested, however, and the remains were recovered and lodged for some time in the governor's office, where Black Hawk's sons were satisfied to allow them to remain. They were later placed in the Geological and Historical Society Museum in Burlington, Iowa. When the museum was burned down in 1855, Black Hawk's ashes were lost among the debris.

# Bogart, Humphrey

Humphrey DeForest Bogart, the film actor who achieved renown in the 1940s and 1950s, was born on January 23, 1899—not December 25, 1900, as film publicists later gave it—in New York City. His father was a doctor, and his mother an illustrator. He became famous for his acting in a series of films which included *Casablanca* (1942), *The Treasure of the Sierra Madre* (1948), and *The African Queen* (1951) for which he won an Academy Award. He was married four times, each time to a

*Humphrey Bogart's death certificate.*          (From the Collection of Mary Ellen Hunt)

Hollywood actress. His fourth wife, who survived him, was Lauren Bacall.

Bogart suffered from cancer of the esophagus for the last two years of his life. He lost considerable weight but, between hospital visits, kept working. In February 1956 he had a malignant growth removed, but recovered. Later in the year he was treated at St. John's Hospital, Santa Monica, California, for nerve pressure caused by scar growth. He died in his sleep in his bedroom at his Holmby Hills home, early on the morning of January 14, 1957.

On January 17, a simple service was held at All Saints Protestant Episcopal Church in Beverly Hills, California. The church was filled to capacity with 650 persons, of whom about 200 were drawn from a street crowd of about 3,000 which had congregated. The officiating clergyman recited the Ten Commandments, saying that they had a "special meaning" to Bogart, and that he "lived by them."

A scale model of Bogart's boat, the Santana, was put on the altar in place of his remains, which were, in accordance with his wishes, being cremated at that time.

His close friend John Huston, who had directed the film The African Queen, eulogized him. Besides his wife, Lauren Bacall, and his family, other notable personalities present from the world of film and entertainment included Spencer Tracy (q.v.), Dick Powell, Danny Thomas, Katherine Hepburn. Marlene Dietrich, Danny Kay, and Ronald Reagan. A minute of silence in tribute to the actor was observed at Twentieth Century Fox and Warner Brothers Studios at 12:30 p.m., the time at which the funeral began.

The ashes were buried in the private Garden of the Sanctuary, Forest Lawn, Glendale, California. Admission to the area is granted only to holders of a special key. Buried with him is a gold whistle from Lauren Bacall, inscribed: "If you need anything just whistle"—a line spoken by her in To Have and Have Not, their first movie together.

Forest Lawn, 1712 South Glendale Avenue, Glendale, California 91205.

# Booth, John Wilkes

John Wilkes Booth, the assassin of President Abraham Lincoln (q.v.), was born on May 10, 1838, near Bel Air, Maryland.

Booth belonged to one of the most distinguished theatrical families of the 19th century. As an actor during the Civil War, he earned an average of $20,000.00 a year, and at the same time served as a secret agent for the Confederacy.

Around 10:00 p.m., on April 14, 1865, Booth entered the Presidential Box at Ford's Theatre in Washington, D.C., where President Lincoln was watching the play Our American Cousin. Booth shot Lincoln in the back of the head, and then jumped out of the box, shouting: "Sic semper tyrannis ('Thus die all tyrants'): the South is avenged." He landed heavily on the stage, breaking a bone in his lower left leg.

On April 26, 1865 a squadron of the Sixteenth New York City Cavalry traced Booth to a barn near Fredericksburg, Virginia. Booth, on crutches in the barn, told them that if they would withdraw one hundred feet he would come out and fight them. The Cavalrymen told him they had come to take him prisoner. After an exchange of words that lasted an hour, the barn was set on fire, flushing Booth out. In the ensuing scuffle, it was never ascertained whether he was shot by one of the cavalrymen, or whether he committed suicide. Reports at the time stated that a

Sergeant Corbett, of English birth, shot him but had only intended to wound him.

Booth's body was placed on the grass outside the burning barn, and he said faintly: "Tell mother I die for my country." The heat from the burning barn became so intense that the body was carried to the porch of a house, and a surgeon sent for. When given some ice-water, he raised his head, in extreme pain, and said: "Kill me! kill me!" He died quickly thereafter. His last recorded words were: "Useless! Useless!" He had been shot at 3:15 a.m. and was pronounced dead at 7:20 a.m.

Booth's body was taken to Washington D.C. aboard the steamer *Ide*. Thousands of persons visited the Navy Yard in Washington where the *Ide* was docked, but none were allowed to see the body, which was covered with a tarpaulin. Rumors abounded as to how it would be disposed of. The Booth family requested that it be given to them for proper burial. Some government sources said that the body would be disposed of in such a way that traces of it could never be found. Later, one source said that, after the surgeon general had performed a post-mortem examination, he dissected the body, and that pieces were sewn up in individual cloth bags and dumped into the Potomac River with heavy weights attached.

Down the years since Booth's death, there has been speculation as to whether the man captured in the barn was indeed Booth, and whether Booth himself might not have escaped from Washington D.C. A man named John St. Johns, claiming to be Booth, died in Oklahoma in 1913. Booth was also reported to have been seen in Canada, France, India, and several other countries. All these claims and allegations remain, however, unsubstantiated. The subject has also lent itself to dramatization, most recently in the form of a book by G.J.A. O'Toole, *The Cosgrove Report* (1980), which fictionalized Booth's escape from Washington.

The purported body is buried in an unmarked grave at Green Mount Cemetery, Greenmount Avenue at Oliver Street, Baltimore, Maryland 21202.

# Borden, Lizzie

Lisbeth A. Borden, better known as Lizzie Borden, was born on July 19, 1860, in Fall River, Massachusetts. She was the focal point of one of New England's most sensational murder trials, and her name entered folklore with the popularization of the jingle:

> "Lizzie Borden took an axe
> And gave her father forty whacks.
> When she saw what she had done
> She gave her mother forty-one."

Her father was a wealthy and retired cotton broker, who had married her stepmother. It was shown by circumstantial evidence that Lizzie wanted to kill both her father and her stepmother so that she could inherit a more sizable portion of the estate. Her parents were found "hacked" to death on August 4, 1892. The autopsies showed that they had been killed with either an axe or a cleaver.

Lizzie was arrested and charged with the crime. Some of the most famous lawyers of the day participated in the ensuing trial. Lizzie was acquitted, and lived the rest of her life in virtual obscurity. In April 1913, her sister Emma broke years of silence and said: "Lizzie is queer, but as for her being guilty, I say 'No' and decidedly 'No.' "

Lizzie never fully recovered from an operation she underwent in 1926. She died alone at her home in Fall River, Massachusetts, at 68 years of age, on June 1, 1927—34 years after her acquittal.

The funeral services, held on June 5, were private. A local newspaper reported that a soloist sang one song, "My Ain Countree." Burial was at Oak Grove Cemetery, Head of Prospect Street, Fall River, Massachusetts 02720.

# Bradford, William

William Bradford, first governor of the Plymouth Colony in New England, was born in March, 1590, in Austerfield, Yorkshire, England.

Bradford supported the Puritan movement in England, and later migrated to the Netherlands in search of religious freedom. He was the organizer of the 100 Pilgrims who came to the New World aboard the *Mayflower*. He was also one of the writers of the "Mayflower Compact" which became the basis for the government of the Plymouth Colony. Chosen as governor of the colony in 1621, he was re-elected 30 times between 1621 and 1656. His writings include *History of Plymouth Plantation, 1620-47*, which dealt with the hardships and struggles of the original settlers.

As Bradford grew older, he remained active, and spent much of his time writing poetry. During most of the winter of 1656-57 he felt ill, and his activities were somewhat reduced. On May 7, 1657 he went to bed feeling weak, and did not have the usual drive that sustained him. He slept soundly, however, and reported having had visions or dreams of warmth that had brought him closer to God. The following day, as he was visited by younger men of the colony who had come to bring news and ask advice, he said: "God has given me a pledge of my happiness in another world." The following day he asked to make his will. As the largest property owner in the colony, his estate was valued at the equivalent (in the 1980s) of more than $200,000.00. He died that evening, May 9, at 9:00 p.m.

When he was buried on a hill overlooking Plymouth, the entire town was in attendance. As the body was lowered into the grave by soldiers, a salute was fired. Cotton Mather (*q.v.*), the famous New England clergyman and writer, said after his death that he was "lamented by all the colonies of New England as a common blessing and father to them all." The exact location of his grave is unknown today, but it is probably in the vicinity of the cemetery where his children are buried, which is Burial Hill Cemetery, School Street, Plymouth, Massachusetts 02360.

# Brady, Diamond Jim

James Buchanan Brady—Diamond Jim Brady, whose name became synonymous with high living—was born on August 12, 1856 in New York City.

Brady was a salesman for Manning, Maxwell, & Moore, a railroad concern. He had such phenomenal sales and investment abilities that, by 1903, he was worth at least $12 million. Brady's two passions were eating well and dressing well. He often wore as much as $2 million in diamond jewelry, and claimed to have a set of jewelry for every day of the month. He gave away or willed fortunes to charities and hospitals, including the Urological Institute of Johns Hopkins in Baltimore, which was named in his honor.

In December 1916, while convalescing from a stroke, he rented a $1,000-a-week apartment on the Boardwalk in Atlantic City. There he spent each day watching the crowds from his glass-encased veranda.

On April 12, 1917, he spent the day on the Boardwalk, and retired feeling "quite well." At 4:30 a.m. on April 13 he called for his servant, and asked for a glass of water, saying a few joking words. They were his last. When the servant tried to awaken him at 8:30 a.m., an hour later than usual, he found him unable to respond. His doctor said that he had been dead less than five minutes.

Funeral services were held in St. Agnes' Roman Catholic Church on 43rd Street, near Lexington Avenue, New York City, on April 16, 1917. The coffin was covered with violets and orchids, and three candles were lit on each side. The choir sang Hammer's *Requiem*. The funeral was attended by more than 1,000 people, drawn from every walk of life, including artists, actors, bankers, and many Broadway actresses.

The body was buried in Holy Cross cemetery in Brooklyn. although one of Brady's last requests, made to Fred Housman, a close personal friend, had been that he be cremated.

Cemetery of the Holy Cross, Tilden Avenue, Brooklyn, New York 11226.

# *Brady, Mathew B.*

Mathew B. Brady, the famous 19th century pioneer portrait photographer, was born around 1823, near Lake George, in Warren County, New York.

He received little formal education. With the help of Samuel Morse, inventor of the electric telegraph, he experimented with daguerrotypes. He opened his own photography business in New York City, and became highly successful. He then set out to make a photographic record of the Civil War. His book, *Brady's National Photographic Collection of War Views and Portraits of Representative Men*, was published in 1870. After the Civil War, he fell into a state of financial ruin, but managed to open a photographic studio in Washington D.C. He gradually faded into obscurity, and at the time of his death was living in near poverty.

On April 16, 1895, Brady was struck by a carriage while crossing a street in New York City. His leg was broken, and a photographic journal later reported that Brady was seen on Broadway, "hobbling with the aid of his cane and wearing thick glasses with blue lens." (sic).

Brady's doctors ordered him to bed in the winter of 1895, at which time he was said to be suffering from a kidney ailment. By December 16 his condition worsened, and he was taken to the indigent ward of the New York Presbyterian Hospital. In the month which followed his condition deteriorated further. He died while in a semi-coma, at 5:00 a.m. on January 15, 1896. The cause of death was listed as "chronic diffuse nephritis."

A close friend sent his body to Washington, D.C., at a cost of $27.10. He was buried in Arlington National Cemetery. The date chiseled on his tombstone in the National Cemetery is incorrect; it records his death date as being in 1895 instead of 1896. Arlington National Cemetery, Fort Myers, Arlington, Virginia 22211.

# *Brice, Fanny*

Fanny Brice, born Fannie Borach in New York City, on October 29, 1891, was a comedienne and singer associated with the *Ziegfeld Follies.* In her early years she was a pianist, singer, and chorus girl. Florenz Ziegfeld *(q.v.),* discovered her in a burlesque house, and hired her for his *Follies* at $75.00 per week. In 1921 she introduced a song, "My Man", which became her trademark. She worked with such stars as W.C. Fields, Will Rogers, and Eddie Cantor *(q.q.v.),* and was the subject of David Belasco's Broadway show, *Fannie* (1925). Her life story was the subject of the Broadway musical *Funny Girl,* which was made into a motion picture in 1968.

On May 25, 1951, when she was 59 years old, Fanny Brice suffered a stroke at her Beverly Hills, California, home. Taken unconscious to the Cedars of Lebanon Hospital, she was put in an oxygen tent. Her doctor said on May 25 that she had suffered a massive cerebral hemorrhage. She never regained consciousness, and died at 11:15 a.m. on May 29. With her when she died were her son, her daughter, and their respective spouses.

Funeral services were held on May 31 at Temple Israel in Hollywood, California. As the body lay in a coffin before the altar a menorah flickered behind. The Hebrew funeral dirge "El Malay Rachamin" ("Lord Full of Compassion") was chanted by a cantor. As the mourners from the world of show business arrived at the temple, an organ softly played "My Man." A spokesman for the entertainment world, George Jessel, said: "She should have been kept longer in this state [of life] to sit in a rocking chair with her grandchildren." She was then eulogized by a rabbi. After the half-hour service, her body was cremated at a local mortuary. Entombment was at the Home of Peace Memorial Park, 4334 Whittier Boulevard, Los Angeles, California 90023.

*The tomb containing Fanny Brice's ashes.*

Photo: Mary Ellen Hunt

# Bryan, William Jennings

William Jennings Bryan, who three times ran unsuccessfully for the presidency of the United States, was born in Salem, Illinois on March 19, 1860.

He grew up in Illinois, and later moved to Nebraska. As an agrarian candidate campaigning about depressed economic conditions, he was elected to the U.S. House of Representatives in 1890. In 1896 he made his famous "Cross of Gold" speech, which won him his nomination as the Democratic presidential candidate. After his unsuccessful bids for the presidency, he was appointed secretary of state by President Woodrow Wilson (q.v.) in 1913. He resigned in 1915, the day after the sinking of the Lusitania, an event which contributed to entry of the United States into World War I. In 1925, on the side of the prosecution, Bryan was one of the participants in the renowned trial of John Scopes, a schoolteacher accused of violating state law by teaching the doctrine of evolution. (Scopes was found guilty, but was later acquitted.)

At the conclusion of the trial, in July 1925, Bryan devoted his time to speechmaking, making a whirlwind tour. In Dayton, Tennessee, on July 25, 1925, he told his wife, Mary: "I have several more years to live." After dinner on the same day, he made some telephone calls to arrange a trip to the Smoky Mountains for himself and his wife, and told her: "Mama, from now on I'm taking care of you." He then said that he felt drowsy, and wanted to take a nap, and that after getting up he would write some letters. On his way to the upstairs bedroom he said to his son: "Seems there's hardly time enough for resting and none at all for dying."

Around 4:00 p.m. his wife sent someone to awaken him. The friend said that Bryan was sleeping so peacefully that it would be a pity to do so. When his wife went upstairs, she found him to be already dead. No doctors were in attendance, and no autopsy was performed. The press reported the cause of death as apoplexy. Later, in a letter to Bryan's daughter, a doctor wrote that the cause of death was "diabetes mellitus," brought on by the fatigue of the Scopes trial.

As the news of his death spread across the countryside, hundreds of mourners, including farmers, shopkeepers, and laborers, came, by auto, foot, horse and mule, to the Tennessee cottage where his body lay. On Tuesday, July 28, 1925, a brief service was held on the lawn of the Rogers' family home, which he had been visiting. A clergyman from the Dayton Methodist Church officiated. After the service, Bryan's body was taken on a five-coach funeral train to services in Nashville, Chatanooga, and Washington D.C. In Washington his body lay in state at the New York Avenue Presbyterian Church, guarded by two Spanish-American War veterans. An estimated 25,000 people filed past his coffin.

The church service on the day of the burial—July 31, 1925—was simple. As the procession left the church, around 4:00 p.m., fog and rain were so heavy that street lamps were turned on. As the crowd of senators, representatives, and government officials stood in the pouring rain, the casket was lowered into the grave, while a clergyman from Birmingham, Alabama, prayed: "We thank Thee for this great hero of the common people."

Arlington National Cemetery, Fort Myers, Arlington, Virginia 22211.

# Buchanan, James

James Buchanan, the 15th president of the United States, who served in office from 1857-61, was born on April 23, 1791, at Mercerburg, Pennsylvania. He was elected to the presidency in 1856 over John C. Frémont, and Millard Fillmore (q.q.v.), although he did not receive a majority of the popular vote. His term of office was marked by the growing national crisis over the issue of slavery, immediately before the outbreak of the Civil War.

In May 1868 Buchanan became seriously ill with a cold, aggravated by the complications of old age. As he worsened, he dictated his final letters and instructions from his upstairs bedroom at Wheatland, his home near Lancaster, Pennsylvania. Besides selling his livestock and making a will, he also made preparations for his funeral. He asked that the ceremony be simple, without pomp, and that his headstone be made of durable marble, with the following inscription and nothing more:

"Here rest the remains of JAMES BUCHANAN, fifteenth president of The United States. Born in Franklin County, Pennsylvania, April 23, 1791; died at his residence at Wheatland, Lancaster County, Pennsylvania on..."

—here he added "with the day of my death, now so near." He also instructed that the Masons could participate in the funeral should they so wish.

He died at 8:30 a.m. on June 1, 1868. His last words were: "Oh Lord Almighty, as Thou wilt."

Buchanan's request for a simple funeral went unheeded, as some 3,000 persons lined the route from Wheatland to Lancaster, a distance of one and a half miles. The body lay in a hall in Wheatland for public viewing, as the family stayed in seclusion in the bedroom where he had died. The ex-president was dressed in a white shroud with a high collar and white tie.

Many local denominations assisted the Masons with the service. A local band played a funeral march on the way to the cemetery.

Woodward Hill Cemetery, Lancaster, Pennsylvania, 17600.

# Buck, Pearl S.

Pearl Buck the Nobel prize-winner, renowned for her novels about China, was born Pearl Comfort Sydenstricker on June 26, 1892, in Hillsboro, West Virginia.

Graduating from Cornell University in 1926, she contributed articles on Chinese life to American magazines in the early 1920s, and won the Pulitzer Prize for literature for her novel *The Good Earth,* in 1932. She was awarded the Nobel Prize for literature in 1938. Altogether she published more than a dozen books, mostly novels. She also established the Pearl S. Buck Foundation to aid illegitimate children of United States Servicemen in Asian countries, to which she contributed more than $7,000,000.00 from her earnings.

In 1972, aged 80, Pearl Buck was admitted several times to a Burlington, Vermont, hospital, where she was treated for removal of her gallbladder, for pleurisy, and for abdominal discomfort. She died on March 6, 1973 in her Danby, Vermont, home.

A private funeral service was held around her plain mahogany coffin in the library of her Perkasie, Pennsylvania, farm, which she had bought in the 1940s. There was no religious service, and no clergyman was present at the ceremony, which was attended by her nine adopted children. She was buried under an ash tree on her farm, a burial site that she had chosen for herself. An afternoon memorial service was held on March 9 at the Pearl S. Buck Foundation in Philadelphia, Pennsylvania. The Pearl Buck Home, Hilltown, Dublin Pike, Perkasie, Pennsylvania 18944.

# *Bunker, Chang and Eng*

Chang and Eng Bunker, the original Siamese twins, were born on May 11, 1811, on a houseboat on the Mekong River, in Siam (now Thailand).

They were joined by a fleshy extension that stretched from breastbone to navel, and that resembled an arm. While on tour in England, Scotland, and Ireland in 1830, they were viewed by more than 300,000 persons, including royalty from France and Germany. They began their American tour in New York City on March 15, 1831. During the next eight years they toured 14 of the 20 states, as well as Canada and Cuba. It has been said that they were discovered by the showman P.T. Barnum (*q.v.*), but in actuality he managed them for only two brief periods. The twins and Barnum had a bitter dislike for each other.

The twins moved to North Carolina and were married to the sisters Adelaide and Sallie Yates in Wilkes County on April 13, 1843. During most of their lives, the twins lived as close to normal as possible, being able to swim, ride horses, and even engage in fistfights. Their personalities were distinctly different, and before the marriage they sought a medical means of separation. They were told, however, that surely one or even both of them would die from such surgery; they therefore adapted as well as they could. They became land-owners, each having a farm one mile from the other in Wilkes County. They alternated between each farm, spending three days in one house and three in the other. They had agreed never to break the arrangement, and held to it despite sickness, holidays, and family deaths. Eng and Sallie had 11 children, while Chang and Adelaide had 10.

In August 1870, Chang suffered a stroke which paralyzed his right side. After the stroke, the twins concluded an agreement that, should one of them die, their doctor would cut the tie, so that the other would have a chance to live. In January 1874, Chang had chest pains and found it difficult to breathe. He coughed up a frothy foam and was diagnosed as having bronchitis, although Eng felt in good health. On January 15, they were to move to Eng's house for three days. Although Eng tried to coax his brother into breaking their agreement this one time, Chang insisted on holding to it. The cold evening ride in the open carriage worsened Chang's condition, and he found it harder to breathe. He slept fitfully and forced his brother out of bed several times in the night, as he could not breathe in a reclining position.

At 4:00 a.m. on January 17, one of Eng's sons checked on his father and uncle. He found Chang dead. The light awakened Eng, and he asked about his brother. Learning that his brother had died, he began to have seizures, and broke out in a sweat. A doctor was summoned so that they could be separated. Eng sat up and said that he was choking. He then pulled his dead brother close to him and said: "May the Lord have mercy upon my soul." He sank into a coma and died two hours later, only minutes before the doctor arrived with surgical instruments to separate them.

During their lives together, the twins had strongly believed that should one of them die, the other would die too. It was felt by their families and their doctor that Eng had died as a result of being frightened by the death of his brother.

Since no means of embalming the bodies was available, they were hermetically sealed in a walnut casket which was then placed in a tin coffin which was enclosed in a wooden box and buried under two feet of powdered charcoal in Eng's basement. The bodies were guarded around the clock as it was thought that they might be stolen and exhibited.

On January 31, a team of doctors from the Mütter Museum of the College of Physicians in Philadelphia arrived at Eng's house to perform an autopsy. The bodies were exhumed and, owing to the sealed coffin and the coldness of the cellar, there was no putrefaction or disagreeable odor. The doctors disrobed the bodies, took pictures, and made a plaster cast. The bodies were then shipped to Philadelphia for a complete post-mortem. The Mütter Museum still has the joined livers, preserved in formalin.

The bodies were then returned to North Carolina in March, and were again interred in Eng's basement, where they were again guarded against theft night and day, for a year. They were then buried in Chang's front yard. In May 1917, the twins' bodies were moved to the churchyard of the White Plains Baptist Church, White Plains, North Carolina 27031.

# *Burbank, Luther*

Luther Burbank, the horticulturalist, was born on March 7, 1849, in Lancaster, Massachusetts. After developing the Burbank potato, he moved to Santa Rosa, California. There he established nurseries and orchards that occupied him for the rest of his life. He developed at least 90 varieties of vegetables, and more than 100 new varieties of plums and prunes. He is most widely remembered for his development of the Shasta daisy.

On March 7, 1926, a birthday party was held for him in Santa Rosa. He was aged 77, and appeared in the best of health. On March 25 he had a slight heart attack, but doctors said that similar previous attacks had been brought on by "overdoing things." In late March he was confined to a bed with a nervous condition which was aggravated by the public outcry when he made a statement that he did not believe in the hereafter. He told his doctor about the beneficial psychological effect of a clean shave, and was allowed to shave, although he had to be helped to do so by two nurses.

In the first week of April, his doctor began issuing daily statements about his health. On April 7, however, his condition was described as "somewhat grave." It was also said that he was unable to assimilate satisfactory nourishment, due to exhaustion of the nervous system. On April 9 his condition was described as critical, and his sister was called to his bedside.

He died on April 11, at 12:13 a.m., in the presence of his wife and sister. He lapsed into a semi-conscious state just before his death, and his last words were: "Oh doctor, I am very sick." It had been raining most of the evening before his death, and many townspeople reported that the rain stopped at the moment of his death.

The funeral was held on April 14, and there was also a public memorial service in Santa Rosa's Doyle Park, at 4:00 p.m., at which the eulogy by Robert Ingersoll (q.v.) on the death of his brother was read.

Burbank was buried in the garden of his home, under a cedar that he had planted from a seed, and that he had used as a shade-tree for many years. Buried with him was a picture of his mother, a porcelain dog that he had liked, two drawings of his niece, and a wooden whistle he had used to call his dog. 2050 Yulupa Avenue, Santa Rosa, California 95401.

# *Burr, Aaron*

Aaron Burr, born on February 6, 1756 in Newark, New Jersey, was the third vice-president of the United States (1801-1805). After a long and tumultuous rivalry with Alexander Hamilton (q.v.), the two men fought a duel in Weehawken, New Jersey, on July 11, 1804. Hamilton was killed, and warrants were issued for Burr's arrest. He fled south, and became involved in treasonable schemes to form an independent empire, formed from territories taken from the United States and Mexico. He was tried for treason in Richmond, Virginia, in 1807, but was acquitted, as he had not committed any overt act. He then traveled to Europe, where he tried to interest Napoleon in a scheme to conquer Florida. Returning to New York in 1812, he practiced law for the remainder of his life, attracting little public notice.

In 1830 he suffered a stroke which left him paralyzed on the right side. After therapy, he recovered enough to regain the use of his limbs. In 1834 he suffered another stroke from which he never recovered. As his health declined, he was cared for by a Mrs. Joshua Webb, who kept a boardinghouse at Broadway, near Bowling Green. When her house was sold in June 1836, he was taken to live with a cousin at Winants Hotel, Port Richmond, Staten Island, New York. Throughout the summer his condition worsened, although he appeared to retain control of his faculties. On September 14 he was asked if he thought that God would see fit to pardon him of his sin. He replied: "On that subject I am coy." A few minutes before his death he reached towards his glasses and said: "Madam"—probably meaning that they were to be given to his companion of his last few years. He died the same day at 2:00 p.m., without a struggle.

Newspapers circulated false accounts of his last moments. In one such story, his doctor supposedly told him that he had no longer than 24 hours to live, and Burr was said to have exclaimed: "Doctor, I can't die, I shan't die. My father and mother, my grandparents, and uncles and aunts, were all pious and godly people; they prayed for my conversion a thousand times, and if God be a hearer of prayer, he is not going to let me die until their prayers are answered. It is impossible that a child of so many prayers will be lost."

A brief funeral service was conducted in the parlor of Winants Hotel, attended by family and friends. Shortly before his death he had requested to be buried at

Princeton, New Jersey, as close to his father and grandfather as possible. Burr's body was sent to Amboy, New Jersey, by boat, and was then taken by train to Heightstown, after which an assembly of people conducted it to Princeton. Burr's body lay in state in the college chapel. Here, at 3:30 p.m. on September 16, the students and faculty, family, and friends gathered to pay honor to him. Dr. James Carnahan, president of the college, delivered a funeral oration, based on First Corinthians, VII:31: "The fashion of this world passeth away."

*Aaron Burr's headstone,*
*Princeton,*
*New Jersey.*

Photo: Princeton Alumni Weekly

Martial music was played, and volleys fired over his grave in the Princeton churchyard. The grave remained without a tombstone for some 20 years, until a relative, Alfred Edwards, had one erected. Besides giving vital statistics, the legend on the stone says: "A colonel in the Army of the Revolution, vice-president of the United States from 1801 to 1805." Princeton Cemetery, Witherspoon Street, Princeton, New Jersey 08540.

# *Byrd, Richard Evelyn*

Richard Evelyn Byrd—renowned as Admiral Byrd, the Polar explorer and navigator—was born on October 25, 1888 in Winchester, Virginia. He became famous when he claimed to have made the first flight over the North Pole on May 9, 1926.

From 1928-57, he made five expeditions to the Antarctic. On his third expedition, from 1939-41, he discovered the southern limit of the Pacific Ocean. From 1946-48 he commanded the United States Navy's Operation High Jump, a project to map large areas of Antarctica. Byrd's last expedition was Operation Deep Freeze—a part of the United States' participation in the International Geophysical Year, 1957-58. After participating in the first phase, he returned to his Boston home.

It was believed that he had been in ill health since an expedition in 1933, in which he was incapacitated by gas fumes leaking from his stove, in a hut located 125 miles south of Little America, Antarctica. In the early part of 1957, rumors circulated that he was hospitalized for a serious heart ailment. Trying to dispel them, he said: "I have been overworked for a long time and finally I have had to take a rest."

He died in his sleep at his Boston home on March 11, 1957. At his bedside when he died were his wife and four children. He had been under the care of Dr. Paul Dudley White, a cardiologist who had attended President Dwight D. Eisenhower.

His funeral service was held at the Fort Myers Chapel in Arlington, Virginia. Captain John D. Zimmerman a Navy chaplain, said at the service that death for Byrd was "only a horizon." The coffin was carried from the chapel to the grave on a horse-drawn, flag-draped caisson. The Navy band served as part of an honor guard along the half-mile wooded path from the chapel to the grave. The day was cloudless and clear; a 13-gun salute was given as the cortege neared the gravesite. A bugler's taps could be heard in the distance as the cortege approached his grave, which is on a slope facing the Potomac River.

Eighteen Americans, on an expedition to the South Pole, kept the flag flying at half-mast for longer than the usual mourning period. It flew until March 20, 1957, when the six-month winter night began at the South Pole. Arlington National Cemetery, Fort Myers, Arlington, Virginia 22211.

# *Calamity Jane*

"Calamity Jane" was born Martha Jane Canary, on May 1, 1852 in Princeton, Missouri. She was also known as Martha Burke. When she was in her early teens, she accompanied her parents on a trip to the West, but both parents died en route. Left without resources, she became a prostitute. Known to dress in men's clothing, often carrying a gun, and with a masculine appearance, she also drank and swore like a man. While in Deadwood, South Dakota, (the region with which she was especially associated), during the smallpox epidemic of 1878, she worked day and night to nurse men back to health, using drugs she had bought with her own funds. As a result, she became a legend, first in Deadwood, and then in the nation. Stories, dime-store novels, and Hollywood scriptwriters have contributed to the myth that she was an Indian fighter, scout, and prospector. There is no evidence to support the belief that, whether dressed as a man or a woman, she ever served in the United States Army.

After the death of Wild Bill Hickock, the famous scout and lawman, in a shooting affray, in 1876, she adopted Wild Bill as her "departed sweetheart," and "mourned" openly for him, although it is doubtful that the relationship between them was ever anything more than casual. Dressed in fancy Western-style clothes, she toured museums, honkytonks, and bars in some of the Western states until the early 1900s.

*Calamity Jane's gravestone, Deadwood, South Dakota.*

Photo: Deadwood Schools, Lead, South Dakota

On July 31, 1903 she appeared at the Calloway Hotel in Terry, South Dakota, very sick and almost blind. The owner—a friend of hers—gave her a room and called a doctor. Her condition steadily worsened. On August 2, she said: "It is the twenty-seventh anniversary of Bill's death. Bury me next to Bill." She died a few hours later, at 5:00 p.m.

Her funeral, on August 4, was one of the largest Deadwood had ever known. The local undertaker, who had been one of the young boys she had helped in the epidemic of 1878, donated the plain white coffin. Funeral services, attended by almost the entire town, were held at the First Methodist Church in Deadwood. She was buried next to Wild Bill Hickock in Mt. Moriah Cemetery, Deadwood, South Dakota 57732.

# Cantor, Eddie

Eddie Cantor, the American entertainer, was born Edward Israel Iskowitz on January 31, 1882, in New York City. Orphaned at an early age, he rarely attended school, preferring to perform on street corners. After breaking into vaudeville, he toured in *Kid Kabaret* with the entertainer George Jessel. He also appeared for several years in *Ziegfeld's Follies* in New York. He had a string of Broadway hits, and appeared in several films, including *If You Knew Susie*, which was the title of his

*Resting place of Eddie Cantor's ashes.*

Photo: Mary Ellen Hunt

theme song. He was well-known for his generosity in contributing his talent to fund-raising benefits. He wrote several works, including an autobiography. Florenz Ziegfeld *(q.v.)* once said that he paid Cantor the highest salary of any comedian "in the history of the world."

He retired in 1953, but his energetic activities worsened a heart condition from which he suffered. He died at the age of 72 on October 10, 1964 in Hollywood, California. A private funeral was held, and the family did not make public the time or place of the service. His remains were entombed at Hillside Memorial Park, 6001 Centinela Avenue, Los Angeles, California 90045.

# *Capone, Al*

Alphonse ("Al") Capone was born on January 17, 1899 in Naples, Italy. His family moved to New York, where he roamed the streets after quitting school in the fourth grade. He subseqently moved to Chicago, where he worked as a professional killer for organized crime. At the same time he organized vice and bootlegging operations in that city. He expanded his bootlegging operations and had agents for his illegal liquor importing trade in California, Florida, the Bahamas, and along the entire Canadian border. In 1929 he staged one of the most famous violent crimes in American history—the machine-gunning to death of members of a rival gang in a Chicago garage. This event became known as the St. Valentine's Day Massacre. During most of his activities he managed to stay clear of the law, but was convicted of income-tax evasion in 1930. He entered the Atlanta penitentiary on May 5, 1932, and in August 1934 was taken to Alcatraz penitentiary in California. In 1939 he was released from prison, and was admitted to the Union Hospital in Baltimore for treatment of paresis, an advanced form of syphilis. He later settled in Miami Beach, Florida.

He suffered a stroke in Miami on January 21, 1947. He was expected to die, and the last rites of the Catholic Church were administered. A dozen or more large and expensive cars assembled outside his villa after this had been announced. His doctor said that he tried to talk, but he was silenced and made to relax. In the days following this stroke, he showed improvement. On January 23, the doctor said that he was out of danger, and that the family could leave if they wanted. On January 24, however, a statement was issued which indicated that recovery was doubtful, due to pneumonia and other complications.

He died very suddenly on January 25, in his Miami Beach home. His entire family was present. His wife, Mae, collapsed, and was said to be in serious condition. On January 26 his lawyer said that Capone had died broke, that his home was heavily mortgaged, and that he had left neither a will nor money. His doctor asked that a post-mortem be performed on the body—especially on the brain for the benefit of science—but the family objected.

His body lay in state in a Miami funeral home until January 30, when his brother Ralph Capone appeared unexpectedly at 3:00 p.m. and said that the family had decided to remove the body. It was then placed in a plain casket and driven away. It was taken to Chicago, with Capone's brother Ralph and an unidentified man taking turns at the driving wheel. The funeral was private, the coffin was sealed, and there were no flowers. Only members of the immediate family were in attendance. Burial was carried out secretly on February 4, in Mt. Olivet Cemetery. A requiem mass was not allowed, but he was buried in the family plot in consecrated ground. The family priest conducted the simple service. In 1952 he was re-buried in Chicago's Mt. Carmel Cemetery. The epitaph on his first grave read: "Qui Reposa," while that on the second reads: "My Jesus Mercy."

Mt. Carmel Cemetery, 1400 South Wolf Road, Hillside, Illinois 60162.

# *Carnegie, Andrew*

Andrew Carnegie, the steel industrialist and philanthropist, was born on November 25, 1835, in Dunfermline, Scotland. In 1848 he emigrated with his family to the United States, and settled in what is now Pittsburgh, Pennsylvania. He started the Keystone Bridge Company and other enterprises which were, in 1901, incorporated as the United States Steel Corporation. He spent most of his later years engaged in philanthropic pursuits, donating to libraries and founding institutions in the United States, the United Kingdom, and other English-speaking countries. In his famous essay, "The Gospel of Wealth," he said that a rich man should, after acquiring his wealth, distribute the surplus for the general welfare.

In 1917 he had an attack of pneumonia, from which he recovered, although he had been on the verge of death. On August 8, 1919 he enjoyed his good health during most of the day, but that evening complained of difficulty in breathing. On August 9 he was able to walk around his Lenox, Massachusetts, home, but felt weak and lethargic. The doctor found him to have a high temperature and pneumonia. His condition rapidly worsened, and he died at his home at 7:10 p.m. on August 11.

In Pittsburgh, Mayor E.V. Babcock ordered all flags in the city lowered to half-mast. The Carnegie Institute was covered with black crepe. After his death, some of his friends and business associates proposed that a public funeral be held in New York City so that his many friends could attend. This idea was, however, rejected by his wife, in keeping with Carnegie's wish to have a simple funeral.

He was placed in a mahogany coffin with gun-metal handles and trimming. A plate of solid silver on the coffin gave his vital statistics. He had been an avid gardener, and his coffin was surrounded by flowers from his own garden. During the day of August 13, the grounds of his Shadowbrook estate, at Lenox, were guarded, and only those bearing a visitor's pass were allowed entry.

On the morning of the funeral, the mansion was only half revealed because of the thick fog. Rain dripped from the English ivy that covered the stone walls. A Presbyterian minister conducted the 25-minute service, which included the reading of the 23rd Psalm, and the singing of Tennyson's poem, "Crossing the Bar." After the service the body was placed on a hearse for the trip to the railroad station. As the party left the mansion, all the servants stood outside in tribute to their late employer.

The body was interred at 5:00 p.m. on August 14 at Sleepy Hollow Cemetery, Tarrytown, New York. The cemetery was closed to the public, and detectives from a private New York City agency were stationed at various points to keep away the curious. It was reported, however, that two women and three girls scaled a monument, and were present at the committal.

The Carnegie plot at Sleepy Hollow Cemetery overlooks the Hudson River. The Pocantico River flows along the east side of the plot, which is adorned with pine trees and shrubbery. The crypt is of reinforced concrete and hollow tiles, built at a cost of $40,000.00. The Carnegie plot is only 900 feet from the spot where the body of Washington Irving *(q.v.)* lies buried. Sleepy Hollow Cemetery, 540 North Broadway, Tarrytown, New York 10591.

# *Carson, Kit*

Christopher "Kit" Carson was a trapper, Indian agent, soldier, and legendary folk hero. He was born on December 24, 1809, in Madison County, Kentucky, and spent most of his early life on the Missouri frontier.

In 1825 he ran away from home to join an expedition to Santa Fe. On the trail he learned hunting and trapping skills, later establishing his base at Taos, New Mexico. He was a guide in the expeditions to the West of John Frémont *(q.v.)* in 1842 and 1843-44. His loyalty, bravery, and devotion to the settling of the West gained him many political allies. Although he was a known Indian fighter, his knowledge of Indians won him the job of Indian agent at Taos in 1854. In January 1868 he was appointed Superintendent of Indian Affairs for the Colorado Territory.

He had suffered from failing health for some time, but in February 1868 agreed to go to Washington, D.C., to negotiate a treaty settlement with the Ute Indians. He consulted medical specialists in New York, Philadelphia, and Boston, but was given no hope of recovery from what appeared to be a heart ailment. In April, he consulted the assistant surgeon at Fort Lyon, Colorado. He tired easily, had a constant cough, and complained of breathing difficulties, especially when lying down. His pain was caused by an aneurysm which pressed on the pneumogastric nerve, and caused bronchial spasms. In the last letter he dictated, on May 5, to a friend, Aloys Scheurich, he said: "I have given the necessary orders to have my own body, if I should die, and that of my wife's sent together to Taos, to be buried in the church."

As his condition worsened, he was moved to Fort Lyon, where he could be under constant medical attention. His bed consisted of a blanket on the doctor's floor. He was not allowed to smoke, and since it was thought that solid foods would worsen his condition, his only nourishment was liquid. He told his doctor several times: "If it was not for this," (pointing to his chest), "I might live to be a hundred years old." He was given chloroform to lessen the pain. During the night of May 22 he coughed up some blood which seemed to indicate that the end was near.

On May 23 he requested a meal of solid foods, and was given buffalo steak and coffee. He then asked for his clay pipe. As he sat smoking and talking to his friend Aloys, he called out: "Doctor, Compadre, Adíos." The doctor rushed to him and found blood pouring out of his mouth. "I supported his forehead on my hand," he said, "while death speedily closed the scene...Death took place at 4:25 p.m., May 23, 1868."

The flag was lowered to half-mast at Fort Lyon. His body was put in a homemade coffin lined with the wedding dress of a captain's wife. Paper flowers from the hats of women at the post were the only floral arrangements. After the funeral, the body was sent to Taos. His grave was largely neglected until 1908, when the Taos Masons erected a tombstone. The cemetery is now surrounded by the Kit Carson Memorial Park, Dragoon and Kit Carson Avenue, Taos, New Mexico 87571.

# Carver, George Washington

George Washington Carver, the black American agricultural chemist, was born of slave parents near Diamond Grove, Missouri, around 1864. He worked his way through high school in Minneapolis, and received bachelor's and master's degrees from the Iowa State College of Agriculture and Mechanic Arts. He was appointed director of agricultural research at Tuskegee Institute, Alabama, by Booker T. Washington (q.v.), the black American educator and spokesman who founded Tuskegee. Carver devoted the rest of his life to agricultural research, being principally concerned with the development of useful by-products from sweet potatoes, soybeans, and peanuts. At a time when the South's economy was suffering from the effects of the destruction of cotton crops by boll-weevils, he was instrumental in convincing farmers to grow other crops. Among the many honors he received were his election as a Fellow of the Royal Society, in London, and the award of the Spingarn Medal.

In December 1942, having been in failing health for some months, he was confined to bed for the last ten days of his life. His breathing became difficult, and he lost his appetite. He was alert during his final days and hours. At 5:00 p.m. on January 5, 1943, he was brought his dinner, but drank only a few sips of milk. He whispered to his servant: "I think I'll sleep now," closed his eyes, and rested. Sometime during the next two hours he died without pain or struggle.

His body lay in state for three days in the Institute's chapel. A white camellia adorned his lapel. Long lines of people from all walks of life filed past his coffin. Funeral services were held at 2:30 p.m. on January 8, in the chapel. Burial was in the cemetery adjoining the chapel, near the grave of his friend Booker T. Washington. His epitaph is: "He could have added fortune to fame, but caring for neither, he found happiness and honor in being helpful to the world." Tuskegee Institute, Tuskegee, Alabama 36083.

# Casals, Pablo

Pablo Carlos Salvador Casals y Defillo, the celebrated cellist and conductor, known for his interpretations of the works of Johann Sebastian Bach, was born on December 29, 1876 in Vendrell, Spain.

He made his debut as a cello soloist in Paris and London in 1898. In 1919 he founded the Pau Casals orchestra, in Barcelona, Spain, to introduce classical music to the working classes. As a protest against the government of Francisco Franco, he refused to return to Spain after the Spanish Civil War (1936-39), settling at Prades in the French Pyrenees, where he held an annual music festival. In 1956 he moved to Puerto Rico, where again he organized an annual music festival. Casals was considered perhaps the greatest cellist who ever lived. In his long career, he played for Queen Victoria at a private recital, and, in the 1960s, for President John F. Kennedy *(q.v.)* in the White House. His friends included kings, queens, philosophers, composers, and musicians.

Towards the end of his life he suffered from heart disease, chronic bronchitis, a kidney shutdown, high fever, and bad circulation. He had a heart attack in early October 1973. On October 16 he lost consciousness. A respiratory machine kept him alive during his final hours. He died of lung complications at 2:05 p.m. on October 22, at Auxilio Mutuo Hospital in Río Piedras, Puerto Rico. His death was officially announced by Elias Lopez Saba, director of the Casals Festival Corporation. Just 35 minutes after his death, his body was taken to a Río Piedras suburban funeral home, where sculptor José Buscaglia made a mask of his face for posterity.

His body lay in state in the rotunda of the Commonwealth legislature. Thousands of Puerto Ricans from all walks of life passed the coffin. Governor Rafael Hernandez Colón decreed three days of mourning and eulogized the musician, thanking him for the contributions he had made to the music of Puerto Rico. The four elected governors of Puerto Rico stood alongside the coffin, which was draped with the Puerto Rican and Catalonian flags. It was the first time all four elected governors had met together publicly.

The state funeral ceremony included a performance of Beethoven's Funeral March movement from the Third Symphony. The Puerto Rican Symphony Orchestra presented two sections of Casal's oratorio *El Pesebre* "The Manger." The Puerto Rican Conservatory of Music chorus sang "The Gloria" and "The Child Jesus Imploration." A requiem mass was celebrated at La Piedad Church during which a recording of Casals' "Song of the Birds," a Catalonian tune, was played.

He was buried near a beach he often visited, in the Cemetery, Río Piedras, Puerto Rico 00928.

# *Cass, Lewis*

Lewis Cass, the first governor of Michigan, who played a prominent role in national and international politics in his day, was born on October 9, 1872 in Exeter, New Hampshire.

He studied law in Marietta, Ohio, and in 1806 became the youngest member of the Ohio legislature. During the War of 1812 he rose to the rank of brigadier general. Because of his valuable service he was made governor of Michigan Territory in 1813. For the next 18 years he oversaw the development of the region, and was widely acclaimed for establishing good relations with the Indians. He was appointed secretary of war in 1831. As U.S. Minister to France (1837-43) he played a major role in perpetuating the transatlantic slave trade by repeatedly thwarting its suppression by the British Royal Navy. Cass represented Michigan in the U.S. Senate from 1845 to 1848, and served as secretary of state under President James Buchanan *(q.v.)* from 1857 to 1860. In 1860 he retired to his home in Detroit, and published studies based on his knowledge of Indian affairs.

He had been quite weak and feeble during the spring of 1866, and on June 16 began to sink rapidly. His family was called to his bedside for what they realized would be their last visit to him. Shortly after 4:00 a.m. on June 17, he grew perceptibly weaker. He rallied once, then, recognizing those around him, asked not to be bothered. He died half an hour later.

His body lay in state in his Detroit home, and the public filed past. The federal and state courts adjourned, and many businesses closed. His funeral service was at 2:00 p.m. on June 20 at the Presbyterian Church on Detroit's State Street. His body was then taken to Elmwood Cemetery in a procession headed by the 17th United States Infantry, and part of the 4th Artillery. At the cemetery, members of the Zion lodge performed the last Masonic rites for a departed brother. A squad of regulars then stepped forward and fired three volleys over his coffin as it was lowered.

Elmwood Cemetery, 1200 Elmwood Avenue, Detroit, Michigan 48207.

# Cerf, Bennett

Bennett Alfred Cerf, publisher, editor, author, and television personality, was born in New York City on May 25, 1898. In 1927 he was a co-founder of Random House, the publishing enterprise. From 1952 to 1968 he was a panelist on the television program *What's My Line?*

He retired in 1970, and in December 1971 underwent major abdominal surgery. He again underwent surgery shortly before his death. He died late in the evening of August 27, 1971 at his Mount Kisco, New York, estate. The cause of death was said to be a heart attack.

The funeral service was first scheduled to take place at Frank E. Campbell's Funeral Home, on Madison Avenue and 81st Street in New York City, but was in fact held at St. Paul's Chapel at Columbia University, on August 31. Random House was closed on that day, in his memory.

Cerf's funeral was attended by distinguished authors, publishers, entertainers, and politicians. His widow and two sons sat in the front pew of the chapel, and wept quietly as John Daly, host of *What's My Line?*, said that Cerf's last 30 years had revolved around "his bride and their family." Daly then read eulogies from publishers, authors, and friends, many of whom attended the service. One such tribute, from James Michener, the author, read: "When the echo of the laughter is forgotten, that excellent row of books will be remembered." Among those present at the service were Frank Sinatra, Danny Kaye, Ali McGraw, Ginger Rogers, Truman Capote, Philip Roth, Ted Geisel (Dr. Seuss), and Rod McKuen. Although it was summer recess at Columbia University, crowds of students waited outside the chapel to catch a glimpse of the personalities inside. The service opened with a medley of Cerf's favorite songs, played by Joe Paposo, a composer for the television show *Sesame Street*, and ended with Phyllis Newman singing "They Can't Take That Away From Me." Following the funeral he was cremated. His ashes were later scattered at his Mount Kisco, New York, home.

# *Chaffee, Roger B.*

Lieutenant Roger Bruce Chaffee, the astronaut, was born on February 15, 1935 in Grand Rapids, Michigan. He logged more than 2,300 hours of flying time, first with the U.S. Air Force, and then with the Air Force Institute of Technology at Wright Patterson Air Force Base in Ohio, before being chosen as one of the third group of astronauts, in October 1963.

On January 27, 1967, three astronauts, including Chaffee, were taking part in a full-scale simulation of the Apollo I launch, scheduled for February 21. At 6:31 p.m. a flash fire ignited by a spark tore through the cabin, which was filled with pure oxygen. No word was picked up by monitors during the fire, and emergency crews were blocked from entering by the thick black smoke coming from the cockpit. The three astronauts were killed instantaneously.

Shortly before the accident, Chaffee was asked if there was anything scary about a first space flight, and answered that there were a lot of "unknowns" and problems. "This is our business, to find out if this thing will work for us. I don't see how you could help but be a little bit excited. I don't like to use the word 'scary.' " On another occasion, he said: "I think we've got an excellent spacecraft. I've lived and slept in it. We know it, we know the spacecraft as well as we know our own homes."

The funeral service was conducted at 5:00 p.m. on January 30 at the Webster Presbyterian Church in Texas. The family requested that instead of flowers, friends and relatives should contribute to the Chaffee Memorial Scholarship Fund at Purdue University, which Roger had attended.

During the service, three astronauts flew white T-38 jets over the church in a traditional diamond-shaped formation with one point missing. Chaffee's body was then flown under miltary escort to Washington, D.C., for burial in Arlington National Cemetery. Fort Myers, Arlington, Virginia 22211.

# *Chrysler, Walter P.*

Walter Percy Chrysler, founder of Chrysler Corporation, the automobile company, was born on April 2, 1875, in Wanego, Kansas. After working as an apprentice in a machine shop, he became plant manager for a locomotive company. He later became first works manager, and then president of Buick Motor Co. He resigned from this last post in 1919 to manage several companies that later merged to become Chrysler Corporation. In 1928 he introduced the Plymouth automobile that became a competitor with the products of the Ford and Chevrolet motor companies.

By 1940, Chrysler had suffered for two years from a circulatory ailment. On August 17, 1940, he had a cerebral hemmorhage, remaining unconscious until his death, late in the afternoon of August 18. His four children and his sister were at his bedside at that time, at his King's Point, Great Neck, Long Island estate in New York.

On August 21, an early morning private service for the family was held at his estate, at which the rector of All Saints Episcopal Church in Great Neck officiated.

At 11:00 a.m. the same day a funeral service was held at St. Bartholomew's Protestant Episcopal Church, at Park Avenue and 51st Street in New York City. The bronze coffin was covered with Easter lilies and smilax, and there were hundreds of floral tributes lining the walls of the church, which was filled to capacity. Hundreds of persons waited behind police barricades on both sides of Park Avenue, as well as on the side streets in the vicinity. Scriptural texts included the 23rd Psalm, and the 14th chapter of John. The honorary pallbearers included many of Chrysler's business associates.

Later, a group of about 75 family members and friends attended the private committal in North Tarrytown, New York, where the coffin was placed in a large granite mausoleum, built about two years earlier.

Sleepy Hollow Cemetery, 540 N. Broadway, North Tarrytown, New York 10591.

# Clark, William

William Clark, the soldier and explorer, who shared leadership of the Lewis and Clark expedition to the Pacific Northwest (1804-06), was born in Caroline County, Virginia on August 1, 1770. In 1792 he was commissioned as a lieutenant in the U.S. Army, serving for four years under the command of "Mad" Anthony Wayne (q.v.). In 1776 he resigned from the army to spend time traveling and tending his estate in Louisville, Kentucky.

In 1803 Captain Meriwether Lewis invited him to share command of a government-sponsored expedition to find a land route to the Pacific Coast. On his return he began to collect the records, maps, and journals of the expedition, which paved the way for publication of the journals in 1814. He was appointed superintendent of Indian affairs, he also showed a personal concern with justice towards Indians, as well as for their well-being.

Clark died on September 1, 1838 after an eight-day illness. He was aged 69. Death occurred at the home of his son, Meriwether Lewis Clark, in St. Louis. A funeral service with Masonic rites was held on September 3 at the farm of his nephew, Colonel John O'Fallon, on the outskirts of St. Louis. His gravesite is today a part of Bellefontaine Cemetery, 4947 West Florissant Avenue, St. Louis, Missouri 63136.

# Cleveland, Stephen Grover

Stephen Grover Cleveland, president of the United States from 1885-89 and from 1893-97, was born on March 18, 1837 in Caldwell, New Jersey. A Democratic candidate, he also served terms as mayor of Buffalo, New York (1881-82), and as governor of New York (1883-84).

In April, May, and June, 1908, rumors persisted concerning his ill health, although these were denied by his family. He died suddenly, at 8:30 a.m. on June 24, in the presence of his wife and three doctors. Death was said to be caused by "failure of heart action and edema." In the 24 hours before his death, he had drifted in and out of consciousness, often talking incoherently. As soon as the "undertaker's wagon" arrived at his house, flags all over Princeton were lowered to half-mast. A typewritten notice by the family said that the funeral would be "strictly private."

The body was placed in a plain quartered-oak coffin with silver handles. A silver name plate bore the inscription: "Grover Cleveland, March 18, 1837-June 24, 1908." Edwin Wilson, a Princeton University sculptor, took a death mask. On the arrival of President Theodore Roosevelt (q.v.) at Cleveland's home, at 5:00 p.m. on June 26, the burial service of the Presbyterian Church was read. There were no hymns or eulogies. The president and a few close friends accompanied the family to the Princeton Cemetery, where a simple prayer was offered. The National Guard kept the crowd at a distance from the funeral cortege.

Princeton Cemetery, Witherspoon Street, Princeton, New Jersey 08540.

# Cobb, Ty

Tyrus Raymond Cobb, known as "Ty," who was perhaps the greatest offensive baseball player in the history of the game, was born in Narrow Banks County, Georgia, on December 18, 1886. He was nicknamed "The Georgia Peach." In the course of his career he amassed 58 offensive records, including total bases stolen (829). He was one of baseball's most feared players, being known for his daring and short temper. After retiring he lived in Atlanta, Georgia, until his death.

Between 1960 and 1961, he showed up frequently at the Emory Hospital in Atlanta. His doctors would keep him in the hospital for a few weeks, but he would often dress himself and leave without notice. On May 15, 1961, when he was 74, he was admitted to be treated for arthritis and diabetes. After undressing, he placed a million dollars in negotiable bonds on his bedside table. He then placed a pistol on top of them. His doctor told him: "Ty, these things might be knocked on the floor. I'll just put them in the hospital safe." Trying to hold on to consciousness, the sick man said: "All right, Maybe that would be best."

His condition seemed to improve on July 15, but he again lapsed into unconsciousness, and his son, two daughters, and first wife came to his bedside. He died on July 17, in a coma-like sleep, without a struggle. The doctors then revealed that he had had cancer of the prostate gland and chronic heart disease, as well as other health problems.

Mickey Mantle, the baseball star, said: "He used to come see me in the dugout when he visited New York and give me some batting tips. He would say 'Come here kid, let me show you what you're doing wrong.'"

His funeral was held at the funeral home chapel in Cornelia, Georgia, on July 19. The services were extremely simple, and were attended by only 150 persons. Only three persons from the world of baseball—Ray Shalk, Mickey Cochrane, and Sid Keener—attended—although condolences were received from scores of others. During the service, his body lay in a bronze glass-topped casket. After, the cortege drove 28 miles to the Cobb family's white marble mausoleum in Royston, Georgia, which Cobb himself had had built several years earlier. En route to the cemetery, the cortege passed a road sign which proclaimed the town of Cornelia to be Cobb's home. About 200 uniformed Little League players lined the entrance to the cemetery as the cortege arrived. Burial was in a mausoleum at Royston Cemetery, Royston, Georgia 30662.

# Cody, "Buffalo Bill"

William Frederick Cody, better known as "Buffalo Bill" Cody, was born on February 26, 1846 in Scott County, Iowa. A buffalo hunter, horse wrangler, plainsman, and Indian fighter, he became a legendary figure. In 1867-68, he hunted buffalo to feed construction crews of the Union Pacific Railroad. During an eight-month period, he killed 4,280 buffalo. He participated in at least 16 Indian fights. In one of these, on July 17, 1876, the Cheyenne warrior Yellow Hair was scalped. As the subject of dime-store novels, he was transformed into an American folk hero. In 1883 he organized his Wild West Exhibition—a touring show which also starred Annie Oakley *(q.v.)* and Chief Sitting Bull. Although his show was popular, he lost his fortune due to mismanagement. His last public appearance was on November 11, 1916, in Portsmouth, Virginia.

On January 3, 1917, accompanied by his sister, he went to the mineral baths at Glenwood Springs, Colorado. On January 7, his doctor announced that his condition was serious, and his wife and daughter were summoned from Cody, Wyoming. On January 8, he played cards with his family, and discussed the future of his Wild West show. He then asked his doctor what were his chances for recovery, and was told that he had at most 36 hours to live. He reportedly took the news stoically. On January 9 he showed so much more vitality that his doctor and nurses expressed amazement, but his heart action was said to be very weak. On that day he was baptized a Roman Catholic. He had had no previous religious affiliation, but was said to be "very devout."

*The bugler at Buffalo Bill's funeral.*

(Colorado Historical Society)

He died of uremic poisoning at 12:05 p.m. on January 10. President Woodrow Wilson *(q.v.)* immediately accepted the vice-presidency of the Buffalo Bill Memorial Association.

His body lay in state in the rotunda of the Colorado State Capitol building in Denver, dressed in a frock coat on which were pinned the badges of the Legion of Honor and of the Grand Army of the Republic. A master of ceremonies, wearing a high silk hat and carrying a cane, implored mourners: "Step lively please, a big crowd's behind, hurry up folks," thus regulating the stream of persons passing the bronze coffin. On January 14, between 9:30 a.m. and noon, 25,000 persons passed his body, including the governors of Colorado and Wyoming, and other officials. Hundreds of children were also among the crowd, which stretched for blocks.

*Buffalo Bill's grave on Lookout Mountain.*

(Buffalo Bill Memorial Museum)

The funeral procession was led by delegations of state officials. Regimental bands from Fort Logan, Colorado, preceded the hearse, and Bill's white horse, "McKinley," followed it, with stirrups reversed. Services were held at Denver Lodge No. 17, Benevolent Protective Order of the Elks. A clergyman from St. Barnabas Episcopal Church read the burial service. A quartet sang Cody's favorite song, "Tenting Tonight on the Old Camp-Ground." The coffin was then stored at a local funeral home to await a spring burial.

On June 3, Cody was buried at the top of Lookout Mountain in Denver. The grave was carved out of granite, and the coffin enclosed in steel and cement vaults, so that the body could not be stolen. The Golden City Lodge of the Free and Accepted Masons read the Masonic burial service and Bill's lambskin apron was dropped into the grave. The chief musician of the Ohio Infantry in the Spanish American War played taps as the American flag was raised. The ceremony ended with an eleven-gun salute, fired by Colorado Battery B.

Buffalo Bill Grave and Museum, Lookout Mountain Park, Golden, Colorado 80401.

# Coltrane, John

John William Coltrane, an innovative and musically controversial black saxophone player, prominent in the 1950s, was born on September 26, 1926 in Hamlet,

North Carolina. In 1947 he played with the "Cleanhead" Vinson group, and then drifted from band to band developing his own style. After attracting attention while working for Dizzie Gillespie (1949-51), he joined Miles Davis (1955-57), and during this period began to develop his own experimental free-style jazz. He was a soloist on the landmark 1956 Miles Davis recording "Kind of Blue," and in 1965 was voted "Jazzman of the Year" by *Downbeat* magazine.

During early 1967 he began to suffer frequent and sometimes debilitating headaches. He refused at first to see a doctor, and began to take very large doses of aspirin. In May of that year he began to have severe and frequent stomach pains. His wife convinced him to see a gastro-enterologist, but after submitting to a biopsy, he refused further testing. On July 16, he was admitted to Huntington Hospital in New York City as an emergency patient. He died the following morning at 4:00 a.m. from complications of liver cancer.

*Coltrane's grave.*

(Douglas L. Dunn)

His funeral was held on July 21 at St. Peter's Lutheran Church, Lexington Avenue at 54th Street, New York City. The "jazz pastor," the Rev. John García Gensel, officiated. Coltrane's body was clothed in a brown and white dashiki, sewn the night before. The brown symbolized the earth, from which he came and to which he would return, and the white symbolized purity. His casket was covered with yellow roses, white lilies, and other flowers, sent by Duke Ellington (*q.v.*), Stan Getz, Nina Simone, and other musicians. Some 650 people filled the pews of the neo-Gothic church, and a delegation of Germans sat in the front pew. Close associates of his from the world of jazz performed, including members of the Albert Ayler Quartet, who were in the balcony overlooking his casket. The Rev. Gensel read chapters from the book of John, from a gold-edged Bible which had been presented to him by Duke Ellington. Gensel said: "I use this bible whenever I conduct a funeral service for a musician." The Ayler Quartet played "Truth is Marching," although the noise of traffic from outside provided a dissonant background. While Ayler was playing a solo, he stopped twice to scream what was described as a "blood-curdling scream." He later said that each scream represented a shout of joy that Coltrane, although dead, would live forever. The closing music, composed "...especially for the funeral," was played by Ornette Coleman, the saxophonist, and was called "Holiday for a Graveyard." As the coffin was being put inside the hearse, a Japanese journalist, who had arrived late, performed a ceremonial bow, explaining that Coltrane was as popular in Japan as he was in the United States.

He was buried in Pinelawn Memorial Park, Farmingdale, New York 11735.

# *Coolidge, John Calvin*

John Calvin Coolidge, the 30th president of the United States (in office 1923-29), was born on July 4, 1872, in Plymouth, Vermont. After serving in the Massachusetts legislature, he became mayor of Northampton and lieutenant-governor of Massachusetts. He was known for his qualities of modesty and unpretentiousness. Serving as vice-president under President Warren G. Harding *(q.v.)*, he became president when Harding died unexpectedly on August 2, 1923. He won renomination, and then the election, in 1924. He followed a policy of international disengagement, and, at home, promoted the interests of business and industry. On leaving office, he retired to his home, The Beeches, in Northampton. Massachusetts.

After New Year, 1933, he complained of indigestion. A recent physical examination had shown no indication of heart disease. On January 5, around noon, his wife returned home after shopping to find the ex-president lying dead on his back in his dressing room. He had a calm expression on his face, as if he had died without pain. Although the entire nation was stunned by the suddenness of his death, the country-folk of rural Vermont, where he had been raised, showed the most sorrow. President Herbert Hoover *(q.v.)* declared 30 days of official mourning. Flags were flown at half-mast. Many Massachusetts and Vermont schools were closed from January 5 to 7, the day of his funeral. His death certificate was filed on that day, listing the cause of death as coronary thrombosis.

At 8:00 a.m. on the 7th, his body was taken from his home to lie in state at the Edwards Congregational Church. The coffin was surrounded by bouquets of flowers. He was dressed in formal attire, and wore a gold ring inlaid with onyx. National Guardsmen stood on each side of the coffin. At exactly 10:30 a.m., President Hoover arrived, and stood by the coffin for five minutes, seemingly in deep thought, before taking a seat in the second pew. During the service there was no eulogy, but readings from Psalms 46 and 121, Corinthians 5, and John 14. At 11:00, as the benediction ended, the sound of a distant church bell blended with the quartet singing the ex-president's favorite hymn, "O Love That Wilt Not Let Me Go."

Rain, hail, and heavy winds marked the 100-mile trip to the hilly cemetery in Plymouth, Vermont. The committal lasted for five minutes, and hundreds of local townspeople stood bare-headed in the rain. As the coffin was lowered, four truckloads of flowers were placed on top. The burial took place in the Coolidge family plot. Later, Mrs. Coolidge explained that she did not want her late husband's grave to look better than those of other townspeople.

Notch Cemetery, Route 100-A, Plymouth, Vermont 05056.

44

FINAL PLACEMENT

# Cooper, Gary

Gary Cooper, (Frank James Cooper), the motion picture actor, was born on May 7, 1901 in Helena, Montana. He gained widespread popular affection for playing slow-spoken characters who with quiet courage made a stand for principle. Among the movies he starred in were *Sergeant York* (1941), and *High Noon* (1953), for each of which he won an Academy Award.

In April 1960 he had prostate-gland surgery and, five weeks later, a major intestinal operation, in Hollywood. A year later, on April 17, 1961, he did not attend the Oscar ceremonies, saying he had a pinched nerve in his back. Instead he sent James Stewart to accept an honorary award on his behalf. On April 19, his family announced that he was critically ill with cancer, that he was confined to his Bel-Air home, and that he knew the nature of his illness. On April 27, his doctor said that his condition was worsening, but that he could be treated at home. On May 7, his 60th birthday, he received scores of cards and letters, but remained heavily sedated.

He died at his home on May 13, 1961. Pope John XXIII sent condolences to his family. His wife requested that, instead of flowers, donations be sent to the Sloan-Kettering Institute for Cancer Research. A high requiem funeral mass was celebrated on May 16 at 10:00 a.m. at the Church of the Good Shepherd in Hollywood. The auxiliary bishop of Los Angeles read the eulogy. It was reported that the roster of stars in attendance was larger than at the funerals of Clark Gable and Humphrey Bogart (*q.q.v.*). Among the pallbearers were movie stars Jack Benny, James Stewart, and Henry Hathaway. Honorary pallbearers included Ernest Hemingway (*q.v.*), (who was not able to attend because of illness), Henry Ford II, and movie stars John Wayne (*q.v.*), Bing Crosby (*q.v.*), Burt Lancaster, Dick Powell, Kirk Douglas, Danny Kaye, Tony Curtis, and Peter Lawford.

The committal service was private, in the Grotto of Our Lady of Lourdes at Holy Cross Cemetery, 5835 West Slauson Avenue, Los Angeles, California 90056

# Crane, Stephen

Stephen Crane, the poet, novelist, and short-story writer, was born on November 1, 1871, in Newark, New Jersey. He had a strict Methodist upbringing, but rebelled at an early age. His post-high school education was sparse. He became renowned for writing the *Red Badge of Courage* (1895), a story of action in the Civil War. From 1897 until his last illness he lived in England with Cora Taylor, a former brothel keeper.

In 1899, he collaborated with other well-known authors, including H.G. Wells, Henry James, and Joseph Conrad, in producing a comedy called *The Ghost*, which was performed on December 28 at Brede, in the county of Kent, in England. The following evening there was a party to celebrate the play's production. While playing his guitar, Crane fell on the shoulder of a guest, and spat up blood. He had collapsed from a lung hemorrhage. Wells rode his bicycle seven miles through the wet night to call a doctor. Crane seemed to recover quickly from this first attack, but the

mittently between 1827 and 1835. After being defeated in the election of 1835, he headed westward to Texas. There he was one of about 200 Texas volunteers who died at the Alamo, a mission station in San Antonio, Texas, fighting to establish the independence of Texas from Mexico.

During the assault, which came on March 6, 1836, at the end of a 12-day siege, the Mexican Army, led by General Santa Anna, butchered the Texan defenders. A Mrs. Dickinson, her son, and a black servant were the only ones spared. Buffalo Bill Cody (*q.v.*), although not himself present, later described the scene: "He was found dead within the Alamo, in an angle made by two houses, lying on his back, a frown on his brow, a smile of scorn on his lips, his knife in his hand, a dead Mexican lying across his body, and twenty-two more lying pell-mell before him in the angle."

The bodies of the defenders were stripped of their clothing, and General Santa Anna thrust his sword through each body before it was put with the others into a pile. Soldiers then poured four cans of camphene on the pile and ignited it. It was reported that the flames rose to an immense height.

Some weeks later, General Sam Houston (*q.v.*) and his troops won the battle of San Jacinto, and secured Texan independence. The smallest group of ashes and bone fragments from the funeral pyre at the Alamo were then later collected, and placed in a coffin, with the name of Crockett, as well as the names of two other defenders, James Bowie, and William B. Travis, engraved on the inside of the lid. The coffin was then taken to the parish church in Bexar, Texas, where a rifle, a sword, and the flag of Texas were placed on top.

At 4:00 p.m. on February 25, 1837, the funeral procession for the three men moved through the streets of the town. Military and civil leaders followed the coffin. Three volleys of musketry were fired, after which Colonel John Seguin made an address in his native Castilian, in which he said that the mighty deeds of the three men and of his compatriots had secured them a high place in the scroll of immortality.

Records from the time reveal that the coffin was buried in a peach orchard near the Alamo, to the northeast. The orchard has long since disappeared, and the exact spot is not known.

# Crosby, Bing

"Bing" (Harry Lillis) Crosby, the singer and entertainer, was born on May 2, 1904, in Tacoma, Washington. In 1925 he was hired to sing in Paul Whiteman's orchestra, and in 1932 he began radio broadcasting, and also appeared in his first movie. His recordings, which included "Buddy Can You Spare a Dime?," "White Christmas," and other songs, made him one of the most popular singers of all time. He made a series of movies with the comedian, Bob Hope, and won an Academy Award for his portrayal of Father O'Malley in *Going My Way* (1944).

In 1977, while taping a television show to commemorate his 50th year in show business, he fell and sustained a back injury. After a tour of Britain in early October, he went to Spain for relaxation. After lunching at La Moraleja golf club with three Spanish friends, on October 14 , he played and won a game of golf. Towards the end of the game he seemed to be favoring his left arm, but he joked as he left the 18th hole. Shortly after, he collapsed, about 20 yards from the clubhouse. He was taken to the Red Cross hospital in Madrid, and was pronounced dead on arrival, from a heart attack. A few hours after learning of her husband's death, Kathryn Crosby said: "I can't think of any better way for a golfer who sings for a living to finish the round." She also wanted it said that Bing had a very good round.

His son, Harry Lillis Crosby, Jr., flew to Madrid to represent the family, and to accompany the body on its trip to Los Angeles.

*Bing*

*Crosby's*

*grave.*

(Mary Ellen Hunt)

As news of his death spread around the world, memorial tributes were published on editorial pages from London to Tokyo. On October 15, an estimated 2,000 persons attended a memorial mass for him at Westminster Cathedral in London. A public memorial service was also held at 12:30 p.m. on October 18, the day of his burial, at St. Patrick's Cathedral in New York City, with Terence Cardinal Cooke officiating, and with an attendance of about 3,000 persons, many of them women.

Earlier that day, a group of 35 family members and close friends attended a predawn requiem mass at St. Paul the Apostle's Church in Westwood, California. The family had decided to have an early funeral to avoid crowds. Among those in attendance were Bob Hope and Rosemary Clooney. Crosby's four sons from his first marriage, and two from his second, served as pallbearers. The cortege drove to the cemetery, just as the sun was rising. His wife told reporters: "He hated funerals. I'm sure he didn't plan to come to this one at all." Minutes after burial, the group left the cemetery, and a group of middle-aged women gathered around the gravesite. Many of them took one of the pink roses that had adorned his plain wooden coffin.

Holy Cross Cemetery, 5835 Slauson Avenue, Los Angeles, California 90056.

# *Currier, Nathaniel*

Nathaniel Currier, the lithographer, who was to gain fame for his part in producing the Currier and Ives prints that were widely popular in the later 19th century, was born on March 27, 1813, in Roxbury, Massachusetts.

In 1852, James Merritt Ives *(q.v.)* became a bookkeeper in Currier's New York City lithography house. In 1857 the two men became partners, and the firm became known as Currier & Ives. The prints they produced sold for from fifteen cents to three dollars each, and found a ready market in the U.S. and abroad. The firm also printed handbills for the showman P.T. Barnum *(q.v.)*. Today, Currier and Ives prints are prized as collectors' items.

In mid-November 1888, Currier caught a severe cold, which developed into pneumonia. His doctor discovered that he also had heart disease. After frequent bouts of unconsciousness, he died at his New York City home, late on the evening of November 20.

An extremely simple funeral service was held in the front parlor of his home at 1:00 p.m. on November 23. The body lay in an oak casket covered by black cloth, with roses and palms on top. The minister from the Madison Square Presbyterian Church conducted the service, and the hymn, "There Is A Green Hill Far Away," was sung.

Green-Wood Cemetery, 17 Battery Place, Fifth and 25th Street, Brooklyn, New York 11228.

# *Custer, George Armstrong*

George Armstrong Custer, born on December 5, 1839, in New Rumley, Ohio, became a general in the U.S. Cavalry during the Civil War of 1861-65. In 1876 he was killed with all the men under his immediate command by Cheyenne and Sioux warriors at the Battle of the Little Big Horn in Montana.

Throughout his career, Custer had disciplinary problems with the U.S. Army authorities. During the Civil War he won a reputation for dash and daring. In 1876 he was placed in command of one of two attack columns sent against Chief Sitting Bull's encampments in Montana. Failing to wait for the second column, Custer divided his forces into three, and then led more than 250 of his men against Cheyenne and Sioux warriors on the banks of the Little Big Horn River on June 25, 1876. After being obliged to make a stand, Custer and all the men with him were killed. His horse Comanche was the sole survivor of this part of the battle, and for some years thereafter appeared saddled but riderless in parades of the Seventh Cavalry.

After the battle, Indian squaws took the clothes from the bodies of the cavalrymen. Indian children found rolls of green and white paper (money) in the dead soldiers' pockets, which they used to decorate their toys. It was two days before the bodies were discovered on the battle ridge by Lieutenant Bradley and 12 mounted infantrymen, and another day or two before the battlefield could be examined in detail. Custer's naked body was found between two other soldiers with his face in the palm of his hand. Lieutenant Edward S. Godfrey said that he looked exactly as he did when he took one of his frequent cat-naps. There was a bullethole in his left breast, and another in his left temple. The position of the body on the battlefield has led to speculation that he may have been killed early in the short battle, and that others subsequently took command. A minor mystery, among the many surrounding this episode, is what happened to Custer's golden spurs. These spurs had been taken from the Mexican general, Santa Anna, by an American officer, during the Mexican War of 1846-48. During the Civil War this officer fought on the Confederate side, and the spurs were taken from him by Custer as spoils of war. Custer was wearing them on the day of his death, but no trace of them has ever been found.

Custer was buried at West Point on October 10, 1877. His coffin was draped with the Stars and Stripes, and a feathered dress-helmet which he had rarely worn. His wife, Elizabeth (Libby), was present at the burial.

Almost all those who fell with Custer are buried on the battlefield. Custer devotees have often taken it upon themselves to care for the graves. In some instances tombstones which were either lacking or weatherworn have been obtained from the U.S. government. The Cemetery, West Point, New York 10996.

# *Daley, Richard*

Richard Joseph Daley, mayor of Chicago from 1955-76, was born on May 15, 1902 in Chicago, Illinois.

Daley grew up in a predominantly Irish neighborhood, and worked in the stockyards while at the same time attending law school at night. By 1950 he became Cook County Clerk, and in 1953 chairman of the County Democratic organization, which he came to dominate. As mayor of Chicago he came to wield an influence which extended far beyond the city itself, and deep into state and national politics. He was regarded as one of the Democratic Party's "kingmakers."

On December 20, 1976, Daley attended the annual Christmas breakfast for City of Chicago department heads, where he was surprised with the gift of two round-trip tickets to Ireland. At noon, he attended dedication ceremonies for a new gymnasium. He was asked to shoot the first basket, and sank the shot on the first try. On his way to lunch, however, he was stricken with a heart attack, and taken to his doctor's office. He died in that office at 2:55 p.m.

At noon on December 21, his mahogany casket was taken from McKeon funeral home to the Nativity of Our Lord Catholic Church. An honor guard of Chicago policemen and firemen accompanied the procession, which passed his Bridgeport area home. At the church, John Cardinal Cody sprinkled holy water on the casket.

Daley lay in state in front of the altar in the same 97-year-old church in which he had been baptized, received first communion, and been confirmed. He was dressed in a dark blue suit, a white shirt, and blue a blue tie. A black rosary was placed in his hands. The church was open all night to accomodate long lines of visitors, estimated to total 25,000, who waited outside despite a wind-chill factor below zero. Early in the evening, 50 members of the Shannon Rovers marched up the aisle playing bagpipes. Two pipers and two drummers stood by the casket and played "Garryowen," one of Daley's favorite songs. Each person received a holy card, imprinted with a picture of Daley and a prayer.

The Secret Service remained in the church throughout the 17 hours that Daley lay in state, to ensure security for President Jimmy Carter. After the night's vigil, on the morning of December 22, the church was closed from 7:00 to 9:00 a.m. for a security check. Carter arrived ten minutes earlier than expected, and sat silently in his limousine, parked in front of the church, until he could enter. Among the other notables who attended the funeral service that followed were religious, business, and political leaders, senators and congressmen, and state governors. A commentator wrote in the *Washington Post* that "To be in Chicago for Richard Daley's funeral is to understand, in a way, what it was like in China when Chairman Mao died." A Dominican priest closed the service by saying: "No man wanted less to die than Richard Daley; he had so much to live for."

A police-escorted funeral entourage took the body to Holy Sepulchre Cemetery for burial. Cardinal Cody, dressed in red and white vestments, performed the committal service in sub-zero temperatures as bone-chilling winds blew, while mourners wept. A crowd of 3,000 stood outside the metal gates of the cemetery and gazed inside as the rites were performed.

Holy Sepulchre Cemetery, 6001 West 111th Street, Chicago, Illinois 60482.

# Davis, Jefferson

Jefferson Davis, president of the Confederate States of America during the Civil War years (1861-65), was born in what is now Fairview, in Kentucky, on June 3, 1808. Before the war he served as a U.S. Congressman and senator from Mississippi, and was appointed secretary of war in 1853. He was elected president of the Confederate States in 1861. Throughout the Civil War he was often in the field with General Robert E. Lee *(q.v.)*. In May 1865, federal troops captured him near Irwinville, Georgia. He was held prisoner for two years, and was then released on bail in 1867. Due to technicalities, he was never tried for treason. He refused offers of general amnesty, and never regained his citizenship.

By 1888 he was in poor health, and by 1889 his wife was answering most of his correspondence. On a business trip to New Orleans in the autumn, he caught a severe chest cold, but refused to see a doctor. When the ship *Leathers* arrived to take him home, he was too ill to travel. Instead, he was taken to the home of a friend, a brownstone stucco building on the corner of First and Camp. A doctor found he had acute bronchitis aggravated by a flare-up of malaria.

During the early part of December, 1889, Davis rallied, and at times was expected to recover. On December 5 he said to his wife: "I want to tell you, I am not afraid to die."

A few minutes before 6 p.m. Davis awoke with a chill, His wife brought medicine to his bedside, but he pushed her hand away and said what were to be his last words: "Pray excuse me. I cannot take it." By late in the evening his breathing had become labored and the doctors moved him onto his right side. Early in the morning of December 6, David died peacefully.

By that afternoon much of New Orleans was in mourning. Black crepe adorned many public buildings and private homes. Telegrams and flowers poured into the home, among them one from the Metarie Cemetery Association, which said: "New Orleans asks that Jefferson Davis be laid to rest within the city where he fell asleep."

Davis's body was placed in a copper-lined casket covered with black velvet. He was dressed in a gray Confederate uniform, with two crossed palms and a sheaf of wheat at his head. A small bunch of rosebuds had been placed in his hands. On the lid of the coffin was a silver plate which said: "Jefferson Davis at Rest."

*Jefferson Davis's Tomb: Hollywood Cemetery, Richmond, Virginia.*

(Theresa Breschel)

At 7:00 p.m. a black horse-drawn hearse took the body to the City Hall, where it was to lie in state. A catafalque set on marbled pedestals supported the casket. Pointing towards the coffin were two twelve-pound howitzers which served as military insignia. The Washington Artillery served as an honor guard as an estimated 150,000 persons passed the glass-covered coffin. Among them was a group of former slaves of the fallen leader. One of them told reporters: "That I loved him this shows, and I can say that every colored man he ever owned loved him." On the first day that he lay in state the funeral director unscrewed the lid to allow the Atlanta sculptor Orion Frazee to make a death mask.

As crowds of people poured into New Orleans, many slept on trains or in the street. Floral tributes arrived from all parts of the country. Among them was a shoe box containing violets packed in damp sponges. With it was a card that bore a South Carolina return address, and which said: "From an old soldier and his son." Another former slave of Davis's, who could not attend, sent a telegram that read: "As the old body servant of the late Jefferson Davis, my great desire was to be the driver of the remains of my old master to their last resting place."

On December 11, at noon, one of the South's most illustrious funeral services began. The sky was clear and the sun warm, even for December in New Orleans.

Delegations from many states, and the governors from eight Southern states, attended. Cannons fired, and bells tolled, not only in New Orleans, but simultaneously in cities from Virginia to San Antonio, Texas. Clergy of all faiths attended. The Rector of the Little Church of the Redeemer in Biloxi, Mississippi, began the Episcopal service. A choir of boy sopranos sang "Through the Valley of the Shadow of Death." Six black horses with silver trimmed harnesses carried the coffin to Metarie Cemetery, where an Episcopal graveside service was conducted. Following the burial, Mrs. Davis received requests from many Southern states that wanted the body to be buried within their borders. A Virginia delegation wrote: " Virginia, holding in her loving embrace the sacred graves of five presidents of the United States, opens wide her arms and asks that she may be permitted to guard the last resting place of the President of the Confederate States."

In late May 1893, Davis's body was exhumed and moved to Richmond, Virginia, to rest in the same cemetery that holds the remains of Presidents James Monroe and John Tyler *(q.q.v.)*. Hollywood Cemetery, 412 South Cherry St., Richmond, Virginia 23220.

# *Dean, James*

James Dean, the motion picture actor, who became a legend after his death at the early age of 24, was born James Byron Dean in Marion, Indiana, on February 8, 1931. For many, in the 1950s, he represented a symbol of rebellion and a semi-Bohemian lifestyle.

Dean was raised by relatives on a farm in Fairmont, Indiana. After playing some bit parts on television and on Broadway, he won the Donaldson and Perry Award in 1953 as the Most Promising Young Actor. He is remembered for his two movies, *East of Eden* and *Rebel Without a Cause*, both made in 1955. The film *Giant*, in which he starred, was released in October 1955, four days after his death.

In 1955 Dean had bought a $6,000.00 Porsche Spyder, which he planned to use for racing. On September 30, accompanied by a friend, Rolf, he started out from Los Angeles towards Salinas, California, to compete in a race. It was a sunny day, and he wore light blue pants, a white T-shirt, and a red nylon jacket. Just south of Bakersfield he was stopped and ticketed for driving at 65 mph in a 45 mph zone. North of Bakersfield, he turned onto Route 46, a two-lane road that stretched through mountainous terrain. The late afternoon sun made driving difficult. Traveling at 85 mph, Dean had far less stopping capacity than a black and white Ford sedan that was approaching in the opposite lane. Dean said to his friend: "That guy's got to stop. He'll see us." But, rather than stopping, the Ford crossed into Dean's lane. The force of impact completely totaled the small sports car. Rolf was thrown clear, but Dean was draped across the steering column, with his head dangling. Another friend of Dean's, photographer Sanford Roth, arrived a few moments later. He afterwards said: "Jimmy was dead in his seat. The impact had thrown his head back too far... I begged the attendant to keep Jimmy under oxygen on the way to the hospital, but it was no use." The 23-year-old college student, who had been driving the Ford, cried at the scene of the accident, saying: "I didn't see them, I swear I didn't." He escaped with only minor injuries: a newspaper reported that he suffered only "a bruised nose." Within half an hour a white Buick ambulance arrived; Dean was placed in its lower rack, and Rolf in its upper. The ambulance attendants, who had little medical training, surmised from their past experiences that Dean was dead. A doctor at War Memorial Hospital in Paso Robles, California, said Dean had died of "a broken neck, multiple broken bones and lacerations over his entire body."

*James Dean's tomb in Fairmount, Indiana: souvenir hunters have chiseled chips off the tombstone, and defaced the inscription.*

(Honor Moore)

Shortly after the accident, Jimmie's father, Winton Dean, drove to Paso Robles and made arrangements for the body to be flown to his boyhood home, in Fairmont, Indiana.

Dean's body lay in state at Hunt Funeral Home in Fairmont. Oddly enough this was not the first time he had been in one of Mr. Hunt's caskets. In February 1955, some six months earlier, while posing for pictures for a *Life* magazine article, he had lain in a casket for a joke. Life ran the article, called "Moody New Star," on March 7, 1955, but did not carry the casket shot.

The funeral was held at the Quaker (Society of Friends) Church on October 8. The Indiana State Police routed traffic through intersections, as by 2:00 p.m. 3,000 people had arrived in the small town. The service was based on James 4:14 "For what is your life? It is even a vapour, that appeareth for a little time and then vanisheth away." One speaker said: "The only worthwhile things are the things that outlast life here. Fame, wealth and pleasure are false goals." A floral tribute sent by Elizabeth Taylor dominated the small church.

Six former high school classmates of Dean's acted as pallbearers. They carried his body to the crest of a small hill in Park Cemetery. The *New Republic* commented: "His death was a fitting culmination to his life, senseless but justified by the story." A year after his death he was still receiving 8,000 letters per week from fans who refused to believe that he was dead. Many of the letters claimed that he had been severely disfigured and was hiding out and on the verge of a comeback. *Life* magazine commented: "That surpasses in fervor and mourning the mass-mourning that attended the death of Rudolph Valentino."

On the 30th of every month, the day of the month in which the crash occurred, flowers were still being put on his grave anonymously in the early 1980s. On what would have been his 25th birthday, 40 baskets of flowers were found on the grave. The granite tombstone has, however, been vandalized by souvenir hunters; pieces of the letters and numbers on the stone have been chipped away.

Park Cemetery, 111 W. Washington, Fairmont, Indiana 46928.

# DeMille, Cecil B.

Cecil B. (Blount) DeMille, the motion picture director and producer, was born on August 12, 1881, in Ashfield, Massachusetts.

*Cecil B. De Mille's tomb.*

(Mary Ellen Hunt)

In 1923 DeMille, the son of a playwright, made *The Ten Commandments*, the first of a series of Biblical movies. In 1928 he joined Metro-Goldwyn Mayer, and in 1932 moved to Paramount Studios. He amassed a personal fortune from such movie successes as *The King of Kings* (1927), and *Cleopatra* (1934). His movie, *The Greatest Show on Earth*, won the Academy Award for best picture in 1952.

On January 17, 1959, DeMille, who had had a heart ailment for several years, was confined to bed. During that week he continued paperwork on the movie *On My Honor.* He died on January 21 of what was termed "heart complications." At his bedside at the time of his death were his wife of 56 years, as well as his daughter and her husband.

On January 23, about 700 onlookers gathered outside St. Stephen's Protestant Episcopal Church in Hollywood, California. During the 12-minute service, which began at 11:00 a.m., the officiating clergyman read from the Book of Common Prayer, and also the 14th verse of St. Paul's Epistle to the Romans. Among the 600 persons present were the comedian Bob Hope, actors Fess Parker and George Seaton, movie producer Hal B. Wallis, and motion picture director Alfred Hitchcock. DeMille's widow did not attend because of ill-health. Family members and friends accompanied the body to Hollywood Memorial Park for burial. Among the pallbearers was producer Samuel Goldwyn.

Hollywood Memorial Park, 6000 Santa Monica Boulevard, Los Angeles, California 90038.

# *Dickinson, Emily*

Emily Dickinson, poet, was born on December 10, 1830, in Amherst, Massachusetts. During her early years she was somewhat outgoing, but later she became something of a recluse. During her lifetime none of her poems appeared with her consent, although a few were published anonymously. After her death her sister Lavinia discovered hundreds of her poems, which were then published in a volume *"Poems By Emily Dickinson,"* in 1890. Although the volume was not well received by critics, sales warranted publishing *"Poems; Second Series"* in 1891, and *"Poems: Third Series;"* in 1896.

Emily
Dickinson's
headstone in
Amherst,
Massachusetts.

(Clive E. Driver)

In April 1884 Dickinson became very ill with Bright's disease, and was confined to bed. The doctor made frequent visits to her house, and, on one occasion treated her for "aching eyes." In June 1884 she became worse: "... I was making a loaf of cake with Maggie, when I saw a great darkness coming and knew no more until late at night. Then I grew very sick and gave the others much alarm, but am now staying. The doctor calls it 'revenge of the nerves'; but who but death had wronged them?"

From that time on she spent most of her time in bed, corresponding with old friends. By 1885 she allowed no visitors outside of the immediate family. She only agreed to let the doctor see her by letting him have a glimpse of her as she passed an open door. In the winter of 1885 she made bundles of her correspondence in a drawer, and instructed that they be burned unopened. It was during this period that she wrote "So Give Me Back to Death"—a short verse in which she expounded her distaste for life. In 1886 she wrote: "I have been very ill, and begin to roam in my room a little." In May she felt that death was approaching. In a letter to her cousins she borrowed the title of a novel *Called Back*, by Hugh Conway. She wrote: "Little Cousins,—Called back, Emily." The words "Called Back," were also used for the inscription on her tombstone.

On May 13, she awoke in much distress and her breathing became difficult. She sank into a coma for some 60 hours, and died quietly at about 6:00 p.m. on the 15th, shortly before the factory whistles of Amherst blew for quitting time.

She was dressed in a robe of soft white flannel made by a neighbor and placed in a small white coffin. She lay in state in the parlor of her house. One neighbor said that, looking at her dead friend, she was impressed by the "wealth of auburn hair and spirituelle face." Another, Thomas W. Higginson, said she "...looked 30, not a gray hair or wrinkle, the perfect peace of the beautiful." A bunch of violets adorned her neck.

On May 19, at the funeral, Higginson read "No Coward Soul is Mine" by Emily Brontë. He wrote in his diary: "The country exquisite, day perfect, and an atmosphere of its own, fine and strange, about the whole house and grounds—a more saintly and elevated *House of Usher*." After the service, six workmen carried the flowered coffin in a slow procession, with mourners following, past the barn and garden to the family plot that also held her mother and father.

The West Cemetery, Triangle Street, Amherst, Massachusetts 01002.

# *Dillinger, John*

John W. Dillinger, Jr., the outlaw and gangleader, designated as "public enemy number one" by the FBI in the 1930s, was born on June 28, 1902, in Indianapolis, Indiana.

Dillinger joined the Navy at 17 but deserted six months later. In 1923 he was imprisoned for robbing a grocery store in Mooresville, Indiana. In 1933 he was paroled. He then formed a gang which terrorized the Midwest, robbing banks in Illinois, Indiana, and Wisconsin. While awaiting trial for the murder of a Chicago policeman, he escaped from jail using a mock pistol made of wood. In March 1934 he was wounded by police in St. Paul, Minnesota, but escaped. To catch him, one of the largest manhunts in modern history was then organized.

After Dillinger was wounded, Attorney General Homer S. Cummings said: "I sometimes wonder if Dillinger is alive. He was wounded, you know, and it isn't possible to get such excellent medical attention while being chased around the country." On May 29, Melvin Purvis of the Chicago office of the FBI said: "I am convinced that Dillinger is dead." He revealed that agents had talked to a Wisconsin doctor who had treated Dillinger a week after the shooting. He also pointed out that any one of the three wounds that the doctor described could have been fatal. Purvis also said that FBI agents were looking for Dillinger's supposed grave in southern Indiana.

On July 22, 1934, Dillinger went to see a movie called *Manhattan Melodrama* at the Biograph theater on Lincoln Avenue on Chicago's North Side. He was disguised, having undergone a face-lift, and having had his naturally reddish hair dyed jet black and his eyebrows plucked. He had also grown a mustache. He was accompanied by two women: Anna Sage and Polly Hamilton. Anna was fighting deportation to her native Romania and had struck a deal with the FBI to help them capture Dillinger. Under the red lights of the theater's marquee, her orange dress looked blood red: hence, as her name was withheld at the time, she became known as the "Lady in Red." While Dillinger was in the theater at least 30 federal agents surrounded the building and others in the neighborhood. It was reported that the agents alarmed passersby, who called the Chicago police to report that a robbery was in progress. Dillinger left the theater two hours and four minutes later, at about 10:30 p.m., and turned into an alley where federal agents fired four shots, three of which hit Dillinger. One shot entered the back of his neck exiting out under his right eye, another entered his left breast, and the third entered his heart. Two women were also slightly injured in the scuffle. The owner of a nearby tavern heard the shots and saw the body lying face down in the alley. He ran to the scene and shouted: "I think that's my brother-in-law." The agents brusquely pushed him aside, telling him he was mistaken. The agents that stood over the body seemed to nod in agreement that the dead man was indeed Dillinger. The body was then placed in an ambulance and taken to Alexian Brothers Hospital. Immediately, souvenir hunters converged on the alley, dipping handkerchiefs in the puddles of blood for keepsakes. At the hospital, the body was put on the grass in front of the building, while four agents stood guard, awaiting the coroner's permission to remove the body to the Cook County morgue. At the morgue it was discovered that Dillinger had used some type of acid to disfigure his fingerprints. As crowds tried to gain entrance to the heavily guarded building, the body was moved to the basement to give the agents more room to work. The body lay on a slab wrapped in a white sheet. Tied to a toe was a tag that said: "No. 116, July, John Dillinger, by District 37, 7-22-34"—meaning that it was the 116th body at the morgue in July, and that it was taken there by the police of District 37.

In Washington, D.C., Attorney General Cummings said: "The news...is exceedingly gratifying and reassuring."

In Mooresville, Indiana, Dillinger's elderly father, John W. Dillinger, Sr. collapsed when he was told the news at his farm on the outskirts of town. He asked in a bewildered fashion "Is it true? Are you sure there is no mistake?...At last it has happened, the thing I have prayed and prayed would not happen. I want the body brought back here. I'm so sick I can hardly talk."

The elder Dillinger and Hubert, a half-brother of the outlaw, arrived in Chicago in an old gray hearse driven by a Mooresville undertaker. They met with federal agents who accompanied them to the morgue to retrieve the body. Dillinger Sr. said: "We aren't sure about the preacher, but he is going to have a good Christian burial, that's certain." Before the body was picked up, word leaked out that he was to be buried in the family plot at Crown Hill Cemetery in Indianapolis. Officials of the cemetery received several telephone calls of complaint and then consulted with an attorney. The president of the cemetery said: "The cemetery has no legal right to object to the burial of Dillinger in the family lot there. John Dillinger Sr. has owned the lot for several years and his wife is buried there. He is a man who bought property from us, and, as the owner of that property, has a legal right to bury the body of his son there."

The body arrived in Moorseville on July 24 and lay in state at a local funeral home. Dillinger's father gave permission for the public to view the body when the local authorities could not control the crowds looking through the windows of the establishment. The crowds were in line at the funeral home until 2:00 a.m.

The private funeral was held in Dillinger's sister's home in Maywood, Indiana, on the afternoon of July 25 and was attended only by the immediate family. The coffin was surrounded by a number of floral tributes, one of which bore a card signed "your friends." As 2,500 people waited outside, a clergyman conducted a simple service. The only hymn sung was "God Will Take Care of Him."

En route to the cemetery there were several scuffles between the police and reporters concerning the taking of pictures of the cortege. Only the family was allowed to enter the cemetery. As a clergyman was saying the words of committal, an intense storm broke out. Rain was said to have come down in torrents; lightning flashed, giving the ceremony a haunting effect; thunder was so loud that the clergyman's final words were lost. A police guard was dispatched to the gravesite to ward off souvenir hunters. Cemetery officials said that the grave would be guarded night and day indefinitely.

The next day, July 26, a car drove around the grave several times. Two women and one man, dressed in black, visited the gravesite and left a note which was found under a nearby rock which said: "I am going to get her, John. So long old boy. J.H." The note probably referred to the "Woman in Red."

On August 1, Dillinger's father sought and obtained permission to exhume his son's body. He would give no reason whatsoever for his action other than saying that it might be as a result of a communication with someone in Chicago. When it was alleged, however, that he had been offered $10,000 for the use of his son's body in a sideshow, he stated: "There isn't enough money in the world to get me to place my boy's body on exhibition."

The following day it was revealed that he had gotten the order so he might be able to check whether or not Dillinger's brain had been returned to his body after an autopsy. Upon learning that it had not, the elder Dillinger decided not to exhume the body. He also said that when he learned that "certain parts" had not been returned to the body he was "rather indignant," but now knew that the removal was not for "malicious purposes" but might aid in gathering "scientific knowledge."

Crown Hill Cemetery 3402 Boulevard Place, Indianapolis, Indiana 46208.

# *Dirksen, Everett McKinley*

Everett McKinley Dirksen, the politician and U.S. senator, famous for his dramatic oratorical style, was born on January 4, 1896, in Pekin, Illinois.

From 1932-48 he served in the U.S. House of Representatives, after which he retired to Pekin for health reasons. In 1950 he was elected to the U.S. Senate and became nationally known for his oratory. He was elected as the Senate Republican leader in 1959.

Dirksen was a frail person, being plagued by illness a good part of his life. In his latter years he suffered from emphysema, a duodenal ulcer, and a fractured hip. In a speech in Peoria, Illinois, in October 1968 he said "Every time I end up in a hospital people get the idea I've got one foot in the grave. But that's not true, I'm not ready and I won't be until the good Lord says so."

On August 9, 1969, Dirksen was admitted to Walter Reed Army Medical Center in Washington, D.C., complaining of a shortness of breath and swollen ankles. A few days later he was operated on for lung cancer.

He seemed to recover rapidly, but on September 4, he suffered extreme confusion and anxiety, and there was speculation that he might have had a minor stroke. His son-in-law, Senator Howard Baker, asked him how he felt. Dirksen replied "Altogether not very well."

On September 7, he seemed to be in good spirits. But after eating lunch at 2:15 p.m., he turned pale and collapsed. Army doctors tried to restart his heart with massage, by electrical shock, and by administering sodium bicarbonate. The doctors massaged so vigorously that five of his ribs were broken, but this was considered of secondary concern in this emergency. At 4:52 p.m., with his wife and daughter at his side, he was pronounced dead.

Word of his death was flashed to the nation by special television bulletins. Networks played prime-time specials which detailed his life, and newspapers ran the story as a page one article. His sudden death surprised his Senate colleagues. Senator James Pearson of Kansas said: "We knew that he was wired together, that he had a bad heart, a bad stomach, and that he didn't take care of himself, yet I was shocked."

Dirksen lay in state in the rotunda of the U.S. Capitol on the same catafalque that had borne the body of Abraham Lincoln (q.v.). The coffin was covered with a blanket of scarlet roses and the seal of the U.S. Senate. Funeral services were held at noon on September 9, and were attended by President Nixon, who eulogized him, as well as by Vice-President Agnew and ranking members of the federal government. His body lay in state for 24 hours.

The funeral service was held on September 10 at the National Presbyterian Church in Washington, D.C., conducted by the Senate's chaplain the Rev. Edward Elson. Former President Lyndon B. Johnson did not attend the service when he learned that the seating arrangements called for him to sit next to President Nixon. On September 11, Dirksen's body was flown to Pekin, aboard the presidential aircraft, Air Force One.

At the Pekin gravesite, where a simple ceremony was held, three volleys were fired by an honor guard, and then a lone bugler played taps. Glendale Memorial Gardens, Rural Route 2, Pekin, Illinois 61554.

# Disney, Walt

Walter Elias Disney, or Walt Disney, the cartoonist and motion picture producer, was born in Chicago, Illinois, on December 5, 1901. In the early 1920s, he worked as a commercial artist and cartoonist, and experimented with animated cartoons. After a few failures he created the character Mickey (originally Mortimer) Mouse. The third film with this new character, entitled *Steamboat Willie*, was a huge success. Disney also created additional characters and drew on familiar fairy tales to bring others to life. In the 1950s he branched out into television, and also created an amusement park in California, called Disneyland. Besides 29 Academy Awards, he received numerous awards from around the world.

On November 2, 1966, aged 64, Disney was admitted to St. Joseph Hospital in Burbank, California, for what was described as "diagnostic" tests and treatment for an old polo-caused neck injury. During the examination, a lesion was found on his left lung, and part of the lung was then removed. Disney Studios refused to reveal whether or not the lesion was malignant. He was released from the hospital on November 21, and returned to his office the following day, for what was called a "limited schedule." He was admitted to St. Joseph again on November 30 for a postoperative checkup. He died at the hospital at 9:35 a.m. on December 15, from what was called circulatory collapse.

*The tomb holding Walt Disney's ashes.*

(Mary Ellen Hunt)

Newspapers the world over carried the news of his death. Many newspapers carried editorial comments. A Paris newspaper said, "all the children in the world are in mourning. And we have never felt so close to them." A Mexico City newspaper reported on the sadness of children and said "More than one tear was seen in the eyes of grown men." His friend former President Dwight D. Eisenhower (q.v.) said: "His appeal and influence was universal. He touched a common chord in all humanity. We shall not see his like again." President Lyndon B. Johnson (q.v.) sent a note of condolence to Mrs. Disney. On the CBS Evening News, Eric Sevareid said: "It would take more time than anybody has around the daily news shops to think of the right thing to say about Walt Disney... He was a happy accident; one of the happiest this century has experienced."

Disney's body was secretly cremated. On December 16 a very private as well as closed funeral service was held at the Little Church of the Flowers in Forest Lawn Cemetery, 1712 South Glendale Avenue, Glendale, California. 91205.

# Doubleday, Frank Nelson

Frank Nelson Doubleday, the publisher, was born on January 8, 1862, in Brooklyn, New York.

He went to work for Charles Scribner's Sons at the age of 15 and advanced rapidly. In 1897, with Samuel S. McClure, he founded the firm that is now Doubleday & Co. He also bought a chain of retail book stores. He was known to have a keen business sense and a warm appreciation for writers. Among the writers he published were O. Henry (q.v.), Booth Tarkington, Sinclair Lewis (q.v.), Joseph Conrad, and Rudyard Kipling. From Kipling he acquired the nickname "Effendi," which is Arabic for "chief."

After some years of ill health, he leased a home in Florida in the Miami suburb of Coconut Grove in the winter of 1933-34. There he died of a heart attack on January 30. His widow, Florence Doubleday, had his body sent to Effendi Hall, his country home in the Mill Neck Colony on Long Island, New York, where it arrived late in the evening of January 31.

The funeral service, attended by 700 persons, was held on February 3, at the Cathedral of the Incarnation at Garden City, Long Island. The cathedral was close to the Doubleday publishing plant, and a line of cars stretched from the cathedral to the gardens of the plant. The coffin was adorned with Prince Camille de Rohan roses, and lilies of the valley. The Bishop of Long Island read the Episcopal burial service. There was no sermon but the choir chanted the Twenty-third Psalm and sang "Abide With Me." Among the writers attending the service were Christopher Morley and Clemence Dane.

Burial was at Locust Valley Cemetery and was attended by only the immediate family and pallbearers.

Locust Valley Cemetery, Ryefield Road, Locust Valley, Long Island, New York 11560.

# Douglass, Frederick

Frederick Douglass, originally called Frederick Augustus Washington Bailey, was born into slavery in Tuckahoe, Maryland, on February 7, 1817. A man of great personal dignity and intellectual brilliance, he was the first black to hold high office in the United States government.

Never knowing his white father, and separated from his mother at an early age, he learned to read as a house servant in Baltimore. In 1838, dressed as a sailor, he fled North, evading slave-hunters by changing his name to Douglass. He became a key figure in the Abolitionist cause, speaking eloquently against slavery, and founding his own anti-slavery newspaper, the *North Star*. In 1845 he wrote his autobiography, published in revised form in 1882 under the title *Life and Times of Frederick Douglass*, which is a landmark in its genre. During the Civil War he was a consultant to President Abraham Lincoln *(q.v.)*, and recruited black troops for military service in the federal cause. After the war he espoused the right of black freedmen. In his later years he received many honors, while also serving as marshall of the District of Columbia from 1877-81, recorder of deeds from 1881-86, and U.S. minister and counsul-general to Haiti from 1889-91.

On February 20, 1895, he was an honored guest at a meeting of the National Council of Women, in Washington D.C. He was invited to the platform, but declined to speak, merely bowing to acknowledge applause. It was a bitter cold day, and when he got home to Cedar Hill, the big white house he owned in Anacostia Heights, Virginia, he shook the snow from his boots and told his wife the events of the day. After supper, he began to walk upstairs, but stopped, seemingly to look at a picture of John Brown, the Abolitionist, who had been a close personal friend. He then said to his wife: "I'm a little tired." This was so unlike him that she turned to look at him. He then fell dead.

A memorial service was held at the Metropolitan African Methodist Episcopal Church in Washington, D.C. Among the distinguished speakers was Susan B. Anthony *(q.v.)*, who came to honor the only man who had supported her demand for the enfranchisement of women when she first made it in 1848.

His body was then taken to Rochester, New York, where he had lived for many years. Here, on February 26, he was buried in Mt. Hope Cemetery.

Mt. Hope Cemetery, 1133 Mt. Hope Avenue, Rochester, New York 14620.

# *Dulles, John Foster*

John Foster Dulles, U.S. secretary of state from 1953-59, was born in Washington D.C. on February 25, 1888. A member of the American delegation to the Versailles Peace Conference, he specialized in international law. After playing a role in the formation of the United Nations, he was appointed secretary of state in 1953, when the Cold War was at its zenith. In the six years that he held that office he was instrumental in forming an anti-Communist system of alliances in Asia.

Dulles died on May 24, 1959 at 7:41 a.m. The cause of death was cancer, complicated by pneumonia. At his bedside were his wife, two sons, sister, and brother. Just before he died, he reached his hand out toward his wife. Although he had been unable to speak for two days before his death, the family was confident that he recognized them. When death came, the family members silently left the room.

The funeral service was held on May 27 at the Episcopalian National Cathedral in

Washington, D.C. Dignitaries from 20 nations were present at the service. The Soviet Union's foreign minister, Andrei Gromyko, said: "I knew Mr. Dulles for a long time... I cannot but recognize that he was an outstanding statesman, and outstanding diplomat." At the request of Mrs. Dulles there was no sermon or formal service, but only prayers and hymns. It was noted that during the prayers Gromyko did not participate but stared passively ahead.

He was buried at Arlington National Cemetery, following the service. Six gray horses drew the body to the top of a hill. The Marine Corps band played "Faith of Our Fathers." President Eisenhower (q.v.) ordered a 19-gun salute, only two less than that reserved for presidents. Arlington National Cemetery, Fort Myers, Arlington, Virginia 22211.

# Durante, Jimmy

Jimmy Durante, comedian, and entertainer was born on February 10, 1893, in New York City. Famous for his radio, television, and nightclub appearances, he was well loved for his straight-forward and warm approach to his audiences. His large nose earned him the nickname "Schnozzola." Many of his routines focused on his own shortcomings and frustrations. His hallmarks were his raspy voice and honky-tonk piano playing. He often composed his own songs.

He died on the morning of January 29, 1980, in Santa Monica, California. He had been admitted to St. John's Hospital in Santa Monica earlier in January for treatment of a form of pneumonia.

Five hundred people attended a rosary at the Good Shepherd Roman Catholic Church on January 31. Comedians Bob Hope and Danny Thomas led the tribute. Other comedians, including Marty Allen, Red Buttons, Bob Newhart, and Don Rickles, were also present. Representing the world of screen and television were Marlon Brando, Desi Arnaz, Ernest Borgnine, Connie Stevens, Angie Dickinson, Fess Parker, and Caesar Romero.

Bob Hope eulogized the dead comedian, saying: "Jimmy, in talking about his looks, once said, 'I know there's a million good-looking guys, but I'm a novelty.' Some novelty! He was one of the greatest human beings to walk this earth!" During the rosary, Monsignor Daniel Sullivan said he was "a man of deep and abiding faith. The greatest tribute I could pay to Jimmy is that his humor was childlike."

The burial service was private, attended by only family and friends. The simple casket was covered with red roses and the comedian's old fedora, which was removed before burial.

Holy Cross Cemetery, 5835 West Slauson Avenue, Los Angeles, California 90056.

# Earp, Wyatt

Wyatt Earp, a legendary lawman of the old West, was born on March 19, 1848 in Monmouth, Illinois.

After holding jobs as stagecoach driver, buffalo hunter, and professional gambler, he moved to Dodge City, Kansas, in 1876, where he served as assistant marshal. He was a close friend of the frontier figure Bat Masterson (q.v.). In 1878 he went to

Tombstone, Arizona, where his brother Virgil was marshal. After a falling out with the gang led by Ike Clanton, Virgil appointed Wyatt and another brother, Morgan, deputies, after which, together with another associate, "Doc" Holiday, they participated in a shoot-out with the Clanton group at the OK Corral in Tombstone that has since become the subject of Western folklore. In this shoot-out, however, Virgil was discharged as marshal, and there was controversy as to whether the Earps had acted as they did to uphold the law, or for personal motives. In 1882 Wyatt moved to Colorado, and then later to Alaska, and, finally, to California, where he lived the rest of his life on income from earlier investments.

He died in Los Angeles on January 3, 1929. He had been bed-ridden for some time, and had left his bed to send a telegram to a sick friend in Florida—an exertion that brought about his final decline. The funeral was held in Los Angeles on January 15. Burial was in the Hills of Eternity Memorial Park, El Camino Real, Colma, California 94014.

# *Eastman, George*

George Eastman, the inventor and industrialist, was born in Waterville, New York, on July 12, 1854.

While working in a bank, Eastman became interested in photography, and in 1880 designed the process for making dry plates. He left the bank and with a partner founded the Eastman Dry Plate Company. In 1888 he introduced the Kodak, a simple and inexpensive camera that was sold pre-loaded with film. It was advertised: "You push the button, we do the rest." By 1900 the firm was recognized as the Eastman Kodak company which became enormously successful worldwide. In later years Eastman devoted much of his time and thought to philanthropy.

Around noon on March 14, 1932, having been in ill-health for many years, he chatted with his doctor and nurses at his Rochester, New York home. Quite suddenly he asked the group to leave the room, explaining that he had a note to write. He then wrote a note which said: "To my friends: My work is done. Why wait? E.G." He then recapped his fountain pen, put out his cigarette, removed his glasses, and shot himself through the heart. His doctor and nurses heard the shot and rushed back in. They found him dead, with the note at his side.

L.B. Jones, vice president of the Eastman Kodak, immediately issued a statement saying: "He should not be misunderstood and so this statement of his end as those of us who worked for him and with him for two-score years see it and understand it: 'George Eastman played the game to the last. By his own hand he lived his life and by his own hand he ended it... He had always expressed a dread of a lingering illness and a life of uselessness... apparently, he planned carefully to end his orderly life in an orderly way.'"

His body lay in state in his Rochester home during the day of March 16. Only those employees who had served Eastman Kodak for 30 years or more were permitted to file past the coffin.

The funeral service was held on March 17 at St. Paul's Episcopal Church in Rochester, New York. The services were simple, consisting of some of Eastman's favorite music and the reading of a Psalm. The church was crowded with distinguished persons from all over the country. Amplifiers carried the service to the 5,000 persons who lined the street in front of the church. In Hollywood, all motion picture production was halted for one minute during the funeral.

After the service the body was cremated at nearby Mt. Hope Cemetery and the ashes, in an urn of solid bronze, were later buried beside the graves of his parents in Mt. Hope Cemetery, 791 Mt. Hope Avenue, Rochester, New York 14620.

# Eddy, Mary Baker

Mary Morse Baker Eddy, founder of Christian Science, was born in Bow, New Hampshire, on July 16, 1821. During most of her childhood she was subject to ill health, nervous seizures and collapse. In 1853 she married a dentist and homeopath named Daniel Patterson, who aroused her interest in natural healing. After studying the New Testament she created her own system of healing. In 1875 she published the first of many editions of *Science and Health* which espoused the doctrine that the mind is the root of all infirmities of the body. After divorcing Patterson in 1873, she married one of her followers, Asa G. Eddy, in 1877. In 1879 she chartered the Church of Christ Scientist. In 1880 she began publishing the *Christian Science Journal,* which later became the *Christian Science Sentinel* and then the *Christian Science Monitor.*

The membership of her church grew rapidly under her direction. In 1889 she retired from Boston to Concord, Massachusetts, then later to Chestnut Hill, near Boston. Although retired, she maintained absolute control of her church even while in ill health.

*Mary Baker
Eddy's tomb.*

(Sammy Edward Baker)

On December 2, 1910 she asked for a writing pad and a pen. She then wrote her last written message: "God is my life." On December 3, she stayed in bed all day but was alert and sent messages to those around her. In one message she said: "Drop the argument, just leave me with the divine love, that is all I need." That evening she ate a small dinner and retired. She passed away at 10:45 p.m. without a sound. The medical examiner recorded the death as due to natural causes—"probably pneumonia." In talking to reporters he said that he did not recall "ever seeing in death before, a face which bore such a beautiful tranquil expression."

The funeral service was held on December 8 at her Chestnut Hill, Massachusetts, home. Approximately 150 persons attended. No curtains were drawn in the home. Her body lay in state in a massive bronze casket in a southeast parlor. Although the casket's lid was closed there was a small viewing window at the top of the coffin.

During the service the Lord's Prayer was read, as well as selections from her book. The 18-minute service was closed by a reading of "Mother's Evening Prayer." Those present were then given the chance to view her features through the glass viewing plate. Her granddaughter was the only person noticed weeping.

After the service her body was taken to a receiving tomb at Mt. Auburn Cemetery. Two "watchers" were placed in the tomb for a time, and were provided with a telephone in case they should need assistance. These precautions, however proved not to be needed. Later her body was moved to a mausoleum, built in a section of the cemetery near such notables as James Russell Lowell and Oliver Wendell Holmes *(q.q.v.)*, Mt. Auburn Cemetery, 580 Mt. Auburn, Cambridge, Massachusetts 02138.

# *Edison, Thomas Alva*

Thomas Alva Edison, the inventor, was born on February 11, 1847, in Milan, Ohio. A technological genius, he was granted more than 1,000 patents, including those for the incandescent light bulb, the phonograph, and the movie projector. He formed various companies to organize and develop his many projects. These companies eventually merged to become the Edison General Electric Company. In 1887 he moved his laboratory to West Orange, New Jersey.

On August 1, 1931, he collapsed in the living room of his home, Glenmont, in the Llewelyn Park section of West Orange, New Jersey. In the days that followed his condition worsened as complications grew. He had been unable to take any nourishment for a week or any liquids for two weeks. On October 15, he lapsed into a coma. World figures such as Pope Pius XI, Henry Ford *(q.v.)* and President Herbert Hoover *(q.v.)* kept in touch with the family. Death came at 3:24 a.m. on October 18. He died peacefully in his sleep, in the presence of his wife, children, and a doctor.

His body lay in state in the library of his laboratory on October 20. Many thousands of persons from all walks of life passed the bier. The funeral service was held on October 23 in the drawing room of his home. Edison's crutches were placed at the side of his coffin during the service. Many of his favorite musical selections were played during the service on an old pump organ. These included "I'll Take You Home Again Kathleen," "Little Gray Home in the West," and the "Moonlight Sonata" by Beethoven.

Thousands of mourners lined the streets of West Orange, New Jersey as the cortege passed en route to Rosedale Cemetery. After a simple service hosted by honor guards, Mrs. Edison leaned over and kissed the metal casket, then stepped back and threw a rosebud on it as it sank from view into the open grave.

Lights across the nation were dimmed at 9:59 p.m. as a tribute to the man who had invented the electric light 52 years earlier to the day. In New York City the lights of Broadway were dimmed, as was the torch of the Statue of Liberty.

Rosedale Cemetery, Linden Avenue, West Orange, New Jersey 07052.

# Einstein, Albert

Albert Einstein, the physicist, who formulated the theory of relativity, was born on March 14, 1879 in Ulm, Germany. As a child he developed a deep interest in mathematics. He completed his schooling in Switzerland where he entered the Polytechnic Academy. After graduation in 1900 he became a Swiss citizen. In 1905 he was awarded a doctorate by the University of Zurich. In that same year he published his papers, which made major contributions to physics—such as the special theory of relativity, the mass-energy equivalence formula; the theory of Brownian motion; and the photon theory of light. In 1921 he was awarded the Nobel Prize for physics. After visiting the United States in 1932, he left Germany, and came to the United States. For the rest of his life he was associated with the Institute for Advanced Study in Princeton, New Jersey, where he lived. He became a U.S. citizen in 1940. His recommendation to President Franklin D. Roosevelt (q.v.) to follow atomic research developments, led to the development of the atomic bomb. Einstein's name is also linked to the opening of the atomic age. In his later years he worked for a number of social and anti-war causes.

Around mid-day on April 13, 1955, Einstein complained of extreme tiredness and lack of appetite. He was found to be suffering from a leakage of blood from a hardened aorta. He was opposed to surgery, and at one point said: "The end comes some time: does it matter when?"

On April 16 he was in extreme pain, and was taken to the hospital. On April 17 his daughter visited him, and later wrote: "I did not recognize him at first, so changed was he by the pain and the lack of blood in his face, but his manner was the same."

Early on the morning of April 18 he died peacefully in his sleep. His literary executor, Otto Nathan, was to write that the less published about his illness and the events that led to his death the better. He could not understand why the public might be interested in the details.

Einstein had asked that there be no funeral service, nor monument, nor grave. He was cremated privately in a place near Trenton, New Jersey. At his own request the manner of the ashes' disposal was kept a strict secret, so that the place could never become a shrine.

# Eisenhower, Dwight D.

Dwight David Eisenhower, 34th president of the United States (1953-61), was born on October 14, 1890 in Denison, Texas. In World War II he was supreme commander of the Allied Expeditionary Force in Europe. After serving as supreme commander of the North Atlantic Treaty Organization (NATO) forces from 1950-52 he was elected to the presidency. During his term of office he brought the Korean War (1950-53) to a close, and the United States experienced a period of prosperity. He retired to private life in 1961.

Throughout the summer and fall of 1968, Eisenhower was confined to Walter Reed Army Hospital in Washington, D.C. because of a series of heart attacks. As the weeks wore on, his condition worsened. On the afternoon of March 28, 1969 he spoke his last words: "I've always loved my wife. I've always loved my children. I've always loved my grandchildren. I've always loved my country." He then died. His wife Mamie was at his bedside at the time.

President Richard M. Nixon described him as being a man "who spoke with moral authority seldom equaled in American public life." He declared March 31 as a day of mourning and ordered flags on all Federal buildings flown at half-mast for 30 days. Tributes were received from ex-Presidents Harry S. Truman and Lyndon B. Johnson, *(q.q.v.)* Vice-President Agnew, British Prime Minister Harold Wilson, Queen Elizabeth II, French President Charles de Gaulle, UN Secretary General U-Thant, and Pope Paul VI.

He lay in state in the Capitol Rotunda in Washington, D.C. in an $80 military coffin dressed in his complete army uniform, including the trim jacket that had made him famous. The flag-draped car carrying his body was placed on board a funeral train which was muted by black morning crepe.

He was given a military funeral on April 2 in Abilene, Kansas, as the Fifth Army Band played "Ruffles and Flourishes," and "Hail to the Chief."

Burial was at the Eisenhower Center, Abilene, Kansas 67410.

# *Ellington, Duke*

Duke Ellington, the composer and jazz bandleader, was born Edward Kennedy Ellington on April 29, 1899, in Washington, D.C. The distinctive style of playing of his orchestra, made famous by recordings such as "Mood Indigo," spread his fame to Europe. He was the recipient of many awards and honors. His music was a characteristic part of the jazz scene for about 50 years.

In March, 1974, he entered the Columbia Presbyterian Medical Center's Harkness Pavilion for treatment of cancer of both lungs. In May he also developed pneumonia. He died in the early hours of May 24.

His mortal remains were taken to the Walter B. Cooke funeral home at 1505 Third Avenue, New York City. On that same night the bodies of two of his friends, the musicians Paul Gonsalves and Tyree Glenn, also lay in the same funeral parlor. Many thousands lined Third Avenue to pay their respects to the man whose music they had loved. His body lay in an open coffin with the Star of Ethiopia around his neck. He also wore the ribbon of the Legion of Honor as well as the Presidential Medal of Freedom. Two Masonic services were held for him at the funeral parlor. Blues singer Joe Williams, in summing up his life, said: "You don't have to say much about Edward because he said it all."

On May 27 his remains were taken to the Cathedral of St. John the Divine, also in New York City. Many of the shops in nearby Harlem were closed to honor him. Thousands lined the rainy streets outside and 10,000 people crowded inside the building. Stanley Dance, the author, gave the eulogy, and spoke of Ellington's music being loved by races and creeds the world over. Jazz singer Ella Fitzgerald sang "Solitude." He was buried in the Wild Rose section of Woodlawn Cemetery, 233rd Street and Webster Avenue, the Bronx, New York 10470.

# *Emerson, Ralph Waldo*

Ralph Waldo Emerson, the essayist and poet, was born on May 25, 1803 in Boston, Massachusetts.

After being ordained as a Unitarian minister in 1829, he resigned from the ministry in 1832, and subsequently became the center of the Transcendentalist literary circle based in Concord, Massachusetts. His literary fame rests on his *Essays*. In his last years in Concord, he became senile.

By April, 1882, he contracted pneumonia in one lung. During the last five days of his life he did not leave his sickroom, but seemed to recognize visiting friends. He died at 8:50 p.m. on April 27.

The funeral services was held on April 30 at the Unitarian Church in Concord. His boyhood friend William Furness officiated. After the simple service, Louisa May Alcott *(q.v.)*, recited a sonnet. He was buried in Sleepy Hollow Cemetery, not far from the grave of Henry David Thoreau *(q.v.)*.

Sleepy Hollow Cemetery, Keys Road, Concord, Massachusetts 01742.

# *Faulkner, William*

William Cuthbert Faulkner (originally 'Falkner'), the novelist, was born in New Albany, Mississippi, on September 25, 1897. His many books included the *Sound and the Fury* (1929), and *As I Lay Dying* (1930). In 1949 he was awarded the Nobel Prize for literature, and in 1955 won a Pulitzer Prize. He was awarded a second Pulitzer Prize posthumously.

On July 6, 1962, Faulkner, aged 64, died in an Oxford, Mississippi, hospital at 2:00 a.m. The cause of death was listed as a thrombosis.

The funeral service was held on July 7, in the living room of the author's antebellum mansion in Oxford. Only immediate family and representatives of Faulkner's publisher were admitted. The body lay in a closed gray metal coffin. A clergyman from St. Peters Protestant Episcopal Church conducted the service.

Few of the townspeople noticed the procession headed by a long black hearse with gray drapes that carried his remains to the hilltop cemetery, which was studded with stately cedars. Less than an hour after the service had begun at the author's home, his body was lowered into the grave.

St. Peters Cemetery, Oxford, Mississippi 38655.

# *Fermi, Enrico*

Enrico Fermi, the physicist who was one of the godfathers to the nuclear age, was born in Rome, Italy, on September 29, 1901. In 1938 he was awarded the Nobel Prize for Physics for his work with neutrons. After accepting the award in Stockholm, he settled in the United States, becoming a professor of physics at Columbia University. Fermi, along with other scientists signed the letter written to President Franklin D. Roosevelt *(q.v.)*, which revealed to him the potential of atomic energy. He later worked on key atomic projects. In 1946 he was awarded the Congressional Medal of Merit.

On November 28, 1954, aged 53, he died at his Chicago, Illinois, home of what was described as stomach cancer. A private funeral service attended only by members of his immediate family was held on November 29. Burial was in Oak Woods Cemetery, 1035 East 67th Street, Chicago, Illinois 60637.

# Fiedler, Arthur

Arthur Fiedler, the musical conductor, was born in Boston, Massachusetts, on December 17, 1894. After playing violin and viola in the Boston Symphony Orchestra in 1929, he organized, a series of free outdoor concerts. In 1930 he became conductor of the Boston Symphony Pops Concerts, which made the orchestra a national institution. In 1965 he and Richard Rogers were the first recipients of the Boston Gold Medal for distinguished achievement. In 1971 he and the Boston Pops were given the Peabody Award for their performances on educational television.

On July 10, 1979, aged 84, he died at his Brookline, Massachusetts, home. The cause of death was listed as heart failure. That evening the Boston Pops Orchestra marked his death by playing his signature piece, "The Stars and Stripes Forever" —without a conductor.

A private funeral service was held on July 12 in Boston. A public memorial service was held on July 24 at the Harvard Memorial Church in Boston. His ashes are buried at St. Joseph's Cemetery, 990 La Grange Street, West Roxbury, Massachusetts 02132.

# Fields, W.C.

W.C. Fields, the comedian, was born Claude William Cukenfield, in Philadelphia, Pennsylvania, on January 29, 1880. He began his career as a juggler, played in the

*The gravemarker of W.C. Fields.*

(Photo: Mary Ellen Hunt)

Ziegfeld Follies, and went on to play in a series of movies that made him one of Hollywood's major stars. His classic comedy films included *My Little Chickadee* (1940), and *Never Give a Sucker an Even Break* (1941).

In a 1925 interview, published in *Vanity Fair*, he said that he would like his epitaph to read: "Here lies W.C. Fields. I would rather be in Philadelphia."

By 1944 his health had deteriorated, and he was in constant pain. He entered a sanatorium spending his better days reading, writing letters and seeing a few close friends. A few minutes after midnight, on December 25, 1946, he woke from a semi-comatose state, put a finger to his lips and winked. A few minutes later he suffered a violent hemorrhage and died.

His will had stipulated that his body was to be taken to a cemetery and immediately cremated, and that under no conditions was he to have any sort of funeral. Two funeral services were nevertheless held. The first was a large public service and the second was a small private Catholic service. It was also decided that his body not be cremated. Only his name and vital statistics are given on his simple grave marker. Forest Lawn Memorial Parks, 1712 South Glendale Avenue, Glendale, California 91205.

# *Fillmore, Millard*

Millard Fillmore, 13th president of the United States (in office 1850-53) was born on January 7, 1800 in Cayuga County, New York. In 1848 he won the vice-presidential nomination and was elected with Zachary Taylor (*q.v.*). Upon Taylor's death, on July 9, 1850, Fillmore became president. The major accomplishment of his administration was the negotiation of a treaty with Japan. His bid for re-election in 1856 was soundly defeated whereupon he retired from public office. He became active in local affairs and founded the University of Buffalo, the Buffalo Fine Arts Academy, and other institutions.

In January, 1874, he said: "My health is perfect. I eat, drink and sleep as well as ever." Five weeks later, on the morning of February 13, as he was shaving, his left hand became numb and useless. The paralysis extended to the left side of his face. Two weeks later he suffered a second attack. His last words, while being offered some food, were: "The nourishment is palatable." He died on March 8.

The funeral service was held on March 10, in Buffalo, and was attended by hundreds of city notables as well as by national figures. Burial was at Forest Lawn Cemetery. His tombstone is a stark obelisk with classic proportions which simply gives his name and vital statistics. Forest Lawn Cemetery, 1411 Delaware Avenue, Buffalo, New York 14209.

# *Fitzgerald, Francis Scott Key*

Francis Scott Key Fitzgerald, the novelist and short story writer, was born in St. Paul, Minnesota on September 24, 1896. His first novel, *This Side of Paradise* was published in 1920, and made him wealthy. Through his short stories, he became a spokesman of youthful rebellion in the 1920s. From the mid-1920s to 1930 he lived in Europe, where he wrote *The Great Gatsby* (1925). His wife, Zelda Sayre Fitzgerald (*q.v.*), became mentally ill while he himself became progressively dependent upon alcohol, and also had financial problems. In his later years he became a Hollywood script writer.

*F. Scott Fitzgerald's grave.*

(Photo: Dan Coffey)

On December 20, 1940, as he was leaving Pantages theatre in Los Angeles, he complained of not feeling well. The following day, while waiting for the doctor, he was sitting by his fireplace eating a chocolate bar. He rose abruptly, and then fell against the mantelpiece before tumbling to the floor. The cause of death was listed as a heart attack.

His body was taken to a mortuary chapel in downtown Los Angeles. One of the few friends who came to see him, said he was "made to look like a cross between a floorwalker and a dummy."

His body was shipped to Bethesda, Maryland. Before dying he had expressed a desire to be buried beside his father and mother in the Cemetery of St. Mary's Catholic Church in Rockville, Maryland, but because he had renounced Catholicism the bishop refused to allow this. The family decided that he should be buried in Rockville Union Cemetery, which was done on December 27, 1940. In 1975 permission was given to remove the remains of both Scott Fitzgerald and his wife to St.

Mary's, which was done. A re-burial ceremony was held there on November 7, 1975, attended by the couple's daughter, Scotty Lanahan Smith.

*F. Scott Fitzgerald's death certificate.*    (The Collection of Mary Ellen Hunt)

Cemetery of St. Mary's Catholic Church, 600 Veirs Mill Road, Rockville, Maryland 20852.

# *Fitzgerald, Zelda*

Zelda Sayre Fitzgerald, wife of F. Scott Fitzgerald (*q.v.*), became a symbol of the flapper and jazz age. She was born on July 24, 1900, in Montgomery, Alabama. She married Scott Fitzgerald in 1920. In 1930 she suffered a mental breakdown, and most of the rest of her life was spent in institutions.

In the fall of 1947, realizing that she needed treatment, she entered a hospital in Asheville, North Carolina. During that winter she wrote many cheerful letters to her family and spoke of being released. But on March 10, 1948 a fire broke out in the kitchen of the hospital. Since it was after midnight, most of the patients were sleeping.

Locked doors and barred windows hampered the rescue attempts. Ten women were trapped on the third story. One of them managed to break a window and jump. Nine others died, among them Zelda. Nothing was left which could positively identify her remains. Some ashes and bone fragments were, however, taken, although they could not positively be identified as hers.

A simple service was held in Rockville, Maryland, on March 17, attended by a small group of friends. An Episcopal minister officiated.

Her remains together with those of her husband, were re-buried at the Cemetery of St. Mary's Catholic Church in Rockville on November 7, 1975 at a ceremony attended by the couple's daughter, Scotty Lanahan Smith. St. Mary's Catholic Church Cemetery, 600 Veirs Mill Road, Rockville Maryland 20852.

## *Flanagan, Edward Joseph*

Edward Joseph Flanagan, the Catholic priest who founded Boy's Town, was born on July 13, 1886 in Roscommon, Ireland. In 1918 he founded Father Flanagan's Boys Home on a small tract of land outside of Omaha, Nebraska. In 1922 the home was incorporated as a municipality, Boys Town. His aim was to take seemingly destitute and aimless boys, and educate them towards useful goals.

While touring Germany for the U.S. government, he died on May 15, 1948, in the 279th Station Military Hospital in Berlin, Germany. A requiem mass was held for him in Berlin on May 17.

His body was returned to the United States aboard a C-47 Army transport plane. It then lay in state at Boy's Town on May 19 and 20. A funeral mass was held at 7:30 a.m. May 21 for staff members and students of Boy's Town. At 10:00 a.m., a public mass was also celebrated. A crowd of about 2,500 persons was present when the Rev. P.A. Flanagan, brother of the famous priest, administered the final absolution. Six Boy's Town seniors then assisted in wheeling the bronze coffin to the rear of the chapel and placing it in a crypt. It had been Father Flanagan's wish to be entombed in the chapel so he could always be near his "boys." The crypt was sealed with a gold engraved slab, on which were the words: "Father Flanagan, Founder of Boy's Town, Lover of Christ and Man."

Dowd Chapel, Father Flanagan's Boys Home, Boy's Town, Nebraska 68010.

## *Flynn, Errol*

Errol Flynn, the motion picture actor, was born in Hobart, Tasmania, on June 20, 1909. He began his professional acting career in 1934 with a repertory company in England, and in 1935 was spotted by a Warner Brothers talent scout. He starred in such films as *Robin Hood* (1938), *The Sea Hawk* (1940), and others. He was married three times, and acquired a reputation for fast living.

On October 14, 1959, while in Vancouver, British Columbia, to sell his schooner, *Zaca,* the 50-year old actor was stricken with a heart attack, and died on the way to the hospital. Funeral services were held in the Church of the Recessional in Forest

*Errol Flynn's
grave.*

(Mary Ellen Hunt)

Lawn Memorial Park, Glendale, California, on October 19. The head of Warner
Brothers studios delivered a eulogy saying that Flynn was a man who "laughed at
himself, but never at acting or the audience." His bronze coffin was covered with
yellow roses.

Burial was in the Garden of Everlasting Peace at Forest Lawn Memorial Park, 1712
South Glendale Avenue, Glendale, California 91205.

# Ford, Henry

Henry Ford, the industrialist, was born on July 30, 1863 near Dearborn, Michigan.
By 1892 he had developed a working gasoline buggy, which he later improved. He

*Mourners
filing past
Henry Ford's
casket, as he
lay in state at
Greenfield
Village,
Dearborn,
Michigan.*

(Photo: Ford Motor Co.)

founded the Ford Motor Company in 1903, and unveiled his masterpiece, the Model T, Ford automobile, in 1908. In 1913 he introduced the conveyor belt assembly line. In 1936 he and his son Edsel established the Ford Foundation which became one of the major philanthropic foundations in the world.

He died on April 7, 1947 at 11:04 p.m. at his estate in Dearborn, Michigan. His body lay in state in the Recreation Hall at Greenfield Village in Dearborn. The lower half of the coffin was not opened. His head rested on a silk pillow and his hands were folded at his waist. More than 75,000 persons filed past the bier.

The funeral service was held on April 10 at St. Paul's Episcopal Church in Detroit. Every industry within the state of Michigan halted production for one minute at 2:30 p.m. when the service began. Every bus and taxi cab, as well as most private vehicles, parked at the curb to honor the industrialist. Floral tributes filled most of the cathedral, with lilies being most in evidence. The 121st Psalm was read, as well as verses from John XIV and Romans 8. His body was interred near the graves of his mother and father at St. Martha's Episcopal Churchyard, 15801 Joy Road, Detroit, Michigan 48228.

# *Foster, Stephen*

Stephen Collins Foster, the composer of popular minstrel songs, was born on July 4, 1826, in Lawrenceville, Pennsylvania (now part of Pittsburgh). In 1846, drawing on folk influences, he began, to write songs which became widely popular, including: "Swanee River," "Camptown Races," and "Beautiful Dreamer." In 1860 he moved from Cincinnatti to New York City. Although many of his songs reflected images of Southern life, he had little knowledge of the South, having made a single visit to New Orleans in 1852.

On January 10, 1864, Foster rose to get a drink of water, but fainted from weakness. He fell against the washbowl which made a long gash in his face and neck. His chambermaid found him lying in a pool of blood. When he was lifted up he said: "I'm done for." He was taken by carriage to Bellevue hospital. He died three days later, at 2:30 p.m. on January 13.

His body was taken to the city morgue and placed in an iron casket, after which it was taken to Winterbottom's undertaking establishment. It was then put on a train to Pittsburgh. En route, on January 17, there was an accident on a bridge four miles east of Tyrone, Pennsylvania. Several cars were thrown into the river, and 21 persons injured. Foster's body, which was traveling in the baggage car, was not injured in any way.

The funeral service was held on January 21 at Trinity Episcopal Church in Pittsburgh. Burial was at Allegheny Cemetery, where a band of musicians had assembled. As the casket was being lowered into the grave, they played "Old Folks at Home" and "Come Where My Love Lies Dreaming."

Allegheny Cemetery, 4734 Butler, Pittsburgh, Pennsylvania 15201.

# *Frankfurter, Felix*

Felix Frankfurter, associate justice of the Supreme Court (1939-62), was born on November 15, 1882 in Vienna, Austria. He came to the U.S. at the age of 12, and became a respected scholar in the field of law. He was an advisor to President Woodrow Wilson (*q.v.*) at the Versailles Peace Conference (1919), and helped found the American Civil Liberties Union (1920). He became nationally prominent with his liberal critique of the Sacco-Vanzetti trial, published in the *Atlantic Monthly*. On the Supreme Court he espoused the doctrine of judicial self-restraint. Notable among his opinions were the *Minersville School District* vs. *Gobitis* (1940), which sustained the flag salute law.

On February 21, 1965 he suffered a heart attack and was taken to George Washington University Hospital in Washington, D.C., where he died the next day, aged 82.

A simple and private funeral service was held in his Massachusetts Avenue apartment. Although he was an agnostic he had made arrangements some years before that a former law clerk, steeped in the Jewish religion, would recite the Kaddish (a doxology expressing praises to God) at his funeral. A former student of Frankfurter's read a passage from John Bunyan's *Pilgrim's Progress*. His body was cremated and the ashes were interred in a crypt in the chapel of Mt. Auburn Cemetery, 580 Mt. Auburn, Cambridge, Massachusetts 02138.

# *Franklin, Benjamin*

Benjamin Franklin—printer, author, inventor, scientist, diplomat and public official, who helped draft both the Declaration of Independence and the U.S. Con-

*Benjamin Franklin's monument, opposite his burial site.*
(Photo: Sammy Edward Baker).

stitution—was born in Boston, Massachusetts, on January 17, (January 6, Old style) 1706. His inventions included bifocal spectacles, the lightning rod, and the Franklin stove. He founded an academy which later became the University of Pennsylvania.

He published some witty and wise sayings in *Poor Richard's Almanack* (1732-57). In 1776 he sought and obtained French support for the American colonies, and after independence was U.S. ambassador to France. His last years were spent quietly and his mind remained active. He invented bifocals at the age of 83.

By 1889 he was bedridden and was in constant pain, for which he took morphine. On April 12, 1790 he had pain in his chest and difficulty in breathing. He insisted on getting up in order to have his bed made, as he wanted to "die in a decent manner." His daughter told him that he would recover and he replied: "I hope not." Soon after, the pain, which had abated, returned, and he was told to change positions so that he would be able to breathe more easily. He said: "A dying man can do nothing easy." He then sank into a semi-comatose state. He died on April 17, 1790 at 11:00 p.m.

Earlier in life, he had jokingly penned his own epitaph, which read:

> The Body of
> B. Franklin,
> Printer;
> Like the Cover of an old Book
> Its Contents torn out,
> And stript of its Lettering and Gilding,
> Lies here, Food for Worms.
> But the Work shall not be wholly lost:
> For it will, as he believ'd, appear once more,
> In a new & more perfect Edition,
> Corrected and amended
> By the Author.

The funeral service was held in Philadelphia, and his death was mourned around the world. He was buried at Christ Church Burial Ground, 302 Arch Street, Philadelphia, Pennsylvania, 19106.

# *Frémont, John*

John Charles Frémont, soldier, explorer, and political leader, was born in Savannah, Georgia, on January 21, 1813. In 1842 he surveyed the route of the Oregon Trail, ascended the Wind River Range, and later explored much of the Northwest, as well as the routes to California. His published accounts of his expeditions made him a popular hero. He played a key role in the U.S. conquest of California. He became a California senator, and the discovery of gold in the state made him a multimillionaire. His widespread popularity won him the presidential nomination of the Republican Party on an anti-slavery platform in 1856, but he lost the election. He was governor of the territory of Arizona from 1878-1883.

While on a visit to New York City in July 1890, he visited the grave of a friend's son. New York was in the middle of a severe heat-wave. Even so, Frémont made the trip to the cemetery in a streetcar. Returning to his hotel room, he felt a drop in his temperature, and became chilled. He sent for a doctor, who diagnosed peritonitis from a ruptured appendix or gastric ulcer. During the early morning hours of July 13 he began to vomit, after which he became peaceful. He said: "If I continue as free from pain, I can go home next week." He then closed his eyes. His doctor asked him which home he meant, Frémont replied: "California, of course." He then died.

Burial was simple. He had requested to be dressed in a plain black suit and placed in a plain pine coffin. He was buried on July 15, on a bluff overlooking the Hudson River in Piermont. The grave is marked by a granite monument on which there is a bronze sword, a flag, and a plaque with a representation of the explorer's head. On the plaque his achievements, titles, and honors are recorded.

Rockland Cemetery, Piermont, New York 10968.

# Friedman, William F.

William Frederick Friedman, the cryptologist and security expert, was born in Kishinev, Russia, in 1891. He came to the U.S. when his family emigrated to Pittsburgh, Pennsylvania in 1920. He and his wife Elizebeth (her mother had insisted on spelling her daughter's name with an "e" in the middle) were the only husband and wife team in cryptology when the U.S. entered World War II. They had spent years studying Shakespeare's works for hidden ciphers to determine whether Sir Francis Bacon (1561-1626) was the real author. They concluded that Shakespeare, not Bacon, was the author, and published the finding in their book *The Cryptologist looks at Shakespeare* (1955). Friedman later led the army task force that cracked the Japanese "purple" code shortly before the United States entered World War II in 1941.

In 1968 he fell ill. On November 2, 1969, aged 78, he had a heart attack, and died within 30 minutes.

The funeral service was held on November 5, at Fort Myers, Virginia. He was buried with full military honors at Arlington National Cemetery on November 6.

Arlington National Cemetery, Fort Myers, Arlington, Virginia 22211.

# Frost, Robert

Robert Lee Frost, the poet, was born on March 26, 1876 in San Francisco, California. He held a succession of professorships and residencies at Amherst, the University of Michigan, Harvard, and Dartmouth. He four times received the Pulitzer Prize for poetry—in 1924, 1931, 1937, and 1943. He was also awarded almost 50 honorary degrees and made a number of goodwill trips abroad for the State Department. In 1958 he was consultant in poetry to the Library of Congress. He made an appearance at the inauguration of President John F. Kennedy *(q.v.)* in 1961, reciting his poem "The Gift Outright." In 1962 he was awarded the Congressional Gold Medal on his 88th birthday.

He entered Peter Bent Brickham hospital in Boston in January 1963. Around the 27th he began to lose strength and it became clear that he would not recover. On January 28 he was unable to eat and doctors were at a loss what to do. That evening he was visited by some friends. Before they left, he said: "I feel as though I were in my last hours." Around midnight several blood clots reached his lungs and he lost consciousness. He died in the early morning hours of January 29. Death was attributed to a pulmonary embolism.

On the afternoon of January 31, a private funeral service was held in Appleton Chapel of the Memorial Church in Harvard Yard, and was attended by 30 of Frost's closest friends and relatives. The minister emeritus of King's Chapel read selections of poetry as well as from the Bible. On the afternoon of February 17, a public memorial service was held at Johnson Chapel, Amherst College, attended by 700 persons. Four months later on June 16, the poet's ashes were buried in the Frost family plot of the Old Bennington Cemetery in Vermont. His epitaph "I had a lover's quarrel with the world" is from his poem "The Lesson for Today."

Old Bennington Cemetery, Bennington, Vermont 05201.

# *Fulton, Robert*

Robert Fulton, the engineer and inventor, was born on November 14, 1765, in Little Britain, Pennsylvania. Fulton was a successful artist and naturalist and in 1786 went to England and studied under the artist Benjamin West (1738-1820). In the 1790s he worked on the development of a submarine. In 1800 he demonstrated a workable submarine, *The Nautilus*, which was also equipped with torpedoes (another of his inventions). He then worked on the development of a steamboat and by 1806 he had finished the *Clermont*. He devoted the rest of his life to overseeing the production of steamboats and the organizing of passenger and freight lines.

*Robert Fulton's grave
in Trinity Churchyard,
New York City.*

(Trinity Church Parish)

In early February 1815 he caught a cold, which became increasingly worse. He died on February 23 from what was called "an inflammation of the lungs and other complications." The funeral service was on February 24. The cortege left his residence at No. 1 State Street, and continued towards Trinity Church. As the body,

which was in a leaden coffin enclosed in mahogany, made its way through the streets
of New York, minute guns were fired from nearby batteries. Burial was in the
churchyard of Trinity Church, 74 Trinity Place, New York, New York, 10006.

# Gable, Clark

William Clark Gable, the movie actor, was born on February 1, 1901, in Cadiz,
Ohio. After winning an Academy Award for his role in the 1934 comedy *It Happened One Night,* his popularity grew. His best known movie roles were *Mutiny on the
Bounty* (1935), and *Gone With the Wind* (1939), although he played in some 70
movies. The prototype of the virile hero, he had box-office appeal to both men and
women. During World War II he served in the U.S. Army Air Corps, and was
decorated for flying bomber missions.

On November 5, 1960, he suffered what he thought was an attack of indigestion.
He took aspirin, but it did not help. He said he felt as though "a huge hand has
crawled inside me and is tearing my rib cage apart." He was rushed to Presbyterian
Hospital in Los Angeles where it was confirmed that he had suffered a coronary
thrombosis. He was given anti-coagulants and sedatives, and was attended by nurses
around the clock. A cardiologist who had been a consultant to President Eisenhower
*(q.v.)* was also brought in. Gable died at 10:10 p.m., on November 16, while reading
a magazine.

Some 500 persons attended a private military funeral at the Church of the Recessional at Forest Lawn Memorial Park on November 19. The coffin was blanketed by
red roses and an Air Force honor guard stood nearby. An Air Force chaplain read the
46th and 121st Psalms. There was no eulogy. A medley of waltzes by Strauss was
played before the Episcopal service. Pallbearers included movie stars Spencer Tracy
*(q.v.),* Robert Taylor, and Jimmy Stewart.

*Plaque marking the resting place
of Clark Gable's ashes.*

Photo: Mary Ellen Hunt

Gable's mortal remains were entombed next to those of his third wife, Carole
Lombard, at Forest Lawn Memorial Park on November 23. He had once told a
reporter that his epitaph would read: "He was lucky and he knew it." There is,
however, no epitaph on the marker on his grave, which bears his name and vital
dates. Forest Lawn Memorial Park, 6300 Forest Lawn Drive, Los Angeles, California
90068.

# *Gardner, Isabella Stewart*

Isabella Stewart Gardner, the socialite and art collector, was born in New York City on April 14, 1840. She was a brilliant woman who was constantly surrounded by actors, authors, musicians, and other artists. She was a patroness of the Boston Symphony Orchestra. She had a deep interest in art, and assembled one of the world's finest collections of Renaissance and Dutch masterpieces. Her art collection, housed in the Isabella Stewart Gardner Museum, was given to Boston as a public institution by a proviso in her will. She stipulated that the collection be kept exactly as she left it, without any additions or subtractions.

On July 7, 1924, in Boston, after having gone for a ride in her Pierce-Arrow auto, she had a severe angina attack. A doctor administered opiates but they did not relieve the pain. On July 14, at 10:40 p.m., death came peacefully.

*Isabella Stewart Gardner's grave.*
(Photo: Kevin Gleason)

She had written directions for her funeral some 11 years before. Her coffin was covered with the same purple pall that had been used for her husband's funeral. Candles were lighted at her head and feet. There was a mirrored door at the foot of the coffin covered with a sheet on which a black crucifix was hung. On July 19, a mass was said, attended only by family and other members of the household. The funeral was held at the Church of the Advent on July 21, at 12:00 noon. Burial was in the Gardner Tomb in Mt. Auburn Cemetery, 580 Mt. Auburn Street, Cambridge Massachusetts 02138.

# *Garfield, James*

James Abram Garfield, 20th president of the United States (in office March 4-September 19, 1881), was born near Orange, Ohio, on November 19, 1831.

On the morning of July 2, 1881, while waiting for a train at the Baltimore and Potomac Station in Washington, D.C., he was shot by Charles J. Guiteau, a deranged disappointed office seeker. The president's hat flew off his head, he threw his arms in the air, and said: "My God. What is this?" As the wounded president was falling, Guiteau fired once again. Garfield remained conscious, but showed all the signs of severe shock. One bullet had grazed his arm and the other had settled about four inches to the right of his spine. He lingered incapacitated for 11 weeks, and died in Elborn, New Jersey, on September 19.

His body was sent to Cleveland, Ohio, where it lay in state in the public square. About 150,000 people (virtually equivalent to the entire population of Cleveland at that time) passed by his bier. The funeral service was held on September 26, and burial was in Lake View Cemetery, 12316 Euclid, Cleveland, Ohio 44106.

# Garland, Judy

Judy Garland, the actress and singer, was born Frances Gumm on June 10, 1922, in Grand Rapids, Minnesota. She adopted the name Judy Garland in 1935 when she began to make movies. The most famous of her many films was *The Wizard of Oz* (1939), which won her an Academy Award. Because of health problems her movie contract with Metro-Goldwyn Mayer was canceled in 1950. She then toured the United States and Europe as a singer, developing a following which was almost a cult. The last 15 years of her life were plagued by drug use and breakdowns.

On June 22, 1969, her husband found her on the bathroom floor of their London, England, home. He said that "her skin was discolored with a red and a bluish tinge and that her face was dreadfully distorted." She had been dead for several hours. The post-mortem showed barbiturates in her blood, and the official ruling was that she had died an accidental death following the incautious use of barbiturates.

Her body lay in state in a small mahogany casket which had been spray painted white because the funeral director did not have a white casket. She wore white gloves, which rested on a small Bible, as well as a chiffon gown, and silver slippers.

*Judy Garland's gravestone.*

(Photo: Eric Mautner.)

The funeral service was held at the Frank E. Campbell Funeral Home on Madison Avenue in New York City, on June 27. It was attended by such notables as Lauren Bacall, Jack Benny, Sammy Davis, Jr., Katherine Hepburn, and other stars of stage and screen. The clergyman closed the services by reading from I Corinthians 13:1-13. Burial was at Ferncliff Cemetery, Hartsdale, New York 10530.

# Garrison, William Lloyd

William Lloyd Garrison, the abolitionist, journalist and reformer, was born on December 12, 1805 in Newbury Port, Massachusetts. He was active in the organization of the New England Anti-Slavery Society in 1832 and of the American Anti-Slavery Society in 1833. During his later years he pressed for prohibition, women's suffrage, and better treatment for American Indians.

By May, 1879, his health was failing rapidly, and he dosed himself with patent medicines. On May 23, while at the home of his daughter in New York City, his doctor asked him: "What do you want?" Garrison replied: "To finish it up." That evening he could no longer speak and slipped into unconsciousness. He died at 11:00 p.m. on May 24.

Everything possible was done to avoid the appearance of mourning at his funeral at the Church of the First Religious Society in Elid Square in Roxbury, Massachusetts. The pulpit was adorned with bright flowers and open blinds allowed the sunshine to enter. His favorite Bible passages were read and black American quartets sang his favorite hymns. He was buried in Forest Hills Cemetery, Roxbury, Massachusetts 02119.

# Gehrig, Lou

Lou Gehrig, the baseball player, was born in New York City on June 19, 1903. He was the American League home-run champion in 1931—tied with Babe Ruth (q.v.). He was named the American League's most valuable player in 1927, 1931, 1934, and 1936. His most remarkable record was in consecutive games played. He did not miss a single game during 14 seasons.

In 1939, after a batting slump, he traveled to the Mayo clinic in Minnesota where it was discovered that he was suffering from a fatal form of paralysis. That same year he was elected to the National Baseball Hall of Fame. By late May he was confined to his bed in his New York home. His condition grew steadily worse as he lost weight and strength. He remained conscious until just before death, which occurred at 10:10 p.m. on June 2, 1941.

The funeral service was private and was held at 10:00 a.m. on June 4 at the Christ Episcopal Church in Riverdale, The Bronx, New York. The service lasted only eight minutes. His body was then taken to the Fresh Pond Crematory, Middle Village, Queens, New York.

On September 13 his ashes were placed in the family vault in Kensico Cemetery, Valhalla, New York 10595.

# Geronimo

Geronimo, the Apache leader, whose Apache name was Goyakla, was born in June 1829 in what is now Clifton, Arizona. Resisting colonization of the Southwest by both Mexicans and Americans, he led Apache raids against white settlers on both sides of the border, thus spreading confusion throughout the region. After what became known as the Geronimo Campaign (1882-86), Geronimo and his band surrendered to U.S. forces. Geronimo was sent first to Florida, and then, in 1894, to Fort Sill, Oklahoma. Here he took up farming, and eventually adopted Christianity.

*Robert Geronimo, last living child of Geronimo, visiting his father's grave. January 13, 1964.*

(Photo: Field Artillery & Fort Sill Museum).

In February 1909 he became drunk, fell from his horse, and lay on the ground so long that he caught pneumonia. He was taken to a hospital, but died at 6:15 a.m. on February 17. The funeral service was on February 18 at 3:00 p.m.

He was buried at the Apache Cemetery, Fort Sill, Oklahoma 73503. In 1931 the Field Artillery School at Fort Sill erected an impressive rock monument in his memory.

# Gerry, Elbridge

Elbridge Gerry, signer of the Declaration of Independence, was born in Marblehead, Massachusetts, on July 17, 1744. A member of the Continental Congress, he served as governor of Massachusetts from 1810-12, during which time the division of the state into new senatorial districts led to the coining of the expression "to gerrymander." From 1812 until his death he served as vice-president of the United States.

In 1813 he suffered a stroke, although he himself characterized it as a "sunstroke." He was described at that time as looking like a "scant old skeleton of a French barber." On November 22, 1814, after reading some documents, he fell ill and retired early. The following morning he complained to his landlady about "strange chest pains." He had his usual breakfast, and left for the Senate at 10:00 a.m. Before arriving, however, his chest pains became more severe, and he returned home. The porter at his door asked him if he felt ill, and his answer was a faint "Yes," this being the last word he spoke. He was carried to his room, and put to bed, but died within minutes.

Burial was at Congressional Cemetery, 1801 East Street, S.E., Washington, D.C. 20003.

# Gershwin, George

George Gershwin, the composer, was born Jacob Gershwin on September 26, 1898, in Brooklyn, New York. He collaborated with his brother Ira and together they wrote scores of successful Broadway shows. Among his other compositions were "The Man I Love" and "They Can't Take That Away From Me." His "Rhapsody in Blue" was commissioned by Paul Whiteman, the orchestra leader. His last major work was the folk opera *Porgy and Bess* (1935).

By June of 1937, Gershwin began to complain of headaches and dizzy spells. Within weeks he could neither walk nor support himself and his food had to be cut up for him. On July 9, he fell into a deep coma from which he could not be aroused and was rushed to the hospital. His doctors diagnosed a tumor of the right temporal lobe and operated on July 11. Five hours after the operation, at 10:35 a.m., he died without regaining consciousness.

Two simultaneous funeral services were held on July 15. One was on the West coast, at Hollywood's B'nai B'rith Temple, and the other at Manhattan's Temple Emanu-El. Gershwin's body had been brought to New York from California, and rested in a flower draped coffin. Notables from the worlds of theater, movies, and politics attended the service. His body was then buried in Mt. Hope Cemetery, Hastings-on-Hudson, New York 10706.

# Goddard, Robert H.

Robert Hutchings Goddard, the physicist and rocketry pioneer, was born in Worchester, Massachusetts, on October 5, 1882. In a paper he published in 1919, "A Method of Reaching Extreme Altitudes," he predicted the development of rockets capable of breaking free of earth's gravity and traveling to the moon and beyond. He was not taken seriously. During the 1920s he worked on the use of liquid fuels, and was granted more than 200 patents in this field. During World War II he moved to Annapolis, Maryland, and worked on the development of rocket engines and jet-assisted take off (JATO) units for aircraft.

By August 1945 he had been ill for eight weeks, and was then hospitalized at University Hospital, Baltimore. He died on August 10, and was buried at Hope Cemetery, Worchester, Massachusetts 01603.

# Goldman, Emma

Emma Goldman, the anarchist and social reformer, was born on June 27, 1869 in Kovno, Lithuania (now in the U.S.S.R.). She came to the United States in 1885, and lived in Rochester, New York; New Haven, Connecticut; then New York City. She was jailed there in 1893 for "inciting a riot" when she told a crowd of unemployed workers to steal bread if they did not have money to buy it. After her release she lectured in the U.S. and in Europe. In 1906 she founded the magazine *Mother Earth*.

She opposed U.S. involvement in World War I and worked against the draft. She was jailed for two years in 1917 for her activities. In 1919 she was declared an illegal alien and, along with 200 others, was deported to the Soviet Union. She became critical of the Russian Revolution, and published her feelings in *My Disillusionment in Russia* in 1923. She later worked for the anti-fascist cause in the Spanish Civil War, and was lecturing on its behalf at the time of her death.

On February 17, 1940 she suffered a stroke in Toronto, Canada, where she was then living. She was admitted to a hospital; was reported to be "seriously ill," and spent several months there. Later she appeared to be improving. She died on May 14, at her Toronto home. Her brother, Dr. Maurice Goldman, and a niece, Mrs. Stella Ballantine, both of New York City, were present at the time of her death.

Her last wish was to be buried beside Fisher, Engel and Parsons, the anarchists who had been hanged for their participation in the Chicago Haymarket riot of 1886. Although Emma was not allowed back into the United States while living, in death the United States authorities allowed her remains to be brought into the country for burial.

A simple funeral service was held on May 17 at Waldheim (now Forest Home) Cemetery, in Forest Park, Illinois. Paradoxically, although she was Jewish she was buried in the German, and not the Jewish, part of the cemetery, in fulfillment of her wish to be laid to rest near her anarchist comrades. The editor of the *Jewish Daily Forward* said that she "was a rebel all her life against injustices, ... were she living to-day, Emma Goldman would be assisting in the present human effort to destroy Hitlerism."

Her attorney and friend, Harry Weinberger, eulogized her saying: "Emma Goldman, we welcome you back to America, where you wanted to end your days with friends and comrades. We had hoped to welcome you back in life—but we welcome you back in death. You will live forever in the hearts of your friends and the story of your life will live as long as the stories are told of women and men of courage and idealism."

Forest Home Cemetery, 863 S. Des Plaines, Forest Park, Illinois 60130.

## *Goldwyn, Samuel*

Samuel Goldwyn, the motion picture producer, was born Samuel Goldfish on August 27, 1882 in Warsaw, Poland. He was orphaned at an early age and emigrated first to London, and later to the United States. In 1917 he formed Goldwyn Pictures Corporation which merged with Metro Pictures in 1924 to become Metro-Goldwyn-Mayer. He introduced many new stars to films, including Will Rogers (*q.v.*) and Ronald Coleman. His films were of high quality, and included *Wuthering Heights* (1939), *The Little Foxes* (1941), and *The Best Years of Our Lives* (1946), for which he won an Academy Award.

He died on January 31, 1973, aged 91, at his Los Angeles home. He had been in ill health for almost ten years and had been released from the hospital only a short time before, after being treated for cancer.

His funeral service was held on February 1, at Forest Lawn, Glendale, attended only by members of his immediate family and presided over by a rabbi. His son, Samuel Jr., delivered a short eulogy. Gates of the cemetery were closed during the ceremony, and security guards kept unauthorized persons away from the grounds. A spokesperson for the family said: "We are grateful for the love of the people who wanted to come but this brief moment is ours." Forest Lawn Memorial Park, 6300 Forest Lawn Drive, Los Angeles, California 90068.

# Gompers, Samuel

Samuel Gompers, the labor leader, was born in London, England, on January 27, 1850. His family emigrated to the United States in 1863 and settled in New York City's lower east side. He helped found the American Federation of Labor (AFL) in 1886, and was president of the organization from 1886 until the time of his death, with the exception of a single year, 1895.

By 1924, aged 74, he was fighting a losing battle against general disorders of aging. In early December, he was in Mexico City, attending a convention of the Pan American Federation of Labor. Due to the effect of altitude on his weakened heart, he became very ill, and was put aboard a special train bound for San Antonio, Texas. It had been his last wish to die on American soil.

He was taken to his hotel in San Antonio on December 13. When surrounded by his friends he gave them some simple directions for his funeral, bade them farewell, turned to a nurse and whispered: "Nurse, this is the end. God bless our American institutions. May they grow better day by day." He then died.

His body was shipped to Washington, D.C. where it lay in state at the AFL headquarters. It was then taken to New York aboard a funeral train. On December 17 he lay in state at the Elks Lodge where his funeral service was held. On December 18, all activity in the U.S. Senate was stopped at the hour of his funeral. All across America workers at factories observed a moment of silence as a tribute to him. He could not be buried in the Jewish cemetery where his parents, his first wife, and two of his children were buried, because of his marriage to a Gentile woman. His body was taken by train to Tarrytown, New York, where a funeral service was conducted by the Masonic Lodge. Burial was at Sleepy Hollow Cemetery, 540 North Broadway, Tarrytown, New York 10591.

# Goodyear, Charles

Charles Goodyear, inventor, was born on December 29, 1800 in New Haven, Connecticut. After opening a hardware store, which failed, in Philadelphia, he devoted his time to finding a way to take the stickiness out of raw rubber, and to make it resistant to heat and cold. By 1844 he had perfected this process and had applied for a patent for the vulcanization of rubber, which made the commercial use of rubber possible. Because of legal technicalities his patent rights were lost in Britain and France, and infringed on in the United States. For a short while he was imprisoned for debt in France. At the time of his death, his family was some $200,000.00 in debt.

In 1859 he bought a home in Washington, D.C. In May 1860, he learned that his daughter Cynthia was gravely ill in New Haven, Connecticut. Since he was too ill to make the trip by train, he traveled to New York aboard the steamship *Montebello*. When he arrived in New York on June 1, he was met at the dock by his son-in-law, who told him that his daughter had died the day before. He wanted to continue on to New Haven for the funeral, but was too weak and was taken to a Fifth Avenue hotel.

As the days wore on, his breathing became heavy and his face yellow and shrunken. His wife arrived in New York on June 7. Goodyear recognized her but was unable to speak. In his delirium he would mutter: "God knows... God knows all." Early on the morning of Sunday, July 1, 1860, as the distant churchbells were ringing, he raised himself from his pillow as if he saw someone in the distance, sank back into bed without a struggle, and died.

The funeral service and burial were in New Haven, at the Grove Street Cemetery, 227 Grove Street, New Haven, Connecticut 06502.

# Grant, Ulysses S.

Ulysses S. Grant, commander of the federal forces during the Civil War (1861-65), was the 18th president of the United States, (in office 1869-75).

*Grant's Tomb, on Riverside Drive in New York City.*

(Photo: Free Library of Philadelphia)

He was born Hiram Ulysses Grant, in Point Pleasant, Ohio, on April 27, 1822. In 1839 he entered the military academy at West Point, where his name was mistakenly entered as "Ulysses S. Grant," a form that he later accepted, stating that the "S" did not stand for anything. During the Civil War, Grant showed himself to be an aggressive commander. He distinguished himself in several battles, and accepted the final surrender of the Confederate forces, under General Robert E. Lee *(q.v.)*, at Appomatox on April 9, 1865. After serving as president, Grant made a world tour, and later retired. At the urging of his friend, Mark Twain, (q.v.), he wrote his memoirs.

He died on July 23, 1885, at his retreat at Mt. McGregor, New York, in the Adirondack Mountains. The family prohibited an autopsy, even though his emaciated body weighed less than 100 pounds. His casket was made of oak with a copper interior, and had silver handles. A gold plaque, engraved "U.S. Grant," was attached to the side. It had a hermetically sealed glass top. The body was dressed in a Prince Albert black broadcloth suit with a white collar.

The funeral service was held on August 4 at Mt. McGregor. His body was then taken via Saratoga, where the cortege switched trains to New York City. There the former president's body lay in state at City Hall. It took 320 policemen to control the crowd of 300,000 people who passed the bier.

The burial took place at Riverside Drive, New York City, in an imposing tomb overlooking the Hudson River. Grant's Tomb is now a New York landmark. Grant's Tomb, 122nd Street and Riverside Drive, New York City, New York 10027.

# *Gray, Asa*

Asa Gray, the botanist, was born on November 18, 1810 in Sauquoit, New York. More than any other botanist, he unified taxonomic knowledge of the plants of North America. His *Manual of the Botany of the Northern United States*, popularly known as *Gray's Manual* is still a standard work. Founder of the National Academy of Sciences in 1863, he was ten years president of the American Academy of Arts and Sciences, and was also a regent of the Smithsonian Institution.

In January 1888, Gray, partially paralyzed, was confined to bed, following a stroke. On January 26 his condition worsened, and he lapsed into a semi-conscious state from which he never emerged. He died at 7:30 p.m. on January 30 at his home in the botanical gardens at Cambridge, Massachusetts.

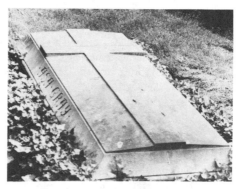

*Asa Gray's tomb in Cambridge, Massachusetts.*

(Photo: Sammy Edward Baker)

A funeral service was held on February 2, at noon, in Appleton Chapel, Cambridge. The service was brief and simple. Interment was at Mt. Auburn Cemetery, 580 Mt. Auburn Street, Cambridge, Massachusetts 02138.

# Gray, Harold Lincoln

Harold Lincoln Gray, the cartoonist, was born on January 20, 1894, in Kankakee, Illinois. A staffer on the *Chicago Tribune,* he was an assistant draftsman for the Andy Gump cartoon strip. He then created a comic strip of his own—"Little Orphan Annie"—which appeared in 1924. It became one of the most popular and long-lived comic strips in American history. More than 300 newspapers eventually carried the strip.

In May 1968, Gray had been ill with cancer for some months, but continued to create the comic strip. He died on May 9, at Scripps Memorial hospital in La Jolla, California.

The funeral service was held on May 11 at 11:00 a.m. in the C.J. Jordan Mortuary in Chicago. Burial took place at Oakridge-Glen Oak Cemetery, Oakridge Avenue and Roosevelt Road, Hillside, Illinois 60162.

# Grey, Zane

Zane Grey, the prolific author of best-selling Westerns, was born on January 31, 1875, in Zanesville, Ohio. He was given the name "Pearl" but later adopted the family name of his mother. After working as a dentist, he took to writing "Wild West" novels. Altogether he wrote 54 novels, which had sales of 15,000,000. His most famous titles included *Riders of the Purple Sage* (1912), *The Lone Star Ranger* (1915), and *West of the Pecos* (1937). He was one of the most popular authors of the 20th century, and also wrote books on outdoor adventure and fishing.

By October 1939 he had been under treatment for a heart ailment, but was in excellent spirits, and continued to write. On October 20, however, he awakened his wife with a pain in his chest. He refused to call a doctor. On October 23, he arose at 7:00 a.m., dressed, and sat on the edge of his bed. Suddenly he gasped and fell to the floor. The family doctor could not be reached although a neighbor, who was a doctor, was called instead. But by the time he arrived, Grey was already dead. Death, which occurred at 7:30 a.m., was attributed to coronary thrombosis.

A private funeral service was held in Pasadena on October 25, and his body was cremated. His ashes lie, together with those of his wife, in Lackawaxen, Pennsylvania, in the same cemetery in which the first Unknown Soldier, killed in the Revolutionary War, is buried. Union Cemetery, Lackawaxen, Pennsylvania 18435.

# Griffith, D.W.

D.W. Griffith, the pioneer motion picture director and producer, was born at Floydsfork (now Crestwood) in Oldham County, Kentucky on January 22, 1875, as David Llewelyn Wark Griffith. He directed or produced nearly 500 films during his career. He is credited with developing some of the basic techniques of cinematography, such as close-ups, fade-outs, and flash-backs. His most famous film *The Birth of A Nation,* opened in 1915 and was a sensational hit. His film, *Intolerance* (1916), is considered by many to be the most outstanding production of the silent film era. He had an eye for talent and the list of stars that he discovered included Mary Pickford, Lionel Barrymore, Mack Sennett, and others. In 1919 he formed the United Artists film distributing company, together with Mary Pickford, Douglas Fairbanks, and Charlie Chaplin. In 1935 the Academy of Motion Picture Arts and Sciences honored Griffith with an award.

After being struck with a massive cerebral hemorrhage on July 22, 1948, he was rushed from the Hollywood Knickerbocker Hotel, where he lived, to Temple Hospital, also in Hollywood. He was comatose, and did not know that his niece and nephew were at his bedside. He died at 8:24 a.m. on July 23.

His body lay in state on July 26, in Hollywood, while hundreds of persons passed the bier. Three hundred persons gathered at the Hollywood Masonic Temple for a memorial service on July 27. Honorary pallbearers included: Charlie Chaplin, Cecil B. De Mille *(q.v.)*, Samuel Goldwyn *(q.v.)*, and Walter Huston. He was eulogized by Donald Crisp, who had played in Griffith's most famous film, *Birth of a Nation*. His body was flown to Kentucky and buried at Mt. Tabor, two miles from his birthplace. Fence rails from his boyhood home surround the grave, and the marker which bears his name and vital statistics.

Mt. Tabor Cemetery, La Grange, Kentucky 40031.

# Grissom, Virgil

Virgil Ivan Grissom, the astronaut, was born April 3, 1926 in Mitchell, Indiana. Nicknamed "Gus," in 1961 he became the third astronaut to travel in space.

On January 27, 1967, at Cape Kennedy, Florida, he participated in a full scale simulation of the launching of Apollo I, which was scheduled for February 21. A flash fire broke out in the cabin at 6:31 p.m. when an electrical spark ignited the pure oxygen inside the cabin. The death of Grissom and his two fellow astronauts was instantaneous.

He was given a military funeral, attended by many political and state leaders, on January 31 at Arlington National Cemetery, Fort Myers, Arlington, Virginia, 22211, where he was also buried.

# Grosvenor, Gilbert H.

Gilbert Hovey Grosvenor, geographer and editor, was born on October 28, 1875, in Constantinople (now Istanbul), Turkey, of American parents. He became president and director of the National Geographic Society in Washington, D.C., in 1899, and began to edit the *National Geographic Magazine* in 1900, at a time when it was only a small technical bulletin. He married the eldest daughter of Alexander Graham Bell *(q.v.)* in 1900. In 1954 he resigned as editor and was elected chairman of the board of trustees.

In 1965 Grosvenor went to his summer estate, Beinn Breagh at Baddeck, on Cape Breton Island, Nova Scotia, Canada, where he celebrated his birthday on October 28. Illness, however, prevented his returning home to Bethesda, Maryland. He died at his estate in Nova Scotia on February 4, 1966, aged 90.

A private funeral service was held on February 6 in Baddeck, and a public service at 2:00 p.m. on February 9, at the National Presbyterian Church in Washington, D.C. The body was interred in the family vault at Rock Creek Cemetery, Rock Creek Church Road and Webster Street, N.W., Washington, D.C. 20011.

# Guggenheim, Meyer

Meyer Guggenheim, the industrialist, was born on February 1, 1820 in Lengnau, Switzerland.

Emigrating to the U.S. in 1847, he established an import firm in Philadelphia. In the 1880s he acquired mining interests, and then specialized in refining and smelting. In 1901 Meyer and his son Daniel gained control of the American Smelting and Refining Company, thereby assuming a leading position in the U.S. mining industry.

He died on March 15, 1905 in Palm Beach, Florida from what was described at the time as a severe cold.

The funeral service was held on March 19 at 10:00 a.m. at Temple Emanu-El at Fifth Avenue and 43rd Street in New York City. Scores of political and industrial leaders attended. Selections sung included "Oh for the Wings of a Dove." The recessional was Chopin's "Funeral March." Interment was in the family plot in Salem Fields, 775 Jamaica Avenue, Brooklyn, New York 11208.

# Gunther, John

John Gunther, journalist and author, was born in Chicago on August 30, 1901. After working for the *Chicago Daily News,* the United Press, and the *New York Daily News,* he wrote a series of sophisticated reportorial books based on exhaustive travel, acute observation, and team research. The series, which included *Inside Europe* (1936), *Inside Asia* (1939) *Inside Africa* (1955), and others, was widely acclaimed.

Gunther died on May 29, 1970 at the Harkness Pavilion of the Columbia Presbyterian Medical Center in New York City after what was described at the time as a brief illness, although he had been in poor health for some years. He was aged 68.

The funeral service was held on June 2, at St. James Episcopal Church, 71st St. and Madison Avenue, in New York City. There was no eulogy. He was cremated in June, and buried in July in the rural cemetery in Greensboro, Vermont. The simple service was attended only by his family. The Cemetery, Greensboro, Vermont 05841.

# Guthrie, Woody

"Woody" Guthrie, the folk singer, guitar player, and composer, was born Woodrow Wilson Guthrie on July 14, 1912 in Okemah, Oklahoma. He wrote more than 1,000 folk songs including: "Hard Traveling," "So Long," and his most famous composition, "This Land is Your Land," which was taken up by the civil rights movement in the 1960s.

His final years were spent in a New York hospital, being treated for the disease called Huntington's chorea. By 1965 he had stopped speaking and could only communicate with his hands due to the almost complete deterioration of nerve relays. When he died, on October 3, 1967, he weighed less than 100 pounds.

His family did not want any type of funeral service, memorial, or religious observance. His body was cremated at a left wing funeral parlor in Brooklyn. Within the week the ashes were delivered to his relatives in a small container. The ashes were then taken to his favorite beach spot at Coney Island, New York, and cast into the ocean.

# Hamilton, Alexander

Alexander Hamilton, the first secretary of the U.S. Treasury, who advocated a strong central government, was born on Nevis in what was then the British West Indies, probably on January 11, 1755. He came to the North American mainland in 1772, fought in the War of Independence, and was a delegate to the Constitutional Convention. He authored two-thirds of the Federalist Papers, and, as secretary of the Treasury, established the credit of the United States government.

Aaron Burr (q.v.) and Hamilton had long been personal enemies, and when Burr campaigned for the New York governorship in 1804, Hamilton's influence was responsible for his defeat. On June 27, alleging that Hamilton had made derogatory remarks about him, Burr challenged him to a duel. The duel was appointed to be held in Weehawken, New Jersey, at 7:00 a.m. on July 11, 1804, at the very place where Hamilton's 19-year-old son had been killed in a duel three years earlier. Both Burr and Hamilton then attended the Fourth of July celebration of the Society of the Cincinnati , and guests later remembered a coldness between the two men. On the morning of the duel, Hamilton set sail, from Manhattan for Weehawken, along with two friends—Nathaniel Pendleton, and Dr. David Hosack, (a surgeon), from the foot of Horatio Street in what is now Greenwich Village. Hamilton told Pendleton that he had made up his mind to fire in the air rather than at Burr. Landing on the New Jersey shore, the duel proceeded. English-made .544 caliber Wogden pistols with nine-inch barrels were used. Before the order to fire was given, Hamilton put on his spectacles.

Hamilton was struck on the right side. He rose to the left, then fell to the ground. Saying: "This is a mortal wound," he lost consciousness. Hamilton's ball hit a tree branch 12 feet off the ground, showing his intention not to shoot Burr.

Hamilton, unconscious, was put aboard a barge and rowed across the river. Approaching the opposite shore in a semi-delirious state he said: "Let Mrs. Hamilton be immediately sent for. Let the event be broken to her; but give her hopes."

Hamilton was taken to a friend's house at 80-82 Jane Street in New York City, and put to bed. He was given wine and water and large doses of anodyne and laudanum to ease pain. Dr. Hosack said his suffering was "almost intolerable."

His wife Elizabeth arrived at noon, and was told at first that the cause of his illness was "spasms." Hamilton's last rational words, spoken to his wife, were: "Remember, my Eliza, you are a Christian."

Bishop Benjamin Moore, a friend of Hamilton, and rector of Trinity Church, after satisfying himself that Hamilton bore no ill will towards Burr, gave him communion. Hamilton died at 2:00 p.m. on July 12, without a struggle. His body was then taken to the house of friends on Robinson Street.

Tomb of Alexander Hamilton in Trinity Churchyard, New York City.

(Trinity Church Parish)

The funeral service was held on July 14. Merchants suspended business that day, and the ordinance prohibiting bell-ringing at funerals was suspended.

Amidst much pageantry the funeral procession, attended by government notables, as well as the president and students of Columbia College, traveled the two miles to Trinity Church in downtown Manhattan. His Majesty's ships *Boston* and *Lord Charles Spencer*, as well as the French frigates *Cybelle* and *Didion*, anchored in the Hook off New York, fired minute guns. The streets of New York City were lined with mourning people. Women wept openly. Hamilton was eulogized by his friend, Gouverneur Morris. Bishop Moore then read the funeral service from the Book of Common Prayer. The service was concluded by troops firing blank musket volleys over his grave in Trinity Churchyard, Broadway and Wall Street, New York City, New York 10006.

# *Hammerstein, Oscar*

Oscar Hammerstein II, the lyricist, was born on July 12, 1895 in New York City. After a career of writing lyrics for Broadway musicals, he teamed up with Richard

Rogers in 1943. They created some of the best musicals to appear on the American stage, including *Oklahoma* (1943), *The King and I* (1951), and *The Sound of Music* (1959).

In September 1959 he visited his doctor for his annual physical, and said he was having stomach pains. X-rays and tests showed he had stomach cancer. Part of his stomach was surgically removed. As the months went on, however, he became weaker, and his deterioration became evident.

He died on August 23, 1960, aged 65, at his Doylestown, Pennsylvania, home. Tributes came from theatrical and artistic personalities. Richard Rogers said: "I am permanently grieved." Mary Martin, who was at the time starring in *The Sound of Music* at the Lunt-Fontanne Theatre, spoke of his "gentleness, his kindness and his greatness of soul." The American Society of Composers, Authors and Publishers (ASCAP), of which Mr. Hammerstein was the director, closed its offices on August 23.

His body was cremated, and a private funeral service was held on August 24 at Ferncliff Cemetery, New York, conducted by the clergyman from the Community Church, Park Avenue at 35th Street, New York, who quoted a line from "I'll Climb Every Mountain"—a song from *The Sound Of Music*. Robert F. Wagner, mayor of New York, asked that all lights on Broadway's theater district be extinguished at 8:57 p.m. on Thursday September 1, so that taps could be played in darkness. London's West End theater district had already paid the same tribute ten days earlier.

Ferncliff Cemetery, Hartsdale, New York 10530.

# *Hancock, John*

John Hancock, first signer of the Declaration of Independence, was born on January 12, 1737 in Braintree (now Quincy), Massachusetts. Because Hancock was the first of the signatories of the Declaration—in itself an act of courage and resolution—and because he used large and distinctive lettering, the name "John Hancock" entered everyday American speech as a popular synonym for a signature.

Hancock had been elected president of the first and second provincial congresses in 1774-75, and from 1775-80 was a delegate to the Continental Congress. His signature of the Declaration took place on July 4, 1776. Upon signing it, he commented: "There! I guess King George will be able to read that!" He subsequently became governor of Massachusetts, and was in his ninth term of office in this post at the time of his death.

During the winter of 1789-90, when he was 53, he became so ill that his signature was almost illegible. His final illness, however, occurred more than three years later. On October 8, 1793, at his home in Quincy, Massachusetts, he experienced trouble in breathing shortly after he got up. A doctor was called, but within an hour he was dead.

His funeral was held at 3:00 p.m. on October 9, in Boston, and was attended by many notables. The funeral procession, in which 20,000 people marched, left his mansion, and went up to the site of the Boston Liberty Tree. It then proceeded around the State Building, and entered the Old Granary Burying Ground, where he was interred.

A century later, the Massachusetts legislature allocated $3,000.00 to erect a memorial shaft over his grave. Since he had no direct descendant, his great-grand-niece, Miss Mary Elizabeth Wood, attended the dedication service on September 10, 1896. Old Granary Burying Ground, Tremont Street, Boston, Massachusetts 02108

# Handy, William C.

William Christopher Handy, the musician and composer, was born on November 16, 1873 in Florence, Alabama. He settled in Memphis, Tennessee, and began developing a musical style of his own, eventually called "blues." He gained fame by composing *St. Louis Blues* (1914). Altogether he composed some 60 tunes.

On March 23, 1958, the 84-year-old composer was admitted to a New York City Hospital suffering from bronchial pneumonia. He died before dawn on March 28, with his wife, his two sons, a daughter, his brother, and a grandson at his bedside.

On March 30 his body lay in state at the Frank E. Campbell Funeral Home in New York City, and was viewed by more than 500 friends and relatives. The sculptor Isaac S. Hathaway, curator of the ceramics department at Alabama State College, made a death mask of the composer for the college's collection.

On April 1, his body was taken to the Prince Hall Masonic Temple at 151st Street, New York City, where it was viewed by another 5,000 persons. There, Masonic rites were held for the composer, attended by about 1,500 Masons. The funeral service was held on April 2, at the Abyssinian Baptist Church at 138th Street, New York City with about 2,500 people in attendance. Jazz trumpeter Cootie Williams, using a muted trumpet, played the hymn "The Holy City," which had been Handy's favorite.

The funeral procession was led by a 30-piece brass band from the Prince Hall Masonic Temple. Burial was in Woodlawn Cemetery, 233rd Street and Webster Avenue, The Bronx, New York, 10470.

# Harding, Warren

Warren Gamaliel Harding, 29th president of the United States, (term of office 1921-23), was born on November 2, 1865, in Caledonia, (now Blooming Grove), Ohio. A Republican, he was elected president in 1920, pledging a return to "nor-malcy" after World War I.

His loosely-run administration led to widespread corruption, that was revealed to the public in 1923. A Senate investigation was launched into what became known as the "Teapot Dome Scandal," in the exposure of which it was established that secret and irregular leasing of federal oil lands by officials in the Harding administration had taken place.

Harding, at this time, undertook a nationwide tour. He had reached Alaska when he received a message in cipher which virtually prostrated him. He then repeatedly remarked that he had been betrayed by his associates. On the train trip from Alaska to San Francisco, he fell ill. One doctor who attended him said that he was suffering from a digestive upset "from eating rotten crabs," although it was later affirmed that crabs had not been on his menu. Another doctor said he had suffered a heart attack.

By August 2, 1923, he had developed pneumonia, and complained of breathlessness and fatigue. Sitting by his bed, his wife read him a favorable newspaper article about himself. After commenting "That's good," Harding suddenly died from an attack of what was described as "thrombosis." Conflicting rumors persisted as to the exact cause of his death.

His body was sent to Washington, D.C., where it lay in state briefly. It was then sent to his home town of Marion, Ohio. The citizens of Marion had expected the body to lie in state at an official location, but instead it lay in the home of his father, Dr. George T. Harding. It was placed in the same room as that in which the bodies of his mother and his sister had lain earlier. About 20,000 people viewed his body.

A private funeral service was held on August 10 at his father's house. A service was also held at Marion Cemetery, opening with the singing of "Lead Kindly Light," and closing with the hymn "Nearer My God To Thee." Among those present were Henry Ford *(q.v.)*, Thomas Edison *(q.v.)*, and Harvey Firestone. He is buried in a ten-acre memorial plot adjoining Marion Cemetery, 620 Delaware Avenue, Marion, Ohio 43302.

# *Hardy, Oliver*

Oliver Nowell Hardy, the film comedian, was born on January 18, 1892 in Atlanta, Georgia. He gave up law for an acting career and teamed up with comedian Stan Laurel *(q.v.)*. From 1926 until the time of Hardy's death they made more than 200 films, many of which were comedy classics. These included *From Soup to Nuts* (1928), *Babes in Toyland* (1934), and *Chump at Oxford* (1940).

Hardy suffered a paralytic stroke on September 12, 1956. He died eleven months later, in the early morning hours of August 7, 1957, at his mother-in-law's home in North Hollywood, California. Stan Laurel, who himself was recovering from a stroke, said: "What's there to say? It's shocking of course. Ollie was like a brother. That's the end of the history of Laurel and Hardy."

A Masonic funeral service was held on August 9 at Pierce Brothers Mortuary in Los Angeles. Stan Laurel was unable to attend the service because of ill health.

Following the service, Hardy's body was cremated, and the remains interred at the Garden of Hope, Valhalla Memorial Park, 10621 Victory Boulevard, North Hollywood, California 91606.

# *Harlow, Jean*

Jean Harlow, the movie actress, was born on March 3, 1911, in Kansas City, Missouri, as Harlean Carpenter. She settled in California, and after a part in the 1929 movie *The Saturday Night Kid*, was chosen by Howard Hughes to star in *Hell's Angels* (1930). She made a series of other movies including *Public Enemy* (1931), and *Bombshell* (1933).

In 1936, while working on the movie *Saratoga,* she suffered an acute case of sunburn and became very weak. Shortly thereafter she contracted a throat infection and stopped work. In early June she was admitted to Good Samaritan Hospital in Los Angeles for the treatment of uremic poisoning. On June 7, she took a turn for the worse, and despite blood transfusions and injections, she died. She was 26 years old.

A private funeral service was held on June 9 in Glendale, California, at the Wee Kirk O' The Heather. About 250 persons, mostly Hollywood stars, attended the 20-minute service. She lay in state in a coffin which bore an engraving of her signature. Singer Jeanette MacDonald *(q.v.)* sang "The Indian Love Call," after which a Christian Science practitioner read the funeral service. Film star Clark Gable *(q.v.)* was both an usher and a pallbearer. The service was closed by Nelson Eddy singing one of Miss Harlow's favorite songs, "Ah Sweet Mystery of Life." Burial was at Forest Lawn Memorial Parks, 1712 South Glendale Avenue, Glendale, California 91205.

# Harrison, Benjamin

Benjamin Harrison, 23rd president of the United States, (term of office 1889-93), was born on August 20, 1833 in North Bend, Ohio. He was the grandson of President William Henry Harrison *(q.v.).* A Republican, he served in the U.S. Senate, and was elected president in 1888. In the election, he failed to gain a popular majority, but received sufficient electoral votes to win. During his administration, U.S. influence expanded abroad, and the first Inter-American Conference was held in Washington, D.C., resulting in the establishment of the Pan American Union. On leaving the presidency, he returned to his law practice in Indianapolis.

In March 1901 he caught a cold, which developed into pneumonia. His private secretary released a statement which described his attack as "quite sudden and unexpected." His condition worsened, and he died on March 13 at 4:45 a.m.

His body lay in state on March 16 at the State House in Indianapolis. The funeral service was on March 17 at the First Presbyterian Church in Indianapolis. Poet James Whitcomb Riley spoke at the funeral. Burial was at Crown Hill Cemetery. His epitaph reads: "Statesman, yet friend to truth of soul sincere. In action faithful and in honour (sic) clear." Crown Hill Cemetery, 700 West 38th Street, Indianapolis, Indiana 46208.

# Harrison, William Henry

William Henry Harrison, ninth president of the United States (in office 1841), was the first chief executive to die in office, expiring after only one month's service. He was born on February 9, 1773, and became an army officer, serving with Anthony Wayne *(q.v.)* at the Battle of Fallen Timbers in 1794. After serving as governor of the Indiana Territory (1800-11), he fought in the War of 1812. He was in command of federal forces which defeated the British and their Indian allies at the Battle of the Thames, in Ontario, in 1813, as a result of which the U.S. gained unchallenged control of the area south of the Great Lakes. He served as a congressman and senator and was nominated as a Whig candidate for the presidency, a post to which he was elected in the 1840 electoral campaign.

Inaugural ceremonies for the incoming president were held on March 4, 1841 in a cold drizzle. Harrison insisted on delivering his inaugural address without a hat or overcoat. He then proceeded to give the longest inaugural address that any president had ever delivered. In consequence, he caught pneumonia, dying a month later, on April 4, 1841.

Not since the death of George Washington *(q.v.)* had the nation mourned so deeply. All the large cities were draped in black. On April 7, as cannons boomed, a military parade defiled down Pennsylvania Avenue in Washington D.C., accompanying the immense funeral car, which was drawn by six pairs of white horses. Old Whitey, Harrison's horse, walked riderless in the procession. The body was then placed in the East Room of the White House, where the calm face of the late president could be viewed through the glass top of the casket. About 40 clergymen were present at the funeral service that was then held, conducted by the rector of St. John's Church.

The casket was then placed in a lead coffin and kept in Washington until late June, when it began its slow and solemn journey back to North Bend, Ohio, by train, and by the Ohio river boat *Raritan*. On the way it lay in state for a short time at the City Hotel in Baltimore. When it reached Cincinnati , it lay for a day at the house of Harrison's son-in-law, Colonel Taylor. Upon reaching North Bend, burial took place on July 7 in a stone vault on a knoll overlooking Harrison's home,—a place that he himself had chosen. It now lies within an Ohio state park called Pioneer Cemetery, North Bend, Ohio 45052.

# Hart, Lorenz

Lorenz Hart, the lyricist, was born on May 2, 1895 in New York City. He collaborated with composer Richard Rogers, and wrote the lyrics for such song hits as "With a Song in My Heart," and "It's Easy to Remember But So Hard to Forget." Rogers and Hart also collaborated on the music and lyrics for several motion pictures.

Hart died in Doctor's Hospital in New York City on November 22, 1943 after a short illness. He was 47 years old.

The funeral service was on November 24 at Temple Emanu-El on Lexington Avenue, New York City. About 300 friends were present, including Richard Rogers and the entire cast of *A Connecticut Yankee*—a show in which Hart had collaborated. Burial was in Mt. Zion Cemetery, 59-63 54th Avenue, Maspeth, Queens, New York 11378.

# Hawthorne, Nathaniel

Nathaniel Hawthorne, the author, was born on July 4, 1804, in Salem, Massachusetts. After early literary successes, he moved to Concord, Massachusetts, in 1842, and became a member of the famous circle of notables which included Ralph

Waldo Emerson *(q.v.)*, Henry David Thoreau *(q.v.)*, and Bronson Alcott. His masterpiece, *The Scarlet Letter,* appeared in 1850. He also wrote many other works.

By April 1864, he had fallen ill, and was too weak to see many of his friends. He refused to see a doctor because of his deep seated mistrust of the medical profession. He had lost weight and was suffering from depression. On May 12, Hawthorne and ex-President Franklin Pierce *(q.v.)* traveled to Concord together. On May 19, between 3:00 and 4:00 a.m., Pierce went into Hawthorne's room and discovered that he had died. It was Pierce's opinion that Hawthorne had died of a disease of the brain or spine because on the last day of their trip he had had only limited use of his hands, legs, and feet.

The funeral service was on May 23, at the Church of Sleepy Hollow in Concord. Pallbearers included Henry Wadsworth Longfellow *(q.v.)* and Ralph Waldo Emerson. Franklin Pierce accompanied Mrs. Hawthorne and her children. Burial was in Sleepy Hollow Cemetery, Keys Road, Concord, Massachusetts 01742.

# *Hay, John Milton*

John Milton Hay, U.S. secretary of state from 1898-1905, was born on October 8, 1838, in Salem, Indiana. He is renowned as the promoter of the Open Door Policy towards China, which upheld equal trading rights for all nations in that country. He also authored several books, and from 1861-65 was private secretary to President Abraham Lincoln *(q.v.)*.

In a letter dated April 12, 1905 he had written: "My doctor here says there is nothing the matter with me except old age."On June 24, when he was in his summer home at Newbury, New Hampshire, doctors were called, arriving on a special train from Boston. They administered medications which had a calming effect. He died at 3:00 a.m. on July 1, 1905. The funeral service was at Lake View Cemetery in Cleveland, Ohio, and was attended by President Theodore Roosevelt *(q.v.)* and all his cabinet. Burial was in Lake View Cemetery, 12316 Euclid Avenue, Cleveland, Ohio 44106.

# *Hayes, Rutherford*

Rutherford Birchard Hayes, 19th president of the United States, (term of office 1877-81) was born in Delaware, Ohio, on October 4, 1822. In 1866 he ran for president against Democrat Samuel J. Tilden. It appeared at first that Tilden had won the election, but then electoral college returns from Louisiana, Florida, Oregon, and South Carolina were contested. A 15-member electoral commission was created, and ruled in favor of Hayes's electors, giving him victory. During his administration, the era of Reconstruction (1865-77) ended, and Hayes withdrew federal troops from the South. Hayes did not seek re-election in 1880, but returned to Ohio and became involved with humanitarian causes. In his later years he developed an interest in socialist philosophies.

On January 17, 1893, after visiting one of his sons in Cleveland, Ohio, he had an attack of angina pectoris at the Cleveland railroad station. He was brought some brandy, and made comfortable in the drawing room of the railroad car taking him home. He said: "I would rather die at Spiegel Grove [his home in Fremont, Ohio] than live anywhere else." He died there that night at 11:00 p.m. of what was described as "neuralgia of the heart."

He lay in state at Spiegel Grove. His cedar coffin was in the center of the room and was covered with three palm branches tied with a ribbon. The funeral service was held on January 20, and was attended by many notables, including President-elect Grover Cleveland. After a funeral procession through Fremont, headed by a military escort, he was buried at Oakwood Cemetery, 1225 Oakwood Street, Fremont, Ohio 43420.

# *Hayward, Susan*

Susan Hayward, the motion picture actress, was born on June 30, 1919, in Brooklyn, New York. Her movies included *With A Song in My Heart* (1952), *I'll Cry Tomorrow* (1955), and *I Want to Live* (1958). She was married twice—in 1944 and in 1957.

*Susan Hayward's grave.*
(Photo: Frances Long)

She had been suffering from a brain tumor when she died in Los Angeles, at 55 years of age, on March 14, 1975. Her doctor said she had suffered a seizure before her death.

The funeral service was held on March 16, at Our Lady of Perpetual Help Church in Carrollton, Georgia. Three priests and a monsignor celebrated the mass. Burial was in the church cemetery. Our Lady of Perpetual Help Church, Center Point Road, Carrollton, Georgia 30117.

# *Haywood, Big Bill*

William Dudley Haywood, the labor leader, also known as "Big Bill," was born on February 4, 1869, in Salt Lake City, Utah. He was born William Richard, but changed his name to that of his father. He began working as a miner at an early age.

After joining and moving up in the ranks of the Western Federation of Miners (WFM), he presided over the founding of the Industrial Workers of the World (IWW) in Chicago in June 1905. Also in 1905, when a WFM member was arrested for the murder of Frank R. Steuneberg, the anti-labor former governor of Idaho, Haywood and others were implicated in the crime and subsequently jailed in Boise, Idaho.

Rallies around the country raised enough money to hire Clarence Darrow as his defense attorney. Haywood was acquitted and became something of a folk hero. He continued to head the IWW, writing and lecturing around the country. In 1917 he and a number of other IWW members were arrested for sedition because of their opposition to World War I. He was sentenced to 20 years in prison. In 1921, while free on bond, he escaped to the Soviet Union where he lived until the time of his death.

In April 1928 he was treated at a Kremlin hospital for an advanced case of diabetes. On May 16 he suffered a stroke, which paralyzed half of his body. He showed improvement, and on May 17 talked with his wife and several friends. That same day he ate a large meal, then died in his sleep. His Russian wife, whom he had married in 1927, burst into tears at the time of his death. In his will he specified that half of his ashes should be buried in Chicago at Waldheim Cemetery near the graves of his comrades who were executed for their participation in the Haymarket Riot. The other half he ordered to be buried in Moscow.

His body was taken to Moscow's Club House of Political Prisoners where 1,000 visitors paid homage. There were no flowers, as Haywood had earlier requested that money for them should go to Lenin's Homeless Children's Fund. On May 19 he was cremated at the municipal crematorium, (formerly the Danskaya Monastery), on the outskirts of Moscow.

There was a special ceremony on August 3 at the Sixth Communist International Congress. At sunset that evening half of his ashes were placed in the Kremlin wall, facing the Red Square, near the grave of American journalist, John Reed. His urn was wreathed with flowers and red ribbons. A large number of police detachments regulated the crowd.

The other half of the ashes were placed in charge of Karl Reeve, an American Communist. They arrived in New York City in the first week of November. They were put on display on November 7 on a small platform in the center of the Manhattan Lyceum at 66 East Fourth Street. Several thousand Communists and representatives of labor organizations paid tribute.

At 9:00 p.m. on that same day the ashes were sent to Chicago, accompanied by an honor guard of the International Labor Defense.

A memorial burial service was held at Waldheim (now Forest Home) Cemetery, near Chicago, on November 18, conducted by the IWW and the Haywood Memorial Committee. Forest Home Cemetery, 863 South Des Plaines, Forest Park, Illinois 60130.

# Hearst, William Randolph

William Randolph Hearst, the newspaper publisher, was born on April 29, 1863 in San Francisco, California. The son of a gold-mine owner, he established a publishing empire, owning and operating newspapers all over the country including the *New York Journal-American*, the *Chicago American*, and the *Boston American*. He also bought several magazines including *Cosmopolitan* and *Harper's Bazaar*. By 1935 he owned 8 newspapers, 13 magazines, 8 radio stations and 2 movie companies. He spent many of his last years in seclusion, at the castle he had build at San Simeon, California.

In 1947 he suffered several heart spasms and during one of them he lost consciousness. His condition was diagnosed as well advanced "auricular fibrillation." After this his condition deteriorated. He lost weight, and his voice became reduced to a whisper, although he was in excellent mental condition. By the summer of 1951 he was left with very little strength and it was clear that death was not too far off. Early on the morning of August 14, he fell into a coma and died painlessly at 9:50 a.m. He was 89 years old.

His heavy copper casket lay in state at the Chapel of Grace at Grace Episcopal Cathedral on Nob Hill in San Francisco. Funeral services were held at the cathedral on August 17. The Episcopal service included neither eulogy nor sermon. The 46th, 121st, and 130th Psalms were read. A choir sang Dvorak's 23rd Psalm, and Ferdinand de la Tombeli's "My Lord and Savior." The service was attended by about 350 persons. Burial was in Cypress Lawn Cemetery, 593 Market Street, San Francisco, California 94105.

# Heinz, Henry John

Henry John Heinz, businessman, was born on October 11, 1844 in Pittsburgh, Pennsylvania. After failing in a venture that sought to produce horseradish, he, together with a brother and a friend, in 1876 formed a company to make pickles, ketchup, sauces, soups, baked beans, and a variety of condiments. In 1896 he first introduced the famous "57 Varieties" slogan. The company incorporated in 1905 as the H.J. Heinz Company, with Heinz as its president.

He died in Pittsburgh on May 14, 1919 at 3:50 p.m. The funeral service was held on May 17 at East Liberty Presbyterian Church in Philadelphia. There was a public showing of his body from 2:00 p.m. till 3:50 p.m. Heinz company plants and offices worldwide were closed on the day of the funeral. Burial was in the family mausoleum in Homewood Cemetery, Dallas and Aylesbord Avenue, Pittsburgh, Pennsylvania 15217.

# Hemingway, Ernest

Ernest Miller Hemingway, author, was born on July 21, 1899 in Oak Park, Illinois. He worked as a reporter for the *Kansas City Star*, and as European correspondent for the *Toronto Star*, and later settled in France. While there he became a member of a group of expatriated American writers and artists living in Paris. His books of novels and short stories included *A Farewell To Arms (1929),* and *For Whom The Bell Tolls* (1940). In 1952 his book *The Old Man and The Sea* won him a Pulitzer Prize. In 1954 he was awarded the Nobel Prize for literature.

*Ernest Hemingway's grave, in Ketchum, Idaho.*

(Photo: Ted Cutler)

In June of 1961 Hemingway was treated for hypertension at the Mayo Clinic and for what a doctor called "a very old case of hepatitis." After being discharged and returning to his home in Ketchum, Idaho, Hemingway, who was six feet tall, became worried about his weight which was 200 lbs. At 7:30 a.m. on July 2, his wife was asleep in an upstairs bedroom in their home when she was awakened by a gunshot. She ran downstairs and found her husband on the floor near a gun rack in the foyer. He was dressed in a robe and pajamas. Beside him lay a 12-gauge shotgun with both chambers discharged. On July 3, the coroner said that an inquest would not be held and that the death certificate would read: "Self inflicted gun shot wounds in the head." Floral tributes and messages poured in from around the world but Mary Hemingway, his fourth wife, asked that instead of spending money on these things mourners make contributions to their favorite charities.

A private funeral service was held in Ketchum, July 6, attended only by his family and close friends. The service was conducted by the pastor of the two Catholic parishes in Ketchum, St. Charles Roman Catholic Church and Our Lady of the Snows. There was no eulogy. As Hemingway had been divorced it was not a formal Catholic ceremony. The officiating priest quoted from Maccabees II 12:46. Burial was only a few feet away from a place where Hemingway had often hunted.

Ketchum Cemetery, Ketchum, Idaho 83340.

# Henry, O.

William Sydney Porter, the author, usually known by his pen name "O. Henry," was born on September 11, 1862, in Greensboro, North Carolina. In 1882 he settled in Texas, but in 1886 was convicted of embezzling funds from an Austin bank. He fled to Honduras but returned because of his wife's impending death. He was sent to prison for more than three years. In prison he began to write short stories. Collections of his short stories include *Cabbages and Kings*, (1904), *The Voice of the City*, (1908), and *Whirlygigs*, (1910). Many of his stories had surprise endings, and were characterized by fate, coincidence, or luck.

On June 3, 1910 he was hospitalized. On the way out of his apartment building, he stopped to talk to elevator operators and bellhops. In the hospital he asked to be called "Dennis," but then decided that the name to go on the hospital records would be "Will S. Parker." He emptied his pockets, saying: "Here I am going to die, and only worth 23 cents." The next day he grew weaker, suffering both diabetes and cirrhosis of the liver. His doctor said that he had "the most dilated heart I have ever seen." On June 4, when a nurse dimmed the lights in his room, she heard him mutter: "Turn up the lights. I don't want to go home in the dark." He died at 7:06 a.m. on June 5. His doctor later said: "He was perfectly conscious until within two minutes of his death and knew that the end was approaching. I never saw a man pluckier in facing it, or in bearing pain. Nothing appeared to worry him at the last."

His funeral service was held on June 7 at 11:00 a.m. at the Church of the Transfiguration on West 29th Street, New York City. By mistake, a wedding party was also scheduled to take place at the church at the same time. As the clergyman

*O. Henry's gravestone, bearing his real name— William Sydney Porter.*

(Photo: Russ Johnson: Hewitt Studios).

read Tennyson's poem, "Crossing the Bar," the wedding party could be heard talking and laughing through the open windows.

Burial was in Riverside Cemetery, Birch Street, Asheville, North Carolina 22802.

# Henry, Patrick

Patrick Henry, political leader and orator, was born on May 29, 1736, at Studley, Hanover County, Virginia. At the revolutionary convention on March 23, 1775, at Richmond, Virginia, anticipating the coming Revolutionary War, he introduced a revolutionary resolution. Defending it, he spoke the words that made him forever famous: "I know not what course others may take but as for me, give me liberty or give me death." He later helped draft the constitution of Virginia, was elected governor in 1776, and served for several terms.

By 1799 he had become very ill. It is now believed that he probably had some type of malignancy. On June 6, as he was sitting in a large comfortable chair at his estate Red Hill, in Charlotte County, Virginia, his doctor prepared to administer a dose of liquid mercury. "I suppose this is your last resort?" Henry asked. The doctor replied that it was.

"What will be the effect of this medicine?" asked Henry, with the vial in his hand.

"It will give immediate relief, or—"

"You mean, doctor, that it will give relief or prove fatal immediately?" The doctor answered: "You can live only a short time without it, and it may possibly relieve you." Henry then pulled his nightcap down over his eyes, and prayed for his family, his country, and his soul. He then took the mercury. His doctor left the house and threw himself under a tree, crying. Regaining his self-control, he returned to the house, and saw Henry still sitting in his chair. By this time, however, his fingernails were turning blue. He then began to lose consciousness, and shortly thereafter died.

At his own request Henry was buried after a simple service at the foot of his garden. A large marble tombstone marks his grave. It is inscribed: "His fame is his best epitaph." Red Hill, Brookneal, Virginia 24528.

# *Herbert, Victor*

Victor Herbert, conductor and composer of operettas and light music, was born on February 1, 1859 in Dublin, Ireland. He emigrated to the United States in 1886, when he was aged 27. After composing operettas for the New York stage, he conducted the Pittsburgh Symphony Orchestra from 1898 to 1904. He also led a campaign for copyright protection of musical compositions which led to the formation of the American Society of Composers, Authors, and Publishers (ASCAP).

On May 26, 1924 he had lunch at the Lamb's Club in New York City with one of the managers of the Ziegfeld Follies. Immediately after lunch he felt ill, and went home. Later, while walking up the stairs to his doctor's office on East 77th Street, he had a heart attack, and died, at about 4:00 p.m.

The funeral service was held on the afternoon of May 28 at St. Thomas Episcopal Church in New York City. It concluded with the playing of "Lead Kindly Light" and a violin solo, the "G String Air," by Bach. At his burial in Woodlawn Cemetery, a squad of the 102nd Engineers fired a volley, and a bugler played taps. Woodlawn Cemetery, 233rd Street and Webster Avenue, The Bronx, New York 10470.

# *Hershey, Milton Snavley*

Milton Snavley Hershey, chocolate manufacturer and philanthropist, was born on September 13, 1857 near Hockersville, Pennsylvania. After some unsuccessful ventures in candy manufacturing, he founded the Hershey Chocolate Corporation in 1903, to make chocolate bars. The company built the largest chocolate manufacturing company in the world, in Pennsylvania, and popularized the candy bar. The town of Hershey grew up around the plant.

A wealthy man, Hershey devoted most of his wealth to philanthropic ventures, such as the Hershey Industrial School for Orphaned Boys, the M.S. Hershey Foundation, and Hershey Junior College.

Hershey died, aged 88, of natural causes, in Hershey Hospital on October 13, 1945. His body lay in state from 9:00 a.m. to 1:00 p.m. on October 17, at the Hershey Industrial School. Funeral services were inter-denominational, and were conducted by a Catholic priest and five Protestant ministers. Services had earlier been held in all the Hershey churches on October 15. Burial took place in Hershey Cemetery. The pallbearers were eight boys from the Hershey Industrial School. Hershey Cemetery, 213 West Chocolate Avenue, Hershey, Pennsylvania 17033.

# Hill, George Washington

George Washington Hill, who introduced "Lucky Strike" brand cigarettes when he was vice-president of the American Tobacco Company, and made their promotion his personal responsibility, was born on October 22, 1884, in Philadelphia. He wrote much of the advertising copy himself, and originated several well-known slogans, such as "It's Toasted," and "Reach for a Lucky Instead of a Sweet." In one of his promotional campaigns, he obtained endorsements from famous women, which contributed to the acceptance of women as smokers.

Hill died on September 13, 1946, of a heart attack, while he was at his private fishing camp in Montepedia, Quebec, Canada.

The funeral service was held on September 16 at St. Bartholomew's Church, Park Avenue at 51st Street, in New York City. About 1,700 persons attended, including executives of the American Tobacco Company, whose offices were closed for that day. Burial was at Sleepy Hollow Cemetery, 540 North Broadway, North Tarrytown, New York 10591.

# Hill, Joe

Joe Hill, originally named Joel Emmanuel Haaglund, the labor organizer and songwriter, was born in Sweden in about 1872. He came to the United States in 1901, and worked in a machine shop in Chicago and in construction camps out West before joining the Industrial Workers of the World (IWW), nicknamed the "Wob-

*Joe Hill's funeral.*

(Photo: Archives of Labor and Urban Affairs, Wayne State University)

blies," in 1910. The songs he composed became famous among union workers. The best known was "The Preacher and the Slave."

He successfully organized workers in Binghampton, Utah, and won them a new wage scale and shorter hours. He was then arrested in Salt Lake City, Utah, and charged with the murder of a grocer named Morrison. The evidence was circumstantial, and the Swedish consul and President Woodrow Wilson (q.v.) tried to get him a new trial, but the supreme court of Utah sustained a verdict of guilty.

He was condemned to death, and kept in jail for about a year, before being taken out to be shot on November 19, 1915. He resisted being taken from his cell, and when the sheriff remonstrated, he replied: "You can't blame a man for fighting for his life." He was strapped into a chair in the prison yard, and a mask was placed over his eyes. He then said: "I will show you how to die. I have a clear conscience." A target was placed over his heart. Hill then smiled, and himself gave the word to fire. A newspaperman reported that it looked as though he had been hit with a heavy weight.

On November 20, his body, dressed in a black suit with an IWW button on the lapel, lay in state at O'Donnell Mortuary in Salt Lake City. Among the selections read at his funeral service was "Crimes of Justice," by Upton Sinclair (q.v.), the novelist. The body was then put on a hearse and taken in slow procession to the Union Pacific Railroad Station to be shipped to Chicago. Many of the marchers sang Hill's songs.

The body arrived in Chicago on November 23, and was taken to the Florence Funeral Parlor, where another viewing was held under IWW supervision. Thousands of people filed past. The cover of the funeral program read: "In Memoriam, Joe Hill, Murdered in the state of Utah, November 19, 1915."

After the funeral service, his body was taken to Graceland Cemetery, Chicago, and cremated. The writer Ralph Chaplain wrote: "Through a slim hole in the side of the furnace each committeeman viewed the flame-drenched casket containing the fine body and placid features of Joe Hill." The ashes were placed in envelopes and distributed to IWW locals in every state except Utah, and were also mailed to unions on every continent.

# Hires, Charles Elmer

Charles Elmer Hires, who popularized root beer, was born on August 19, 1851 in Bridgeton, New Jersey.

Hires improved upon a concoction of sassafras bark, sarsaparilla root, juniper berries, and other herbs, and named it "root beer." He introduced it at the Centennial Exposition in Philadelphia in 1876. He was president of the Charles E. Hires Company, the world's leading producer of root beer, from 1896 to 1918.

On July 30, 1937, Hires suffered a stroke as he was leaving his home for a fishing trip. He died the following day, July 31. A private funeral service was held on August 3 in Philadelphia, and was attended only by his family and close friends. Burial was at Westminster Cemetery, Manayunk, Philadelphia, Pennsylvania 19127.

# Hoffa, James R.

James Riddle Hoffa, the labor leader, was born on February 14, 1913 in Brazil, Indiana. After joining the International Brotherhood of Teamsters in 1932, he became the president of its Detroit Local 299 in 1935, and chairman of the Central Confederation of Teamsters in 1935. After the Teamsters' Union was expelled from the AFL-CIO in 1957, following charges of corruption, he played a role in making it the most powerful single union in the country.

In 1967 he began to serve a prison sentence for mail fraud. In December 1971 President Richard Nixon ordered the remainder of his sentence to be commuted on condition that Hoffa not be involved in union activities for eight years.

On the afternoon of August 12, 1975, Hoffa left his home near Detroit, Michigan, and drove about 40 miles to keep a 2:30 luncheon appointment at the Red Fox Restaurant, north of downtown Detroit. The last time he was seen was at 2:45 p.m. that day in the restaurant parking lot. After that, no trace of him was found. There was widespread speculation that he might have been killed by underworld figures, and his body disposed of. In June 1982, it was alleged in testimony that the underworld had Hoffa "ground up in little pieces, shipped to Florida and thrown into the swamp."

# Holiday, Billie

Billie Holiday, the jazz singer who became famous in the 1930s, was born as Eleanora Holiday on April 7, 1915, in Baltimore, Maryland. Later in her career she was nicknamed "Lady Day." She developed an intimate singing style that made her famous, and that was in contrast to the blues shouting of the 1920s.

In her teens she was a prostitute, but soon rejected prostitution and sought other work. Her first singing job was in a Harlem night club in 1931. By 1935 she had become recognized, and toured briefly with the orchestras of Count Basie and Artie Shaw. Her career flourished, but she became addicted to heroin, and in 1947, after an incident in Philadelphia, she was arrested in New York, and sent to a West Virginia reformatory for a year. Her autobiography, *Lady Sings the Blues*, written with W. Dufty, was published in 1956, and later, in 1972, was made into a film. She disliked the title, since her singing style was upbeat, and the antithesis of the blues. By the later 1950s her health problems, aggravated by her heroin habit and her resort to alcohol, had become acute. Her singing also deteriorated markedly.

In late May, 1959, she collapsed, and fell into a coma. She was admitted to Metropolitan Hospital in New York City, suffering from a liver ailment and cardiac failure. On June 12, the police raid found a small packet of heroin in her possession, which was confiscated, together with her radio, flowers, comic books, and chocolates that friends had brought to her bedside. On July 11, she was placed in an oxygen tent. She received the last rites of the Roman Catholic Church on July 15, and died at 3:10 a.m. on July 17. It was found that she had only seventy cents in her bank account, but she had $750.00 in fifty dollar bills taped to her legs—an advance on a series of articles she had been commissioned to write. In the year following her death, however, royalties from sales of her records totaled more than $1,000,000.

More than 10,000 persons viewed her body when it lay in state at the Universal Funeral Chapel on Lexington Avenue in New York City. The funeral service was held at St. Paul the Apostle Roman Catholic Church on July 21, and was attended by many famous names from the world of jazz, such as Benny Goodman, Gene Krupa (q.v.), and Roy Eldridge. Burial was in St. Raymond's Cemetery, 1201 Balcom Avenue, The Bronx, New York 10465.

# Holmes, Oliver Wendell

Oliver Wendell Holmes, physician, educator, and author, was born on August 29, 1809 in Cambridge, Massachusetts. A graduate of Harvard Medical School, of which he later became dean, he was renowned alike for his medical research and teaching, as well as for his witty "Breakfast-Table" series of essays. He also wrote poems, as well as three novels.

*Gravestone of the elder*
*Oliver Wendell Holmes.*

(Photo: Sammy Edward Baker)

He became ill with flu in November 1893. His weight dropped, but he seemed to recover. On October 7, 1894, while napping in a chair, his head fell forward onto his chest, and he died from what were called "natural causes."

He was placed in a simple black cloth covered coffin which bore a plain nameplate. Funeral services were held at King's Chapel in Boston on October 10, The service consisted of scriptural readings and a prayer. Musical selections included "The Lord is My Shepherd," and the hymn "Oh Paradise." Burial was at the Jackson lot at Mt. Auburn Cemetery, 580 Mt. Auburn Street, Cambridge, Massachusetts 02138.

# Holmes, Oliver Wendell

Oliver Wendell Holmes, son of the author of the same name, and justice of the Supreme Court, was born on March 8, 1841, in Boston. After serving in the Civil

War, he became a lawyer. He authored legal works, and became Weld Professor of Law at Harvard. He served on the Massachusets Supreme Judicial Court from 1882-1904. In 1902 President Theodore Roosevelt *(q.v.)* named him to the U.S. Supreme Court, where he served until 1932. Known on the Court as "the Great Dissenter," he became memorable for establishing the concept of "clear and present danger" as the only valid reason for limiting free speech.

He became ill in early March, 1935, and died on March 6 in Washington, D.C. at 2:15 p.m. A simple funeral service was held on March 8 at All Souls Unitarian Church. The officiating clergyman then recited one of Holmes's favorite sonnets—"Tonight," by Joseph Blanco White. At the end of the short service, Holmes was eulogized in a single sentence: "He never turned his back but marched straight forward." During the burial at Arlington National Cemetery there was a sleet storm, caused by low hanging clouds. A transport plane, trying to land at a nearby airfield, flying at treetop level, buzzed over the head of President Franklin D. Roosevelt *(q.v.)*, who was in attendance. Arlington National Cemetery, Fort Myer, Arlington, Virginia 22211.

# *Homer, Winslow*

Winslow Homer, the painter, was born on February 24, 1836 in Boston. After working as a lithographer, he began his artistic career as an illustrator. While under contract to *Harper's Weekly*, he was sent to Washington to sketch Lincoln's inauguration, and then covered the war for *Harper's* as an artist-correspondent. His first paintings were heavily influenced by what he had seen during the Civil War.

*Headstone of the Homer family, in Cambridge, Massachusetts. Among others, it marks the last resting place of Winslow Homer's ashes.*

(Photo: Sammy Edward Baker)

After a trip to Europe he turned to landscapes. "Snap The Whip," showing children frolicking, was exhibited at the 1872 Centennial Exposition in Philidelphia. In 1873 he began to paint watercolors, in which he captured much of the moodiness of the sea, and from this time on seascapes formed the dominant theme in his work. In 1883 he moved to Prouts Neck, a fishing village in Maine, where he lived until his death.

By 1910 he had become very ill, and was suffering from a variety of ailments and internal pains. Early in September he had a hemorrhage and became delirious. On September 17 he was visited by a nephew and Homer asked him: "How soon will I be able to have a drink and a smoke?" It was thought that he was recovering, when he died suddenly, on September 29, 1910, at his home in Prouts Neck.

His body was taken to Cambridge, Massachusetts, where a brief private ceremony was held on October 3. He was then cremated, and buried in Mt. Auburn Cemetery, 580 Mt. Auburn Avenue, Cambridge, Massachusetts 02138.

# *Hoover, Herbert C.*

Herbert Clark Hoover, 31st president of the United States, (in office 1929-33), was born on August 10, 1874, in West Branch, Iowa. A mining engineer, he gained international relief experience in the Boxer Rebellion in China in 1900, and in 1914, on the outbreak of World War I, was appointed chief Allied relief administrator. In 1917, when the U.S. entered the war, he was appointed U.S. food administrator. After serving as secretary of commerce in Republican administrations, he was elected to the presidency on the Republican ticket in 1928. With the onset of the Great Depression in 1929, however, his humanitarian image became tarnished by his failure to alleviate unemployment and other economic ills by conventional methods. In the presidential election of 1932, he was overwhelmingly defeated by Franklin D. Roosevelt (*q.v.*). He then retired to New York City where he lived in a suite in the Waldorf Towers.

On October 17, 1964, at 3:55 p.m., he was stricken by a massive internal hemorrhage. He was given blood transfusions, but his condition remained critical. By October 19, he had slipped into a mild coma, and his two sons came to his bedside at the hotel. He slipped into a deeper coma the following day, October 20, and died painlessly and effortlessly at 11:35 a.m.

On October 21, his body lay in state at St. Bartholomew's Episcopal Church in New York City. His flag-draped coffin was surrounded by a military honor guard, directly in front of the green marble altar. About 2,500 mourners passed his coffin each hour. The following day, October 22, a private 25-minute funeral service was held, attended by many notables. The rector of the church read from the Episcopal Book of Common Prayer.

*Herbert Hoover's grave (left).*

Photo: Herbert Hoover Presidential Library)

On October 23, the coffin was driven to Pennsylvania Station in New York City, and from there was taken by train to Washington, D.C. where it lay in state in the rotunda of the Capitol on the same catafalque on which the bodies of Presidents Lincoln and Kennedy *(q.q.v.)* had rested. Two days later, Hoover's remains were flown to West Branch, Iowa, where he was buried on a grassy knoll overlooking the cottage where he was born. About 75,000 mourners were at the graveside, where a short ceremony was held, consisting of a prayer and a eulogy. Herbert Hoover Historic Site, Park Lite Drive, West Branch, Iowa 52358

# Hoover, John Edgar

John Edgar Hoover, director of the Federal Bureau of Investigation for almost half a century, was born on January 1, 1895 in Washington, D.C. In 1924 he was appointed to the directorship of the Bureau of Investigation (as it was known until 1935, when the prefix "Federal" was added), and succeeded in freeing the organization from the disrepute into which it had earlier fallen. By exercising care in the screening and training of personnel, building the world's largest fingerprint collection, and introducing other crime-detection techniques, he transformed the Bureau into an effective and widely respected institution. In the final years of his directorship, however, he was subjected to some criticism for authoritarianism, and for some methods used by the Bureau.

By 1972, he had for some time been suffering from a heart ailment. On May 1, after working a full day at his office, he returned home and went to bed. Sometime in the early morning hours of May 2, he died of a heart attack caused by hypertension. His body was found beside his bed by his housekeeper at 8:30 a.m.

On May 3, his flag-draped coffin lay in state in the rotunda of the Capitol Building—thus making him the first civilian to be accorded this honor. It lay on the same catafalque that had borne the bodies of Presidents Lincoln, Kennedy, and Hoover *(q.q.v.)*. The rotunda was open all night.

The funeral service was on May 4 at the National Presbyterian Church in Washington, D.C., and was attended by many politicians and government officials. President Richard Nixon gave a short speech. Burial was next to the graves of Hoover's parents, at the Congressional Cemetery, 1801 East S.E., Washington, D.C. 29993.

# Hoppe, William Frederick

William Frederick Hoppe, the outstanding billiard player, was born on October 11, 1887, at Cornwall-on-the-Hudson, New York. He gained a position of almost total dominance in international three-cushion (carom) billiards, and won 51 world titles between 1906 and 1952, the year of his retirement. At that time he was acknowledged to be the greatest player in the history of the game.

On September 18, 1958, he suffered a heart attack. He was taken to St. Francis Hospital in Miami, Florida, where he died on February 1, 1959, at 4:00 p.m., from gastric hemorrhage. His body was flown to Philadelphia, where a requiem mass was held at St. John's Catholic Church on February 5. Burial was at Whitemarsh Memorial Cemetery, 1169 Limekiln Pike, Prospectville, Pennsylvania 19077.

# Hopper, Hedda

Hedda Hopper, the actress and gossip columnist, was born Elda Furry on June 2, 1890 in Holidaysburg, Pennsylvania. She made her debut on Broadway in *The Motor Girl* (1909), and later met De Wolf Hopper whom she married in 1913. She appeared in the film *Virtuous Wives* (1915), but was never a successful star. She subsequently became a nationally syndicated gossip columnist, covering Hollywood. In this capacity, she became, for several decades one of the most influential—and feared—personalities in the nation's movie capital.

On January 28, 1966, the 75-year-old columnist contracted a viral infection. Her condition worsened on January 30, and she was admitted to Cedars of Lebanon Hospital in Hollywood. A hospital spokesman said that she was ill with pneumonia, and that her condition "remained critical and the prognosis is very grave." She died on February 1. Death was attributed to double pneumonia and resulting heart complications.

Her body was cremated and there was no funeral ceremony. The ashes were buried three months later, on May 3, beside the graves of her mother and father, in Rose Hill Cemetery, 1207 12th Avenue, Altoona, Pennsylvania 16601.

# Hornsby, Rogers

Rogers Hornsby, the baseball player, was born on April 27, 1896, in Winters, Texas. He was widely considered to be the greatest right handed hitter in baseball history, and his lifetime batting average was .358, second only to that of Ty Cobb (*q.v.*). While with the St. Louis Cardinals in 1924 he batted .424, which in the 1980s was still the 20th century record.

In the summer of 1962 he underwent a cataract operation, and a few days later suffered a mild stroke. On January 4, 1963 his lungs became congested, and he developed a fever. He died of a heart attack on January 6, in Wesley Memorial Hospital in Chicago, aged 66. His family asked that no flowers be sent, and that instead money be sent to the Heart Fund.

The funeral service was held in Chicago on January 8, at Drake and Son's Funeral Home. Burial was on January 10 at Hornsby-Bend Cemetery, Travis County, Texas 76688.

# Houdini, Harry

Harry Houdini, the magician and escape artist, was born on April 6, 1874 in Budapest, Hungary, as Ehrich Weiss. (He was later legally to change his name to Houdini.) His family brought him to the U.S. shortly after his birth. In 1894 he married Wilhelmina Rahner, who assisted him in his stage acts. His escapes from shackles and locked mechanisms gained him a reputation which became international when, in 1900, he proved he could escape from the custody of Britain's famed Scotland Yard.

While he campaigned against spiritual charlatanism, in books and lectures, in his later years he became obsessed with premonitions of his own death.

In October 1926, he had had several sleepless nights sitting up to nurse his wife, who was sick with ptomaine poisoning. He was also recovering from a broken ankle. It was under these circumstances that, when he was backstage after one of his shows at the Princess Theatre in Montreal, Canada, he was approached by J. Gordon Whitehead, a student from McGill University, who asked him if it was true that he could withstand a blow to the stomach. When Houdini told him "Yes," Whitehead asked to strike him. Houdini, who had been distracted by reading his mail, and who was also at the same time sitting for a portrait, began to rise to his feet. Before he could brace himself, Whitehead struck his stomach with four blows, causing him great pain. Others present restrained him before he could strike further blows. Houdini assured them that he was all right, but that night he was in pain, and could not sleep. The next day, with a temperature of 102°, he took the train for Detroit. A doctor met the train at London, Ontario, examined him, and said he should be hospitalized at once. Houdini refused, as he had a show to give in Detroit. In great pain he gave the show, but at 3:00 a.m. on the 25th, he was taken to Detroit's Grace Hospital. That afternoon he went into surgery, and his ruptured appendix was removed, but it was too late. Peritonitis had spread poison through his body. He was given 12 hours to live. His wife collapsed at this news. Houdini nevertheless lived for several days before abandoning his fight to survive. He said to his brother, Dash, who was at his bedside: "I'm tired of fighting, Dash. I guess this thing is going to get me." He then lay quietly, and stared at his wife a long while. Then his head fell back on his pillow. He died at 1:26 a.m. on Sunday, October 31. It was Halloween Night.

He was placed in the same bronze coffin that he had bought for one of his escape routines. He had earlier left a sealed letter giving instructions for his burial. He had always worshipped his mother, and after her death in 1913 he had tried to visit her grave daily while in New York, his home base. He often visited her grave at dawn, or at fifteen minutes after midnight, the hour of her death. Now he asked that his body be embalmed and buried next to his mother's grave, which was done. Under his head was placed a black bag, containing all the letters his mother had ever written to him.

His funeral took place on November 4 at the Elks' Clubhouse on 43rd Street in Manhattan. He was buried in the Machpelah Cemetery in Brooklyn, New York. The past president of the Society of American Magicians was present, and broke a wand over his grave.

Before his death, he had reached agreement with his wife that the first of the two to die would communicate with the survivor. Several years went by without any message being received from him, and after a time his wife declared the experiment to be a failure. She herself died in 1943.

From time to time there were published reports that hidden clues or codes had been buried with the magician. On April 10, 1975, the stone bust of Houdini that had dominated his burial plot was destroyed with hammers by vandals.

Machpelah Cemetery, 82-30 Cypress Hills Street, Brooklyn, New York 11358.

# Houston, Samuel

Samuel Houston, leader of the U.S. emigrants who struggled to gain control of Texas and make it part of the United States, was born on March 2, 1793, in Lexington, Virginia. Of a frontier family, he was raised in Tennessee. After fighting in the War of 1812, he was assigned to help supervise the removal of the Cherokees from Tennessee to Arkansas. Later he was himself adopted into the Cherokee tribe. In 1827 he was elected governor of Tennessee. In 1832 President Andrew Jackson (q.v.) sent him to Texas, then a Mexican province, to negotiate Indian treaties for the protection of American traders. He arrived in Texas when the struggle between American settlers and the Mexicans was approaching its height. Houston was chosen as leader of the settlers, and assumed military command when the settlers rebelled against Mexico in 1835. On April 21, 1836, Houston and a force of 800 won a decisive victory at San Jacinto, securing the independence of Texas. Houston was elected president of the new state, and served twice in that office before Texas was accepted into the United States in 1845. He later served as senator and governor, but was deposed from office for his pro-Union views on the outbreak of the Civil War in 1861.

He spent the last two years of his life living quietly at home in Steamboat House, Huntsville, with his wife, Margaret, and family. In July of 1863 he caught pneumonia. His condition worsened, and his family gathered at his bedside. At one point he said: "Tell my enemies I am not dead yet." On July 26, as his wife read him the Bible, he spoke his last words: "Texas—Texas—Margaret!" He died quietly at sunset.

He was buried, seemingly the next day, during a rainstorm, in a small cemetery within sight of his house. His coffin was made by the ship's carpenter of the *Harriet Lane*, a Union prisoner of war on whose behalf Houston had interceded. His grave was marked by a simple stone, bearing only his name and vital statistics. A generation later it was replaced by a more grandiose marker—a piece of Texas granite 25 feet high, with the epitaph: "The world will take care of Houston's fame." Oakwood Cemetery, Huntsville, Texas 77340.

# Howard, Oliver Otis

Oliver Otis Howard, a Union officer who headed the Freedman's Bureau after the Civil War, was born on November 8, 1830, in Leeds, Maine. A colonel in the Maine militia, he fought in many battles, losing an arm at the Battle of Fair Oaks (Seven Pines). He was in command of the Army of Tennessee and marched through Georgia to the sea during the 1864 campaign of General William T. Sherman (q.v.). In 1865, President Andrew Jackson (q.v.) appointed him commissioner of the Freedman's Bureau. Howard University, chartered in 1867, of which he was third president, was named in his honor. After returning to military service, he fought against Indians in the West, and was superintendent of West Point from 1880-82.

On October 26, 1909, after eating breakfast at his Burlington, Vermont, home he had chest pains and nausea. Shortly after noon, while dictating an article about the changes in warfare in the 50 previous years, he felt sharp chest pains again. The doctor insisted that he be put to bed, which was done. Around 5:00 p.m., his doctor gave him nitroglycerine tablets. After the family dinner, his daughter-in-law took him some broth, which he sipped, but could not keep down. He then fell backward onto the bed, pinning his daughter-in-law so that she could not move. She called for help, but by the time others came, Howard was already dead.

Immediately, an honor guard from the 10th Cavalry—a black regiment—was positioned outside his house. The funeral service was held at the Burlington Congregational Church on October 29 with full military honors. A cavalry horse with reverse stirrups walked behind his flag-draped casket. Three volleys were fired, and a black bugler played taps as the casket was lowered into the grave. Lake View Cemetery, 455 North Avenue, Burlington, Vermont 05405.

# Hughes, Howard Robard

Howard Hughes, the industrialist, aviator, and motion picture producer, was born on December 24, 1905 in Houston, Texas. He inherited a tool company from his father, and at 20 years old went to Hollywood to produce motion pictures. Among his hits were *Hell's Angels* (1930), starring Jean Harlow *(q.v.)*, which won an Academy Award, the gangster movie *Scarface* (1932), and *The Outlaw* (1941). He organized the Hughes Aircraft Company, and while working for it as president, set the world's airspeed record of 352 miles per hour, (1935). In January 1937 he broke his own transcontinental flying record with a new time of 7 hours, 28 minutes.

In 1938, he circled the Earth in the record time of 91 hours, 14 minutes. By 1959 his tool company had acquired three-fourths of all TWA stock. He also owned the famous strip of hotels and casinos in Las Vegas. In 1950 he went into seclusion, and later became the subject of many bizarre rumors.

On April 5, 1976, officials of the Methodist Hospital in Houston, Texas, received some telephone calls from aides of Hughes. Hospital officials were informed that Hughes would be arriving that afternoon, and were also asked about possible medical treatment. A hospital official said: "We were aware it was an emergency but we did not know what the nature of the problem was." That same day a very ill Howard Hughes was flown from Acapulco, Mexico, en route to Houston. He died over southern Texas at 1:27 p.m. According to spokespersons from his company, the cause of death was a "cerebral vascular accident"—a stroke.

At the Houston airport an unmarked ambulance met the plane. After customs clearance, in which officials of the Summa Corporation showed the inspector only a birth certificate of Hughes, the body was taken to Methodist Hospital. An autopsy was performed on April 6. The body weighed only 90 lbs., and was frail and dehydrated. Hughes had grown a partial beard and a mustache. His measurements had shrunk two inches from his former stance of 6 feet 4 inches. Fingerprints were taken and sent to the FBI who used them to identify the remains. The cause of death was said to be kidney failure.

There was no funeral but instead a simple graveside ceremony was held on April 7 at Glenwood Cemetery, in Houston. There were no pallbearers, but instead funeral home attendants placed the copper-colored coffin on a support above the open grave. Two dozen white roses were on top of the coffin. The service was attended by 20 mourners, mostly distant cousins of Hughes, who heard the Episcopal burial rites, and readings from the Book of Common Prayer. The eight-minute ceremony ended at 8:02 a.m., after which the coffin was lowered into the vault and covered with earth. Glenwood Cemetery, 2525 Washington, Houston, Texas 77007.

# *Humphrey, Hubert H.*

Hubert Horatio Humphrey, vice-president of the United States from 1965-69, was born on May 27, 1911 in Wallace, South Dakota. In 1945 he was elected mayor of Minneapolis, and in 1948 was elected to the U.S. Senate as a Democrat, serving there until 1961, after which he became assistant Senate majority leader. After his term as vice-president, he contested the 1968 presidential election as the Democratic nominee, but lost.

In 1967, while he was vice-president, it was discovered that he had a disease of the urinary bladder that had the potential to become malignant. In the mid 1970s, some malignant cells were discovered, and in August 1976 a biopsy showed that he had cancer. After undergoing surgery for this condition at Sloan-Kettering Cancer Center in New York City, he returned to Washington, D.C. and began chemotherapy. In February 1977 his right leg began to swell because of pressure from the tumor. He did not, however, curtail his schedule of meetings at the White House or in the Senate. In August 1977 he began to develop nausea and abdominal pain. A tumor was found in his abdomen, and a colostomy was performed. During his final months he had a whirlwind schedule of public appearances, dedicating public buildings that were named after him, and making speeches. On January 13, 1978, at Waverly, near Minneapolis, he slipped into a coma and died.

President Carter dispatched Air Force One to Minnesota, after having seats removed so that the body would not be carried in the baggage compartment. On January 14 the body, accompanied by his family, was flown to Washington, D.C., and was taken to the Capitol rotunda, where a small service was held. An official service was held on January 15, attended by President Carter, and former Presidents Ford and Nixon. Barbara Merrill sang "America the Beautiful." On July 16 the body was flown back to Minnesota, where it lay in state in the rotunda of the state capitol in St. Paul. Despite the icy cold winter, 40,000 people waited to view the coffin. A funeral service was held at Hope Presbyterian Church in Minneapolis, at which vice-president Walter Mondale spoke. Musical selections included "Ave Maria," and "A Mighty Fortress is Our God," which had been requested by Humphrey before his death. A black choir from the Sabathani Baptist Church of Minneapolis then sang. The burial took place the same day at Lakewood Cemetery, 3600 Hennepin Avenue, Minneapolis, Minnesota 55409.

# *Ingersoll, Robert G.*

Robert Green Ingersoll, the 19th-century politician, orator and lecturer, known as "the great agnostic," was born on August 11, 1833, in Dresden, New York.

A lawyer, he served in the Civil War (1861-65), and was attorney general of Illinois from 1867-69. A Republican, he did not gain a cabinet post because of his unorthodox religious views, but his lectures, which were highly paid, attracted a large attendance. In 1885 he moved his practice to New York City.

On July 21, 1898, while living in Dobbs Ferry, New York, he awoke at 1:00 a.m. with abdominal pains, which he attributed to indigestion. When daylight came he telephoned his doctor for an appointment the following day, and was advised to take nitroglycerin tablets every 15 minutes until the pain subsided. After talking with his family, he took a nap in the early afternoon. When he awoke a family member noted that his tongue was coated, but he smiled and replied: "I'm better now." Then his eyes recessed deeply into his head and his mouth fell open. Thinking he had only fainted, his family gave him a little brandy and a hot foot bath, and then a hot mustard bath. Within a few minutes of this, a neighboring doctor arrived, and pronounced him dead. Attempts, a few minutes later, by other doctors to give him oxygen and artificial respiration met with no success. Death was attributed to angina pectoris.

A funeral service was held on July 25, at 4:00 p.m., in Ingersoll's bedroom. His body was wrapped in a linen cloth and lay on a flower-covered bier. A red rose lay on his chest. Forty friends gathered in the darkened room, but there was no eulogy nor any formal rites. Instead, the group read from Ingersoll's own writings.

His body was cremated on July 27, and the ashes were placed in a bronze urn, inscribed on one side with his name, and on the other with these words, in French: "The urn holds the dust, the heart, the memory." The urn remained in his wife's possession at the Ingersoll estate in Dobbs Ferry until her death in 1923 when the ashes were buried under a granite monument in Arlington National Cemetery, Fort Myer, Arlington, Virginia. 22211.

# *Irving, Washington*

Washington Irving, author of *The Sketch Book* (1819-20), which contained such tales as "Rip Van Winkle" and "The Legend of Sleepy Hollow," was born on April 3, 1783 in New York City. He wrote a number of other works. From 1826-32 he was attached to the American Legation in Spain, during which time he wrote books on Spanish subjects, including *Columbus* (1828), and *A Chronicle of the Conquest of Granada* (1829).

In his later years he settled in "Sunnyside," the house he had built in Tarrytown, New York. (The house may still be visited, but the land it stands on is now in Irvington, New York.) His final years were spent writing a *Life of George Washington*, published in five volumes between 1855-59. This task became a race against death, and when he had completed it, he fell into a depression, compounded by fatigue and bad health. He only wished to die. Already, in 1858, he had said: "I am getting ready to go. I am shutting up my doors and windows." On the evening of November 28, 1859, one of his nieces brought medicine to his bedroom. He sighed and asked her: "You cannot tell how I have suffered. When will this ever end?" He then raised himself up, clutched at the bedpost, and fell to the floor, dying.

Flags in New York City were lowered to half-mast at the news of his death. On December 1, after a private service at Sunnyside, an Episcopal funeral service was held at 1:00 p.m. at Christ Church in Tarrytown. After a reading from Corinthians, 150 carriages and more than 500 pedestrians accompanied the body to the place of burial, passing along the picturesque route that Irving had made famous in his story *The Legend of Sleepy Hollow*. Sleepy Hollow Cemetery, 540 North Broadway, North Tarrytown, New York 10591.

*Washington Irving's headstone, in Sleepy Hollow Cemetery, Tarrytown, New York.*

(Photo: Marc Loonan)

# *Ives, Charles Edward*

Charles Edward Ives, the composer, was born on October 20, 1874 in Danbury, Connecticut. He received a Pulitzer Prize in 1947 for his *Third Symphony*. His music is often said to be dissonant and disjointed, combining polytonal and polyrhythmic structures with popular melodies, marching music, or hymns. Besides chamber music and symphonies, he also wrote piano and violin sonatas. His compositions, which were often on characteristically American themes, included: "Harvest Festival" (1898), "Decoration Day" (1912), and "Fourth of July" (1913).

He died at 1:45 p.m. on May 19, 1954, at Roosevelt Hospital, New York City, of complications after an operation. The funeral, at which his brother-in-law, a Congregational minister, officiated, was held at his home in West Reading, Connecticut. Burial was at Wooster Cemetery, 20 Ellsworth Avenue, Danbury, Connecticut 06810.

*The headstone of Charles Edward Ives.*

(Photo: Donna Hibbert)

# *Ives James Merritt*

James Merritt Ives, the lithographer, who, together with Nathaniel Currier *(q.v.)*, gained fame for his part in producing the Currier and Ives prints that were widely popular in the later 19th century, was born on March 5, 1824 in New York City.

In 1852, Ives became a bookkeeper in Currier's New York lithography house. They became partners in 1857, and proceeded to produce the series of hand-colored prints that are now collector's items. Ives's special contribution was to select subjects that were popular. The prints were generally used for wall decorations. More than 7,000 subjects were produced altogether, either by the Currier firm or by Currier and Ives. The firm also printed hand-bills for the showman P.T. Barnum *(q.v.)*.

Ives died in Rye on January 3, 1895. While, according to the newspaper account, he died at midnight, his death certificate states that he died at 6:30 p.m. Cause of death was enlargement of the heart. The funeral service was held at Christchurch Episcopal Church in Rye, and the hymn "Abide With Me" was sung. Burial was in the same cemetery as Nathaniel Currier, in Brooklyn. Green-Wood Cemetery, 17 Battery Place, Fifth and 25th Street, Brooklyn, New York 11228.

# *Jackson, Andrew*

Andrew Jackson, seventh president of the United States, (in office 1828-37), was born on March 15, 1767 in Washaw, in what is now South Carolina. After representing Tennessee in Congress and the Senate, Jackson became major general of the Tennessee militia. In the War of 1812, he distinguished himself in campaigns against the Creek Indians in Alabama (1813-14), by marching into Florida, and by defeating the British at the Battle of New Orleans (1815). In 1817-18 he served in Florida, helping to pave the way for its acquisition by the United States. He failed to gain the presidency in the 1824 election but, as the Democratic nominee, was elected president in 1828. The first president from the west of the Appalachians, he came to epitomize populist and democratic sentiment. On leaving the presidency, he retired to his home, the Hermitage, in Nashville, Tennessee, leaving behind him a strong and well organized Democratic Party.

By 1845 he was suffering from dropsy, and his body was almost twice its normal size. He also had frequent tubercular hemmorhages, and coughed day and night. One lung was useless, and the other was affected. His mental faculties may have been impaired, for he sang incessantly—his shrill voice echoing through the Hermitage as he sang "Auld Lang Syne," or perhaps a hymn.

When word spread that he was near death, numbers of people came to see him, entering his bedroom two or three at a time. Jackson received them while lying in bed, usually smoking a small silver pipe, while being fanned by a black servant boy.

On June 8, 1845, it became obvious that death was near. Hearing servants moaning, Jackson said: "Please don't cry. Be good children, and we'll all meet in heaven." He closed his eyes and began to breathe shallowly. At 6:00 p.m. his head fell forward, and death came.

At his own request the funeral, held on June 10, was as simple as possible. It was attended by 3,000 people from the surrounding countryside. The text of the sermon was: "These are they which came out of the great tribulation and washed their robes white in the blood of the lamb." A spectator wrote "I never witnessed a funeral of half the solemnity." In March 1845 he had been offered an Oriental sarcophagus, said to have once contained the bones of the Roman emperor Alexander Severus, to be used for his own remains. He refused it, saying: "My republican feelings and principles forbid it. The simplicity of our system of government forbids it."

He was buried beside his wife in the grounds of the Hermitage, Rachel Lane and Lebanon Road, Highway 70, Old Hickory, Tennessee 37138.

## Jackson, Mahalia

Mahalia Jackson, the gospel singer, was born on October 26, 1911 in New Orleans, Louisiana. In 1934 she recorded "God Separate the Wheat From the Tares," a popular gospel song which led to a series of hits, including "He's Got The Whole World In His Hands." She refused to sing in nightclubs, or in any place where liquor was served. She sang at the inauguration of President John F. Kennedy (q.v.) in 1961, and in her later years was associated with the civil rights movement.

By 1972 she had been in ill health for several years. She died on January 27, of a heart seizure, in Little Company of Mary Hospital, Evergreen Park, Illinois.

The body lay in state on January 31 at Greater Salem Baptist Church in Chicago and was viewed by approximately 50,000 people. A memorial service was held in Chicago on February 1, attended by many notables including Mrs. Martin Luther King, Jr., Ella Fitzgerald, the Rev. Jesse Jackson, and Chicago's Mayor Richard Daley, (q.v.). Actor Sammy Davis, Jr. arrived in a helicopter, bearing a message of condolence from President Richard Nixon.

Emotions ran high among the mourners, as gospel singers sang, and many nurses attended those who fainted. At the conclusion, Detroit-based gospel singer Aretha Franklin sang "Precious Lord" and "Take My Hand."

Jackson's body was sent to New Orleans, where it arrived on February 3. The coffin had been damaged en route, at Chicago's O'Hare Airport. It lay in state, while at least 70,000 people filed past. Mahalia was dressed in a blue gown, laced with gold. The funeral was held at Rivergate Center. The remains were then taken to Providence Memorial Park and Mausoleum. A memorial service was also held on July 9 in New York City at the Cathedral Church of St. John the Divine. It was attended by almost 3,000 people, including jazz musician Duke Ellington. Providence Memorial Park, 8200 Airline Highway, Metairie, Louisiana 70003.

## Jackson, "Stonewall"

Thomas Jonathan Jackson, the Confederate general, celebrated as "Stonewall" Jackson, was born on January 21, 1824 in Clarksburg, Virginia, (now West Virginia). After fighting in the Mexican War of 1846-47, he taught at the Virginia

Military Institute from 1851-61. On the outbreak of the Civil War in 1861, he joined the Confederacy. He commanded Confederate troops at the First and Second Battles of Bull Run, and in the Seven Days Battles. At the First Battle of Bull Run, a dying Confederate officer exclaimed: "See, here stands Jackson like a stone wall"—thereby giving him the name by which he is remembered.

At the battle of Chancellorsville, on May 2, 1863, Jackson, returning from pursuing the enemy, was caught by rifle fire from his own men. He had to have his left arm amputated. On May 7, at Guiney's Station, Virginia, he awakened nauseated, and wet towels were applied to his chest and head, thereby worsening his condition. Pneumonia developed, he became delirious, and was given morphine. On May 10, the day of his death, his doctor told him he would soon be in heaven, and asked him if he wanted to go. He replied: "Yes, I'd prefer it, I'd prefer it." Later he said: "It is the Lord's Day, my wish is fulfilled. I have always wanted to die on Sunday."

At the funeral service, held on May 15 in the Presbyterian Church of Lexington, Virginia. The Twenty-third Psalm was read. Burial took place the same day, in what is now the Stonewall Jackson Cemetery, on the east side of South Main Street, in the 300 block, Lexington, Virginia 24450.

# James, Henry

Henry James, the novelist, was born on April 15, 1843, in New York City. He was the younger brother of the philosopher William James (*q.v.*). He alternated his residence between the United States and Europe, until 1876, when he settled in London, where he lived until his death. He became known as a master of literature. His many novels included *The American* (1877), and *The Golden Bowl* (1904). His most

*The headstone of Henry James.*
(Photo: Kevin Gleason)

famous short story is *The Turn of the Screw* (1898). In sympathy with the British cause in World War I, he became a British subject in 1915.

In late 1915 and early 1916, James had had a series of strokes, and embolic pneumonia, as well as a blood clot on the brain and another on the lung. On February 2, 1916, his nephew Harry wrote: "Physically he's near helpless, being completely paralyzed on the left side... He's very confused in mind, drowsily wandering almost all the time and cognizant of nothing except that he's ill." In the middle of February he fell into a coma and in one of his last conscious moments said: "Tell the boys to follow, to be faithful, to take me seriously." He died painlessly, without regaining consciousness, around 7:00 p.m. on February 28, 1916. According to his sister-in-law, Alice James: "He just gave three sighs and went."

The funeral service was held on March 3 at Old Chelsea Church, London, England. His body was cremated, and the ashes returned to America, where they were buried in the family burial ground in the Cambridge Cemetery in Massachusetts. His tombstone reads: "Henry James, O.M. [Order of Merit]. Novelist-Citizen of two countries, interpreter of his Generation on both sides of the sea." His family also placed a memorial at Old Chelsea Church which read: "Lover and interpreter of the fine amenities, of brave decisions and generous loyalties; a resident of this parish who renounced a cherished citizenship to give his allegiance to England in the first year of the Great War." Cambridge Cemetery, 76 Coolidge Avenue, Cambridge, Massachusetts, 02138.

# *James, Jesse*

Jesse Woodson James, one of the most famous outlaws of Western lore, was born on September 5, 1847, near Centerville, in what is now Kearney, Missouri. After fighting as part of a Confederate guerrilla gang during the Civil War, he was declared an outlaw in 1866. The following year, together with his brother Frank, he formed the James gang, which committed many robberies and murders, held up banks and stage coaches, and introduced the practice of robbing trains. During an abortive raid on a Northfield, Minnesota, bank in 1876, all of the gang except the James brothers were captured or killed. The brothers were protected from capture by the authorities by the people of their region.

After a $10,000.00 reward was offered for Jesse, however, a newly-recruited member of the gang, Robert Ford, sought to gain it. Jesse was then living in St. Joseph, Missouri, under the assumed name of Thomas Howard. Ford visited him at his home. Picking one of Jesse's pistols off the table, he shot him in the back of the head, killing him instantly, as he was straightening a picture on the wall. Ford later said: "The ball struck him just behind the ear and he fell like a log, dead."

The shooting took place on April 3, and the funeral service was held on April 6, 1882, at the Baptist Church in Kearney, Missouri. At the grave, which was at the farm owned by James's mother, a group sang "We Will Wait Until Jesus Comes."

In later years, Frank James, who had surrendered, and been tried and acquitted, earned money by showing tourists his brother's grave, and selling them pebbles from it as souvenirs. He was subsequently re-buried in Mt. Olivet Cemetery, on the south side of Missouri Highway 92, Kearney, Missouri 64060.

# James, William

William James, the psychologist and philosopher, older brother of the novelist Henry James *(q.v.)*, was born in New York City on January 11, 1842. Associated with Harvard University, he was the leader of a philosophical movement known as Pragmatism. A pioneer in physiological psychology, he wrote *The Principles of Psychology* (1890). He also wrote *The Varieties of Religious Experience* (1902), an empirical approach to religious studies.

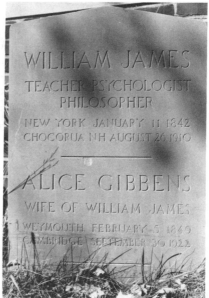

*The headstone of William James.*
(Photo: Kevin Gleason)

From 1907 onwards, he suffered from increasing ill health caused by a heart problem. He died at his home in Chocorua, New Hampshire, on August 26, 1920. A funeral service was held on August 30, at 4:00 p.m., in the Appleton Chapel in Harvard Yard, in Cambridge, Massachusetts. His casket was covered with palm branches and an asparagus fern. The organist played Chauvet's *Funeral Prelude*. The body was then cremated at Mt. Auburn Cemetery in Cambridge. The ashes were taken back to Chocorua, where they were scattered in a mountain stream.

# Jarrell, Randall

Randall Jarrell, the poet, critic, and novelist, was born on May 6, 1914, in Nashville, Tennessee. He wrote some of the most celebrated American wartime poetry to be published during and after World War II. He also taught at universities in New York and North Carolina.

On October 14, 1965, he was walking along the heavily-traveled Chapel Hill bypass highway in North Carolina when he was hit by a car. Witnesses later reported that he had lunged into the side of the car that struck him. On November 8 the Orange County medical examiner's office ruled that the death was accidental.

The funeral service was held on October 17 at the Holy Trinity Episcopal Church in Greensboro, North Carolina. After the simple service, attended by close friends and family, his remains were cremated and then buried at New Garden Cemetery, Guilford College, Greensboro, North Carolina 27410.

# *Jefferson, Thomas*

Thomas Jefferson, third president of the United States, (in office 1801-09), was born on April 2, 1743 in what is now Albemarle, Virginia. A delegate to the Continental Congress, he was on the committee that drafted the Declaration of Independence, and was chosen to do the writing. His draft, with only minor changes, became the text that was approved on July 4, 1776. In 1790 he became the first U.S. secretary of state. When the presidential election of 1800 went to the House of Representatives for decision, Jefferson, Democrat-Republican, was chosen. In 1804 he was re-elected to a second term.

*Thomas Jefferson's grave, at Monticello, Virginia.*

(Photo: Thomas Jefferson Memorial Foundation)

During his presidency, Jefferson authorized the Louisiana Purchase from France in 1803. He also succeeded in keeping the United States out of the Napoleonic Wars during his presidency. In 1809 he retired to his estate, Monticello, in Virginia, where he worked on many projects, including drafting the charter of the University of Virginia, and the architectural design of the state capitol of Virginia. During his later years he conducted a voluminous correspondence with John Adams (*q.v.*) of Quincy, Massachusetts. Both men died on July 4, 1826, on the 50th anniversary of the adoption of the Declaration of Independence. Jefferson's death occurred a few hours before that of Adams.

By 1826, Jefferson was suffering from arthritis, rheumatism, and diarrhea. His doctor wrote that by July 3rd he had fallen into an almost permanent stupor. About seven o'clock in the evening he woke and, seeing the doctor at his bedside, asked in a husky indistinct voice whether it was July the Fourth. He was told that it was not yet, but that it soon would be. "These," wrote the doctor, "were the last words I heard him utter." At 9:50 a.m. on July 4 he died peacefully.

His body was placed in a shroud, and late in the afternoon of July 5 was given a simple Episcopal funeral at Monticello. Before dying he had designed his own tomb, which was surmounted by an obelisk. It bore the inscription: "Here was buried Thomas Jefferson, Author of the American Declaration of Independence, of the Statute of Virginia for religious freedom, and Father of the University of Virginia." Burial took place in the rain at his plantation, Monticello, near Charlottesville, Virginia. Monticello Memorial Park, Route No. 1, Charlottesville, Virginia 22901.

# Johnson, Andrew

Andrew Johnson, seventeenth president of the United States, (in office 1865-69), was born on December 29, 1808, in Raleigh, North Carolina. After serving in Congress from 1843-53, he was governor of Tennessee from 1853-57. In 1864 he was elected to the vice-presidency on the Republican ticket with President Abraham Lincoln *(q.v.)*. When Lincoln died, on April 15, 1865, he succeeded to the presidency.

Johnson's lenient Reconstruction policy towards the South immediately after the Civil War brought him into sharp conflict with radical Republicans in Congress. This came to a head with a clash with his opponents over the Tenure of Office Act (1867) and his right to dismiss from office Secretary of War Edwin M. Stanton. This led to impeachment proceedings being opened against Johnson. In May 1868, however, his enemies failed by a single vote to secure his impeachment, but his political credibility on the national level had crumbled.

On July 30, 1875, Johnson was in the mountains of Carter County, Tennessee, about 40 miles from Greenville, visiting his daughter. He was suffering from a prevailing heat wave. After lunch he was talking with his granddaughter in his bedroom. As she was leaving she heard a thump, looked around, and saw her grandfather lying on the floor. He had had a stroke. He was put to bed, but refused to allow a doctor to be called. On the afternoon of July 31, he had a second stroke, fell unconscious, and died before a doctor could arrive.

He had once said: "When I die, I desire no better winding sheet than the Stars and Stripes, and no softer pillow than the Constitution." His body, wrapped in the American flag, was placed in a coffin with a copy of the Constitution beneath his head. Special trains brought mourners to Greenville, Tennessee, where the funeral service was held on August 2. His grave is marked by a monument decorated with the Stars and Stripes, an eagle, and a hand resting on the Constitution. It bears the inscription: "His faith never wavered." The Andrew Johnson National Historic Site, Greenville, Tennessee 37743.

# Johnson, Jack Arthur

Jack Arthur Johnson, the boxer, whose professional career lasted from 1897 to 1928, was born on March 31, 1878, in Galveston, Texas. He won the world's heavyweight title from Tommy Burns in Sydney, Australia, on December 26, 1908, thus becoming the first black boxer to hold the title. (He lost it to Jess Willard in Havana, Cuba, in 1915.) In 1912 he was convicted of violating the Mann Act by transporting his wife across state lines before they were married. He fled abroad while out on bail, but returned to the U.S. in 1920, to serve a one-year sentence on this charge. In his later years he earned his living by appearing in carnivals and at vaudeville theaters.

On June 10, 1946, while driving on U.S. Highway 1, north of Raleigh, North Carolina, he lost control of his car, which hit a light pole and overturned. Thrown from the car, he was taken to St. Agnes Hospital in Raleigh, where he died at 6:10 p.m. He was aged 68. His body was sent to Chicago where the funeral service, attended by 2,500 people, was held at the Pilgrim Baptist Church on South Indiana Avenue. He was buried at Gracelands, near the grave of Bob Fitzsimmons, a world boxing champion whom Johnson had defeated in 1907. Gracelands Cemetery, 4001 North Clark, Chicago, Illinois 60613.

# Johnson, Lyndon Baines

Lyndon Baines Johnson, 36th president of the United States, (in office 1963-69), was born on August 27, 1908, near Stonewall, Texas. After serving in the Congress and Senate, he became Senate whip in 1951, and was Senate majority leader from 1955-61. He was elected vice-president in 1960, and succeeded to the presidency on

the death of President John F. Kennedy (q.v.) in 1963. He was re-elected to the presidency in 1964 with the largest popular vote recorded up to that time. He introduced a program of domestic reform aiming at the establishment of what he called the "Great Society." The legislation he piloted through Congress included measures con-

*Lyndon Baines Johnson's gravestone.*

(Photo: Frank Wolfe)

cerned with civil rights and welfare. His policy of increased intervention in the undeclared war in Vietnam, however, which sharply divided the nation, eroded much of his popular support. In 1968 he announced that he would not seek a further term as president. On leaving office, he retired to his ranch near Johnson City in Texas.

On January 22, 1973, while lying in the bedroom of his ranch, he picked up the telephone and called the Secret Service agent assigned to guard him, whispering: "Send Mike immediately!" Another Secret Service agent rushed into the room and found Johnson unconscious on the floor. He died in a plane en route to a San Antonio hospital, where he was declared dead on arrival.

On January 23 his remains lay in state at the Lyndon B. Johnson Library at the University of Texas, Austin. The following day, January 24, they were removed from the Library at 9:00 a.m., and flown to Washington, D.C. on the same plane in which he had been sworn in as president after the assassination of President Kennedy in 1963. His body then lay in state in the Capitol rotunda. A state funeral service was held on January 25 at 10:00 a.m. at the National City Christian Church in Washington, D.C. Hymns sung included "Onward Christian Soldiers," and one of Johnson's favorites, "In Christ There Is No East or West." Burial took place on January 25, at his Texas ranch on the northern branch of the Pedernales River. The Rev. Billy Graham spoke at the burial service. The LBJ Ranch, Ranch Road No. 1, Stonewall, Texas 78671.

# *Jolson, Al*

Al Jolson, the musical comedy singer, was born Asa Yoelson, on May 26, 1886, in St. Petersburg (now Leningrad), Russia. He came to the U.S. at the age of seven, and grew up in Washington, D.C. He became a popular entertainer, sometimes appearing as a blackface comedian. After appearing in Broadway musicals and other shows, he appeared in a short talking picture, *April Showers* (1926). He starred in the first feature-length talking picture, *The Jazz Singer* (1927). Other movies followed, including *The Jolson Story* (1946). He also hosted a radio program.

On October 23, 1950 he was in San Francisco to record a guest appearance on the Bing Crosby radio program. While playing a game of cards at the St. Francis Hotel, he fell ill. A doctor was called. Shortly after, he said: "Well boys, this is it. I'm going. I'm going." He then died.

More than 10,000 persons crowded in front of Temple Israel on Hollywood Boulevard, in Los Angeles. About 2,500 people were able to enter the temple to view the body. The temple closed at 11:00 a.m. but re-opened at noon to admit 1,500 mourners to the service, at which entertainer George Jessel delivered a eulogy. The service closed with the Kaddish (a Jewish doxology). The body was then taken to Beth Olan Cemetery in Los Angeles, where it was temporarily buried. Later, a crypt was built at the Hillside Cemetery, and his remains transferred there. Hillside Memorial Park and Mausoleum, 6001 Centinela Avenue, Los Angeles, California 90045.

# *Jones, John Paul*

John Paul Jones, naval hero of the U.S. War of Independence (1775-83), was born under the name of John Paul on July 6, 1757 at Kirkbean, Kirkcudbrightshire, Scotland. He went to sea at the age of 12. In the West Indies in 1773, while master of his own ship, he killed the ringleader of a mutiny, and fled to Fredericksburg, Virginia, to escape trial. It was because of this incident that he changed his name to "John Paul Jones."

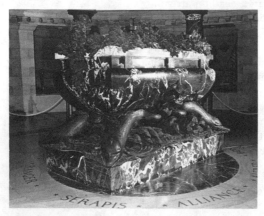

*The grave of John Paul Jones at Annapolis, Maryland.*

(Photo: U.S. Naval Academy)

On the outbreak of the War of Independence, he was commissioned an officer in the Continental Navy. During the war he distinguished himself in action, sinking a number of British vessels, and making prizes of others. In 1779 , in command of the *Bonhomme Richard* and other ships, he fought and won one of the most famous engagements in naval annals, against British men-of-war off the coasts of Scotland and Ireland. For this he received the thanks of Congress. He was then sent to Denmark on official business. He was later appointed a rear-admiral in the Russian Navy, but his last years were filled with disappointment.

He died in Paris, on July 18, 1792, while sitting in a chair. The cause of death was said to be dropsy of the breast, and jaundice. A funeral service was held on July 20. His body was taken from his home at 42 Tournon Street to the cemetery reserved for foreign Protestants.

In 1905 the U.S. government set out to find his grave, which had been forgotten as a result of the growth of Paris in the intervening years. Documents showed that his body had been placed in a leaden coffin. When the ground was excavated, five lead coffins were found, of which three had nameplates. Another contained the remains of a man more than six feet tall, who could not have been Jones. A team of 12 doctors and other specialists unanimously agreed that the remaining body was that of Jones. Although deterioration of the body made analysis impossible, leisons of the kidneys presented the appearance of nephritis, a condition which might have led to his death. In July 1905, a squadron of American warships brought his body back to the United States. Commemorative services were held at the U.S. Naval Academy in Annapolis in April 1906, where his tomb is now a national shrine. The United States Naval Academy, Annapolis, Maryland 21401.

# *Jones, Mother*

Mary Harris Jones—nicknamed "Mother Jones"—the labor leader was born on May 1, 1830, in Cork, Ireland. Her maiden name was Harris. She came to the U.S. in 1835. After Mr. Jones, her husband, and four children died in a yellow fever epidemic in Memphis, Tennessee, and she had lost her possessions in a Chicago fire, she devoted her life to union organizing. For most of her life she appeared wherever there were labor troubles, and was present at the Pittsburgh Railroad Strike (1877), the Chicago Haymarket Riot (1886), and the Copper Mine Strike in Colorado (1913). She was also active in garment workers' strikes in New York City in 1915 and 1916. In 1923, aged 93, she was still working with striking coal miners in West Virginia.

*The grave of
Mother Jones*
(Photo: Carl Dettmaier)

She died of natural causes on November 30, 1930 at her home in Silver Springs, Maryland. A funeral service was held on December 3 at St. Gabriel's Church in Washington, D.C. Her body was taken to Mt. Olive, Illinois, where it lay in state at the Oddfellows Temple. The Rev. J.W.R. McGuire of Kankakee, in a eulogy which was broadcast over radio station WCFL, said: "Wealthy coal operators and capitalists throughout the United States are breathing sighs of relief while toil-worn men and women are weeping tears of bitter grief. The reason for this contrast of relief and sorrow is apparent. Mother Jones is dead." She was buried on December 8. Miner's Union Cemetery, Mt. Olive, Illinois 62069.

# *Joplin, Janis*

Janis Joplin, rock and blues singer of the 1960s, was born in 1943 in Port Arthur, Texas. Her energetic and husky style of singing the blues was often compared to that of blues singer Bessie Smith. She inspired a following among the young during the late 1960s. She joined a rock band called Big Brother and the Holding Company, later sang with the Kozmic Blues Band, and then organized her own group, The Full Tilt Boogie Band.

On October 4, 1970 she was found dead in her Hollywood, California, hotel apartment by her guitarist. The police determined that she had been dead about 12 hours. The Los Angeles county coroner stated at a news conference on October 5 that a hypodermic needle had been found in her bedroom, and that a white powder, "probably heroin," had been found in the trash can. He excluded the possibilities of suicide or homicide.

A private funeral service was held on October 7, at the Westwood Village Mortuary in Los Angeles. In accordance with Janis Joplin's wishes, her remains were then cremated and the ashes scattered at sea off the Marin County coast, north of San Francisco.

# *Joplin, Scott*

Scott Joplin, called the king of the ragtime piano players, was born on November 24, 1868, in Texarkana, Texas. His most famous composition was "Maple Leaf Rag." He also wrote two ragtime operas, *A Guest of Honor*, and *Treemonisha*.

In December 1917, suffering from tertiary (terminal) syphilis, he was admitted to Manhattan State Hospital, on Ward's Island. Paralyzed, and unable to recognize visiting friends, he lay dying in his bed. The *New York Age*, in its March 29 issue, reported that he had been hospitalized "with mental troubles." He died on April 1.

A modest funeral service was held at the S.O. Paris Funeral Home at 116 West 131st Street, New York City on the afternoon of April 5. His body was buried in a common grave at St. Michael's Cemetery, in Queens, New York. Joplin had asked his wife that "Maple Leaf Rag" be played at his funeral. She did not honor this request, and later bitterly regretted that she had not done so. After his death, a popular legend, that had no foundation, was circulated that at his funeral there was a big procession, with prominent musicians attending, and with large banners displaying the names of the famous rags that he had composed. St. Michael's Cemetery, 72-02 Astoria Boulevard, East Elmhurst, New York 11370.

# *Keaton, Buster*

Buster Keaton, the film comedian, was born Joseph Francis Keaton on October 4, 1895, in Piqua, Kansas. At the time of his birth his parents were on tour with magician Harry Houdini (q.v.). He received his nickname when Houdini said of him: "What a Buster!" He was known as one of the great clowns of the early silent screen, but failed to make a successful transition to talking pictures. In his later years he reappeared in films, and his silent films were revived, renewing some of his former popularity.

By October 1965 he had become tired and weak. His "cigarette cough" had become almost constant. A checkup showed that he had terminal cancer, and doctors gave him no more than three months to live. His family did not tell him of this diagnosis. At one point they suggested that he use a heating pad to relieve pain, but he replied that this would not do any good. It was then they realized he knew the truth. On January 30, 1966 he was playing a game of bridge, but had trouble concentrating. He left the game, and went into another room. Half an hour later he began choking and gasping, and fell unconscious. Taken to hospital, he kept asking the nurse: "Why don't I just give up? Why don't I?" He died at 6:30 a.m. on February 1 at his Hollywood home.

A funeral service was held on February 4 at 1:30 p.m. at Church of the Hills in Los Angeles. Burial was at Forest Lawn Memorial Park, 6300 Forest Lawn Drive, Los Angeles, California 90068.

# Kefauver, Carey Estes

Carey Estes Kefauver, public official, was born on July 26, 1903, in Madisonville, Tennessee. After serving in Congress, he was elected to the Senate in 1948, where he served until his death. He gained national attention when he conducted a Senate investigation into organized crime in 1950-51. He supported civil rights legislation, and made several attempts to gain the Democratic presidential nomination.

On August 8, 1963, while on the floor of the Senate, he had what he thought was an attack of indigestion. He was urged to seek medical help, but replied: "No, I've got to keep going." He was later admitted to Bethesda Naval Hospital and the "indigestion" was diagnosed as a heart attack. On August 9 it was discovered that he had an aneurysm. At 3:40 a.m. on August 10 he died quickly and peacefully.

A simple Baptist funeral service was held on August 13, in Madisonville, Tennessee, attended by local people as well as such dignitaries as then vice-president Lyndon Johnson (q.v.), Adlai Stevenson (q.v.), senators, congressmen, and other politicians. Burial was in the family cemetery in Madisonville, Tennessee 37354.

# Keller, Helen

Helen Adams Keller, a blind, deaf, and mute person who became an outstanding public figure, was born June 27, 1880, near Tuscumbia, Alabama. Through study at Boston's Perkins Institution, and at the Horace Mann School for the Deaf, she learned to speak, and to read Braille and lips. She graduated cum laude from Radcliffe College in 1904. She wrote books and articles about blindness, and traveled the world on lecture tours promoting the better treatment of the handicapped. She was awarded the Presidential Medal of Freedom in 1963. Her story was made the subject of a film, *The Miracle Worker*.

On June 1, 1968 she died at her Westport, Connecticut, home, aged 87. Her companion for the previous 11 years, Mrs. Winifred Cornbally, was at her bedside at the time of death. She said: "She drifted off in her sleep... Miss Keller died gently."

A funeral service was held on June 5, 1968 at the Washington National Cathedral.

*LEFT: An effigy in stone of Helen Keller's head, in Washington National Cathedral.*

(Photo: Byron Chambers)

*BELOW: The Choir of the Perkins Institute for the Blind, Watertown, Massachusetts, in the cloister of Washington National Cathedral, before Helen Keller's funeral.*

(Photo: Morton Broffman)

The eulogy was translated into sign language, and a blind choir made up of students from Perkins Institute for the Blind of Watertown, Massachusetts, sang hymns. Following the service her ashes were interred in a crypt in the cathedral, next to those of Ann Sullivan Macy, her first teacher, who had been sent to her by Alexander Graham Bell (*q.v.*). Washington National Cathedral, Massachusetts and Wisconsin Avenues, N.W., Washington D.C. 20016.

# Kennedy, John F.

John Fitzgerald Kennedy, 35th president of the United States, (term of office 1961-63), was born on May 29, 1917 in Brookline, a suburb of Boston, Massachusetts. After representing a Boston district in Congress from 1946-52, he was elected to the U.S. Senate in 1952. In 1960 he was nominated as Democratic candidate for president, and won the election by a narrow margin of the popular vote. He was the first Catholic to become president. During his administration he dealt with confrontations with the Soviet Union over the building of the Berlin wall (1961), and the placing of missiles in Cuba (1962).

At 12:30 p.m. on November 22, 1963, while riding in a motorcade in Dallas, Texas, he was shot by rifle fire. Bullets struck him in the head and at the base of the neck. He was rushed to Parkland Hospital, where he was pronounced dead on arrival at 1:00 p.m. Lee Harvey Oswald (q.v.) was accused of the shooting, but was himself shot by a nightclub owner two days later before he could make any public statement or be brought to trial.

Kennedy's body was flown back to Washington, D.C. on Air Force One, and was taken to Bethesda Naval Hospital. Later it was taken to the White House where his body lay in state in a closed flag-draped coffin in the East Room. On November 24 the body was taken from the White House to the Capitol where it lay in state in the rotunda.

As the nation felt the effects of the assassination, 300,000 people lined Pennsylvania and Constitution Avenues and thousands more filed past the slain president's bier. By November 24, foreign dignitaries began arriving in the United States for the funeral, including France's President Charles de Gaulle and Ethiopia's Emperor Haile Selassie.

*The coffin of assassinated President John F. Kennedy in Washington, D.C.*

(Photo: National Archives)

On November 25, as television cameras rolled, the body was taken from the Capitol to St. Mathew's Cathedral on a horse-drawn caisson. At the cathedral, Cardinal Cushing said a low pontifical mass. A million people watched in the streets, and millions more on television, as the cortege traveled to Arlington National Cemetery. As the body reached the gravesite, 50 jet planes (one for each state) flew overhead, cannons fired a 21-gun salute, and taps were played.

According to the U.S. State Department the funeral was attended by representatives from 92 nations, 5 international organizations, and the papacy. These included 8 heads of state, 10 prime ministers, and royalty. It was one of the most dramatic and most publicized deaths and funerals of the 20th century. To Kennedy's generation, the recall of those three days in Dallas and Washington continued to evoke many clearly defined images which the years did not dim.

*John F. Kennedy's coffin at the gravesite. Among the mourners may be seen French President Charles de Gaulle, and the Emperor of Ethiopia, Haile Selassie.*

(Photo: National Archives)

Incoming President Lyndon Baines Johnson (q.v.) named a commission of inquiry, headed by Supreme Court Justice Earl Warren, which examined evidence of the assassination and concluded that Oswald was the killer and acted alone. Many questions nevertheless have remained unanswered, and doubts that all the facts have been made public have persisted.

Arlington National Cemetery, Fort Myer, Arlington, Virginia 22211.

# *Kennedy, Robert Francis*

Robert Francis Kennedy, younger brother of President John F. Kennedy (q.v.), was born on November 20, 1925 in Brookline, a suburb of Boston, Massachusetts. After working for the criminal division of the Department of Justice, he managed his brother's political campaigns for the Senate and the presidency. When his brother became president, he was appointed as U.S. attorney general. After his brother's assassination, in November 1963, he continued as attorney general under President Lyndon B. Johnson (q.v.), but resigned in 1964. In November 1964 he was elected senator from New York. Both in the Justice Department and the Senate, he championed civil rights, supported the cause of the young, poor, and black, and combated organized crime. In March 1968 he announced his candidacy for the Democratic presidential nomination.

After winning five out of six presidential primaries, he was shot on June 5, 1968 by Sirhan Sirhan, a Jordanian living in the United States. The shooting occurred in the Ambassador Hotel in Los Angeles. He was taken to General Receiving Hospital, then transferred to Good Samaritan Hospital. He died at 1:44 a.m. on June 6, with his family at his side.

His body was flown to New York City where, on June 7, it lay in state at St.

Patrick's Cathedral. Lines stretched for a mile and a half as 100,000 people waited to pass the African mahogany casket in which he lay. A short private ceremony was conducted by Cardinal Terence J. Cooke.

A requiem mass was celebrated at the cathedral on June 8, attended by more than 2,300 people, including President Lyndon B. Johnson. Cardinal Richard Cushing of Boston officiated. His younger brother, Edward Kennedy, eulogized him, saying: "My brother need not be idealized, nor enlarged beyond what he was in life." Robert Kennedy's body was then taken by train to Washington for burial near the grave of his brother, John F. Kennedy. Arlington National Cemetery, Fort Myer, Arlington, Virginia 22211.

# Kerouac, Jack

Jack Kerouac, author and spokesman of the "Beat" movement, was born Jean-Louis Kerouak on March 12, 1922, in Lowell, Massachusetts. After traveling through the United States and Mexico, he published his first novel, *The Town and the City*, in 1950. His most famous book, *On the Road*, was written in 1951 during a three-week period, during which he typed it on strips of pasted art paper. After publication, he became the spokesman of the "Beat Generation,"—a Bohemian movement which offered an alternative and unconventional lifestyle. Other novels followed.

On October 20, 1969, Kerouac, who was in St. Petersburg, Florida, was suffering from a hernia and had not felt well for weeks. He became nauseated, and began to bleed internally from a ruptured vein. An ambulance was called and he was rushed to St. Anthony's Hospital, where emergency surgery was performed for massive abdominal hemorrhaging. He did not survive the operation but died, at 5:30 a.m. on October 21.

His remains were sent to Lowell, Massachusetts, where his open casket was on display at the Archambaud Funeral Home. He was dressed in a checkered sports jacket and a red bow tie. Rosary beads were draped over his folded hands.

The funeral service was held on October 24 at St. Jean Baptiste Roman Catholic Church in Lowell. The priest, who had known Kerouac as a child, read a quotation from Ecclesiastes.

Burial was in Edison Cemetery, Lowell, Massachusetts 01853.

# King, Martin Luther

Martin Luther King, Jr., the black civil rights leader, was born on January 15, 1929, in Atlanta, Georgia. After receiving a doctorate from Boston University in 1955, he became a Baptist minister in Montgomery, Alabama. When the Southern Christian Leadership Conference was formed in 1957, King was elected its president. Through the organization he became known as an activist, preaching non-violence. In the late 1950s and the 1960s he organized a mass civil rights movement for racial equality. He organized voter registration drives in Alabama and Georgia, and, in

1963, the massive March on Washington. He was awarded the Nobel Peace Prize in 1964.

On April 4, 1968, while in Memphis, Tennessee, to organize striking sanitation workers, King, who was staying in room 306 at the Lorraine Motel, stepped out on the balcony. He leaned over the railing to talk with his associate Jesse Jackson, who was below, standing in the parking lot. Jackson introduced Ben Branch, a musician who was to play at that evening's rally. King said: "Yes that's my man!" Then shots rang out, and King fell to the walkway. His necktie was torn off his shirt by the blast. It was a few minutes after 6:00 p.m. He was still living when he arrived at the emergency room at St. Joseph's Hospital but, despite emergency surgery, was pronounced dead at 7:05 p.m. (His assassin, James Earl Ray, was later caught in Europe, and was returned to the United States to face trial. In 1969 he pleaded guilty to the murder charge, and was sentenced to 99 years in prison.)

Memorial marches, services, masses and vigils of prayer were held all over the country. On April 8, King's body lay in state at Sister's Chapel, on the campus of Spellman College, Atlanta, Georgia. A private funeral service was held at his father's church, Ebenezer Baptist Church, in Atlanta at 10:30 a.m. on April 9. His body was then taken to Morehouse College, Atlanta, where King had once been a student. It was taken on a crude farm wagon, pulled by two Georgia mules, followed by a procession of mourners, black and white, estimated to number 100,000. On arrival, in South View Cemetery, Atlanta, a public service was held at 2:00 p.m. During the burial rites the Rev. Ralph Abernathy said: "The cemetery is too small for his spirit but we submit his body to the ground. The grave is too narrow for his soul but we commit his body to the ground. No coffin, no crypt, no stone can hold his greatness but we submit his body to the ground." The epitaph on his tombstone reads: "Free At Last; Free At Last; Thank God Almighty I'm Free At Last."

On January 12, 1970 his remains were reburied at the Martin Luther King Memorial Center, 449 Auburn, Atlanta, Georgia 30312.

# *Kinsey, Alfred Charles*

Alfred Charles Kinsey, the zoologist and researcher on human sexual behavior, was born on June 23, 1894, in Hoboken, New Jersey. A professor of zoology, he became director of the Institute for Sex Research at Indiana University in 1942, holding this position until his death. By interviewing thousands of American men and women, he and his aides compiled extensive statistical data on the sexual activities of Americans. His book, *Sexual Behavior in the Human Male* (1948), shattered many myths surrounding human sexual practices. In 1953 he published *Sexual Behavior in the Human Female*, and had plans to publish further volumes dealing with the sexual behavior of men in prison, of Europeans, and of animals, but died before these could be researched.

By August 1956 he had been in ill health for almost six months. He was admitted to Bloomington Hospital in Bloomington, Indiana, on August 22, and by August 24 his condition was considered critical. On August 25 he died from a heart ailment and pneumonia.

A funeral service was held at 10:30 a.m. on August 27 at the Day Funeral Home in Bloomington. Burial was in Rose Hill Cemetery, 416 East 2nd, Bloomington, Indiana 47403.

# Krupa, Gene

Gene Krupa, the most famous of jazz drummers, was born on January 15, 1909, in Chicago. After working with Chicago jazz bands in the 1920s, he began working for the Red Nichols orchestra in 1929. After working with various groups, he starred with Benny Goodman from 1934-38. After recording "Sing, Sing, Sing" (1938) he became famous. From 1938 to 1951 he led his own successful band. He appeared in many films and recorded the soundtrack for an allegedly biographical movie *The Gene Krupa Story*, (1959).

Krupa, who had been suffering from benign leukemia since the mid 1960s, entered a Yonkers hospital in early October 1973 for treatment of a heart problem connected with the leukemia. He died at his Yonkers home on October 16, 1973, aged 64.

A funeral mass was held at St. Denis Roman Catholic Church in Yonkers on October 18. There was no eulogy but one of those attending, jazz musician Bennie Goodman, said: "Gene was a perfectionist." The parish priest said: "There was a modest man—one deeply attached to his community."

His body was flown to Chicago on Friday, October 19, where the funeral was held on October 20 at the Immaculate Conception Church. Burial took place in the Immaculata section of the Holy Cross Cemetery, Burnham Road and Michigan, Calumet City, Illinois 60409.

# La Follette, Robert Marion

Robert Marion La Follette, Wisconsin politician, and founder of the U.S. Progressive movement, was born on June 14, 1855, in Primrose, Wisconsin. He served in the House of Representatives from 1885-1891 and was governor of Wisconsin from 1900-06. He was a senator from Wisconsin from 1907-25. Although he ran as a Republican he stayed fiercely independent of party, and championed the cause of the common man against privilege. In 1924 he was nominated as the Progressive Party candidate for president. He and his running mate received more than 5,000,000 votes, but gained only the electoral votes of Wisconsin.

By 1925 he had suffered from angina pectoris for about ten years, and in April he became seriously ill. He died, at 1:21 p.m. on June 18, at his Washington, D.C., home, of "heart disease complicated by bronchial asthma and pneumonia." His body was sent to Madison, Wisconsin, by train, arriving there on June 20. On June 21 it lay in state in the Capitol rotunda from noon till 8:00 p.m. Thousands of persons passed the bier. The funeral service was held there on June 22. After a funeral oration, the burial service of the Unitarian Church was read, and "America" was

*LaFollete's funeral procession in Madison, Wisconsin.*

(Photo: State Historical Society of Wisconsin).

sung. Burial was in his family plot in Forest Hill Cemetery, 1 Speedway Road, Madison, Wisconsin 53705.

# *Laurel, Stan*

Stan Laurel, the movie comedian, was born Arthur Stanley Jefferson on June 16, 1890, in Ulverston, England. He came to the United States in 1910. In 1917 he joined the Hal Roach studio as a writer and director. He teamed up with the comedian Oliver Hardy *(q.v.)*, to form a highly successful partnership, with Laurel playing the skinny partner, and Hardy the fat one. In 1926 they made their first film together, *Putting Pants on Phillip*. During a period of 25 years they made about 200 films, with Laurel doing most of the editing. Among their popular films were *Double Whoopee* (1929), *Pack Up Your Troubles* (1932), and *Way Out West* (1937). After Hardy died in 1957, Laurel rarely made public appearances, preferring to stay in his Santa Monica apartment watching television.

He had a heart attack in mid February 1965. On February 23 he knew that he was dying. He motioned a nurse to his bedside, and said: "I'd rather be skiing than doing this." She asked him: "Do you ski Mr. Laurel?" He replied: "No, but I'd rather be doing that than this." He died a short while later.

Three hundred friends and relatives gathered on February 26 at Forest Lawn's Church of the Hills to pay him tribute. An organist played the Laurel and Hardy theme song, "The Cuckoo Song." Comedian Dick Van Dyke eulogized him as "the greatest comedian of all." Among the many others present was comedian Buster Keaton *(q.v.)*. Immediately after the service his body was cremated and the ashes buried at Forest Lawn Memorial Park, 6300 Forest Lawn Drive, Los Angeles 90068.

# Lawrence, D.H.

David Herbert Lawrence, the English novelist who pioneered the treatment of explicit sexual themes in 20th century literature, was born on September 11, 1885, in Eastwood, Nottinghamshire, England. In 1914 he married Frieda Weekley, a German. Among his most famous works are *Sons and Lovers* (1913), *Women in Love* (1916), and *Lady Chatterley's Lover* (1928). This last work was banned as obscene in several countries. In his work Lawrence also explored the ills of modern industrialism.

In 1930, suffering from pleurisy, he was taken to a sanatorium near Cannes, France. The doctor noted that "both lungs appear to be affected... his appetite is poor and he does not respond to treatment." On March 1, his wife moved him to a rented villa in Vence, France. He went into the house and lay down on the bed in which he was to die, exhausted. The next day, Sunday, he asked his wife not to leave him. After lunch he began to suffer very much. Then the doctor came and gave him a morphine injection. After a little while he said: "I am better now." He died that day, March 2.

On March 4 he was buried in a plain oak coffin at the cemetery in Vence. Frieda said: "We buried him very simply like a bird... we put flowers into his grave, and all I said was 'Goodbye Lorenzo,' as his friends and I put lots and lots of mimosa on his coffin."

On March 13, 1935 his body was disinterred and cremated in Marseille. On April 4 the urn of ashes was put aboard the ship *Conte de Savoia* at Villefranche. After arriving in New York the ashes were sent west. Frieda was to collect them at the rail station in Lamy, New Mexico, but by error she left the urn of ashes on the platform at the station. She did not discover the loss until she was 20 miles away, and had to return. The ashes were then buried at Frieda's Taos, New Mexico, home. The D.H. Lawrence Ranch, Taos, New Mexico 87571.

# Lee, Gypsy Rose

Gypsy Rose Lee, the most famous of American striptease artists, was born Rose Louise Hovick, on February 9, 1914, in Seattle, Washington. At the age of 15 she took strip tease lessons from a lady known as Tessy the Tassel Twirler. Her act was distinguished by grace and personality. By 1931 she was doing shows at Minsky's and other burlesque houses in New York City. She wrote a best-selling murder mystery, *The G-String Murders* (1941), starred in several movies. In the 1960s she had her own television talk show.

She underwent cancer surgery in 1966. On April 27, 1970, she died at the UCLA Medical Center in California, aged 56. A memorial service was held on April 29 at 10:00 a.m., at Pierce Brothers in Beverly Hills. Her remains were cremated at Pierce Brother's Chapel of the Pines Crematory. The ashes were then given to the family, and taken to New York, where they were reportedly buried in a Brooklyn cemetery.

# Lee, Robert E.

Robert E. Lee, commander of the Southern forces during the Confederacy, was born on January 19, 1807, in Stratford, Westmoreland County, Virginia. After serving with General Winfield Scott during the Mexican War of 1846-48, he became superintendent at West Point in 1852. On the outbreak of the Civil War, Lee, while opposing secession, resigned from the U.S. Army, and took command of Virginia's forces. In 1862 he became military adviser to Jefferson Davis (q.v.). Subsequently he became commander of all Confederate armies. He was the most talented and successful of the Confederate generals, and gained several victories. His surrender to General Ulysses S. Grant (q.v.) at the Appamatox Courthouse on April 9, 1865 marked the end of the Civil War. After the war he became the idol of the defeated Southern cause. He held the position of president of Washington College in Lexington, Virginia.

From 1866 onwards, Lee began to talk of getting old, and of only having a short while to live. By winter 1869, exercise was painful, and he had difficulty breathing. In February 1870 he was unable to walk more than 200 yards without discomfort.

(Photo: Washington and Lee University)

*Vigil over Lee's body at Washington and Lee University.*

On October 12, 1870 he died at 9:30 a.m. at his residence, the house of the college president, in Lexington, Virginia. At the time of his death his doctors reported that the cause of death was "mental and physical fatigue... which... gradually caused cerebral exhaustion and death." It now seems fairly certain that Lee suffered from angina pectoris and arteriosclerosis.

At first a coffin for Lee could not be found. Three caskets that an undertaker had ordered from Richmond had reached Lexington, but had been washed away by flood waters. Two boys later found one of the coffins and, being undamaged, it was used for Lee's body. It was, however, slightly short for him, and for this reason he was buried without shoes. These circumstances are also the origin of the myth that the coffin that he was buried in appeared mysteriously floating down the river.

A memorial service was held on October 14 at 9:00 a.m., at which Psalm 37, verses 8-11 and 28-40 were read. At 1:30 p.m. on that same day his remains, clothed in plain black civilian clothes, were moved from his home to the chapel in Lexington, where they lay in state till 10:00 a.m. on October 15. Because of the floods it was impossible for him to be buried anywhere else but in Lexington. The flood also kept away many who wished to attend the funeral. Memorial services were held throughout the South, as well as in New York City. Burial was at Washington and Lee University, Lexington, Virginia 24450.

# *Lennon, John*

John Lennon, songwriter, cultural hero, and leader of the "Beatles" musical group, was born on October 9, 1940 in Liverpool, England. The Beatles, the British rock group which he led, and which became famous in the 1960s, became the most musically influential act of its generation. Along with his Beatle partner Paul McCartney, Lennon wrote such songs as "Michelle," "Strawberry Fields Forever," and "Lucy in the Sky With Diamonds."

On December 6 and 7, 1980, a 25-year-old ex-mental patient, Mark David Chapman, visited the gate of Lennon's apartment building, the Dakota, on Manhattan's upper west side. Chapman asked the doorman and other employees about Lennon. On December 8, at about 4:00 p.m., Chapman approached Lennon as he was leaving for a recording session, asking him to autograph an album. Lennon complied. Lennon and his wife, Yoko Ono, returned home shortly before 11:00 p.m. As they walked into the Dakota's large archway, Chapman stepped out from a vestibule on the left where he had been hiding. He called out "Mr. Lennon." With both feet spread and both hands on a .38 caliber revolver, he fired four bullets, which entered Lennon's back, leg and arm. Lennon slumped over, shouting: "I'm shot." He staggered up the stairs into the guard's office, and fell to the floor in a pool of blood.

Arriving police officers found Chapman reading a book, a few feet from the wounded musician. Chapman told the officers: "I didn't have anything against him, I don't know why I did it." Lennon was taken to the emergency room at Roosevelt Hospital in New York City, where he was pronounced dead on arrival. Immediately, distraught Beatle fans began to gather outside the Dakota in a candle-light vigil, singing Beatle songs.

Radio stations worldwide abandoned their normal programming. Many switched to programs of continuous Beatle music. Former Beatle Ringo Starr and his fiancee, Barbara Bach, visited the Dakota on December 9, but both refused to comment on the shooting. Former Beatle Paul McCartney said: "Lennon is going to be missed by the whole world." George Harrison, another former Beatle, said: "I am shocked and stunned... To rob life is the ultimate robbery." On December 14 the *New York*

*Times* commented that the display of sympathy seemed to be "the most extensive since that following the assassination of President John F. Kennedy in 1963."

Yoko Ono released the following statement: "I told Sean [Lennon's five-year-old son] what happened... Sean cried later. He also said: 'Now daddy is part of God. I guess when you die you become more bigger because you're part of everything.' "

On December 9, Lennon's body was taken to the city morgue and photographed. A picture of his head appeared in The *New York Post* on December 11.

Late on the afternoon of December 10, his body was taken to the Frank E. Campbell Funeral Home at Madison Avenue and 81st Street, and placed in a coffin. Two hearses were used. The first hearse was used as a decoy for the press, and drove around the block, while Lennon's body, in the second, was taken to the Ferncliff Crematorium in Hartsdale, New York, for cremation. Since it was feared that his ashes might be stolen by fans outside the Dakota building, the ashes were disguised as a Christmas package and taken back to his widow, Yoko Ono.

No funeral service was held, but Yoko Ono asked those who wished to pay their respects to Lennon to pause for 10 minutes at 2:00 p.m. Eastern Standard Time on Sunday December 14 in a "silent vigil." This silent tribute was observed throughout the world. At least 100,000 people gathered in New York City's Central Park. During the vigil a 19-year-old Brooklyn man was shot in the chest in a scuffle. In the early 1980s the ashes were believed to be in the possession of his widow, Yoko Ono, at the Dakota building in New York City.

# *Lewis, Meriwether*

Meriwether Lewis, the explorer, who, with William Clark *(q.v.)*, led the first overland expedition to the Pacific Northwest in 1804-06, was born on August 8, 1774, in Albemarle County, near Charlottesville, Virginia. He was private secretary to President Thomas Jefferson *(q.v.)* from 1801-03, and the president groomed him for a journey of exploration across the continent. At his request William Clark was

*Meriwether Lewis's gravesite.*

(Photo: National Park Service)

appointed to share the command with him. The two men, with a party of 40, set out in 1803. They reached the Pacific coast in November 1805. They began their return trip in March 1806, arriving in St. Louis in September. The journals of the expedition, constituting a classic work of its kind, were later published. They contained much vital information which later facilitated the movement of westward expansion.

In November 1806, Lewis was appointed governor to the Louisiana Territory.

En route to Washington, Lewis either committed suicide or was murdered on October 11, 1809, at an inn on the Natchez Trace, near Nashville, Tennessee. The circumstances have remained mysterious and controversial. One account says that he was lodging in the home of a Mrs. Robert Grinder with some of his men, and that she heard gunshot in the middle of the night, and a heavy object hitting the floor. She then heard words "Oh Lord" and another shot. According to this account, he committed suicide, and his last words, as the sun was rising, were: "I am no coward, but I am so strong. It is so hard to die."

Burial was in Meriwether Lewis Park, Route 3, Hohenwald, Tennessee 38462.

# *Lewis, Sinclair*

Harry Sinclair Lewis, novelist and social reformer, was born on February 7, 1885, in Sauk Centre, Minnesota. His first major work, *Mainstreet* (1920), won him instant fame and a literary reputation. His subsequent works included *Babbitt* (1922), *Arrowsmith* (1925), and *Elmer Gantry* (1927). In 1930 he became the first American to be awarded the Nobel Prize for literature.

*Sinclair Lewis's grave.*
(Sinclair Lewis Foundation, Inc.)

In 1950 he went to Europe for an extended stay. He was experiencing heart and lung trouble, and in January 1951 he entered the Villa Electra nursing home in Rome. Most of the time in the two weeks before his death he was unconscious. Franciscan nuns who attended him in the hours before he died said he often awakened and said: "I am happy, God bless you all." He died on January 10. The cause of death was said to be paralysis of the heart.

When news of his death reached Sauk Centre, Minnesota, the town he had satirized in *Mainstreet,* the mayor said: "All of us love him. We were proud to call him our own, no matter what he wrote." According to Lewis's instructions, his body was cremated on January 13 without a religious service. After the cremation the ashes were placed in the chapel of the Protestant cemetery until the following week, when they were flown to the U.S.

A funeral service was held on January 28 in Sauk Centre. One service, held at the Sauk Centre High School, included readings from some of his writings. There was also a graveside service at Green Wood Cemetery where his ashes were scattered in a grave containing some of his novels. Green Wood Cemetery, Sauk Centre, Minnesota 56378.

# *Lincoln, Abraham*

Abraham Lincoln, 16th president of the United States, (in office 1861-65), was born on February 12, 1809, near Hodgenville, Kentucky. The most respected of U.S. Presidents, he preserved the Union during the Civil War of 1861-65, and emancipated the slaves in 1863. After being raised in near poverty in an Illinois frontier log cabin, he was self-educated. He studied law and was admitted to the Illinois bar in 1836. He served in the state legislature from 1834 to 1841, and in Congress from 1847-49. In 1856 he became a Republican. Subsequently his political debates with Stephen A. Douglas gained him a national reputation. In 1860 he was elected to the presidency. His term of office virtually coincided with the duration of the Civil War, and he was wholly preoccupied in saving the Union during its time of greatest trial. He was re-elected president in 1864 by a large electoral vote and a small popular majority.

*A drawing showing Lincoln's coffin and its escort on the funeral train.*

(National Archives)

One night in the second week of April 1865—the very week that General Robert E. Lee *(q.v.)* surrendered at Appomattox—Lincoln had a dream which seemed to foretell his assassination. In relating it to his wife and others he said: "I kept on until I arrived at the East Room [of the White House], which I entered... Before me was a catalfaque on which rested a corpse wrapped in funeral vestments... 'Who is dead in the White House?' I demanded of one of the soldiers. ' The president,' was his answer; ' He was killed by an assassin!' "

On Good Friday, April 14, 1865, Lincoln was seated in the presidential box at Ford's Theatre in Washington, D.C., to see the play *Our American Cousin*. Shortly before 10:00 p.m., a 26-year-old actor, John Wilkes Booth *(q.v.)*, a Southern sympathizer, entered the box and shot the president. Booth then jumped on to the stage, breaking his left leg. Yelling: "Sic semper tyrannis" [Ever thus to tyrants], he then ran out of the theater. The bullet from the brass derringer pistol he had used had entered the back of Lincoln's head. Later examination showed that its course "was obliquely forward toward the right eye, crossing the brain in an oblique manner and lodging a few inches behind that eye." In the track of the wound were found fragments of bone, which were imbedded in the anterior lobe of the left hemisphere of the brain.

The mortally wounded president was taken to a room in a private house, 453 Tenth Street, across the street from the theater, where he died the following morning, April 15, at 7:22 a.m.

His body was returned to the White House that day. It was embalmed, and lay in state in the East Room (as in his dream) on April 17. His mahogany coffin was lead lined and covered with black broadcloth. On April 18, about 25,000 people came to view the body.

During the day of April 19, 60 clergymen and President Andrew Johnson attended the funeral service in the East Room of the White House. On the evening of April 19 his body was taken to the rotunda of the Capitol, where all the next day it lay in state. Thousands more people, including the war wounded, passed the fallen president's bier. His remains were placed on board a seven-car funeral train on Friday, April 21, at 8:00 a.m. The officer in charge of the funeral train said: "History has no parallel to the outpouring of sorrow which followed the funeral cortege from Washington to Springfield." The train reached Baltimore, Maryland, and Harrisburg, Pennsylvania, on April 21; Philadelphia on April 22; New York on April 24; Albany on April 25; Buffalo on April 27; Cleveland on April 28; Columbus on April 29; Indianapolis on April 30; Chicago on May 1; and, finally, Springfield, Illinois, on May 3 at 8:00 a.m.

His body lay in the State Capitol in Springfield, where 75,000 people passed the bier. On May 4, a funeral procession moved from the State Capitol to Oak Ridge Cemetery, where thousands of mourners listened to hymns and heard prayers. The stone floor of the vault was carpeted with evergreen and the coffin was set in a black walnut receptacle.

On November 7, 1876, a gang of thieves and counterfeiters broke into the tomb. They forced open the sarcophagus and pulled Lincoln's casket partially out. Their plan was to cart the casket away on a wagon, hide it in the sand dunes of Indiana, and then demand $200,000.00 ransom as well as the release of Benjamin Boyd, a counterfeiter serving time in the penitentiary at Joliet, Illinois. They had confided their plans to a Pinkerton detective who had agreed to help them. Instead, he notified the Secret Service, and the gang was arrested. At that time there was no penalty for body stealing, so they were convicted of breaking the lock on the tomb and sentenced to one year in prison.

On April 24, 1901, Lincoln's remains, and those of his wife, were moved to a marble tomb and cemented inside. This was done without ceremony, but was witnessed by the governor of Illinois and other officials.

*Lincoln's tomb in Springfield, Illinois.*
Photo: Illinois Dept. of Conservation)

On June 6 that year, Robert Todd Lincoln told of having visited the monument disguised as a workman, and said that his father's remains were in danger of being stolen. He called for heavy cement over the casket to secure it against theft. Lincoln's body was then placed 13 feet in the ground and surrounded by more than 6 feet of solid cement. This work was completed in September 1901.

Oak Ridge Cemetery, 1441 Monument Avenue, Springfield, Illinois 62702.

# Lindbergh, Charles

Charles Augustus Lindbergh, the aviator who made the first non-stop solo flight across the Atlantic, was born on February 4, 1902, in Detroit. After training at army flying schools in Texas in 1924 and 1925, he worked as an airmail pilot on the St. Louis to Chicago route. When a $25,000 prize was offered for the first non-stop trans-Atlantic flight from New York to Paris, Lindbergh bought a Ryan monoplane which he christened *The Spirit of St. Louis.* He left Long Island's Roosevelt Field on May 20, 1927, and 33½ hours later arrived at Le Bourget airfield near Paris. After a reception by the French government, he was received as a hero when he returned to America. He was nicknamed "Lucky Lindy" and "Lone Eagle," and was awarded the Congressional Medal of Honor. In 1932 his son was kidnapped and murdered. Lindbergh later became politically controversial when he advocated a policy of neutrality for the U.S. in World War II. He then became a consultant to industry and to the U.S. Department of Defense, and flew combat missions in the Pacific. In 1953 he won a Pulitzer Prize for his book *The Spirit of St. Louis.*

On August 17, 1974, after a 26-day stay in Columbia Presbyterian Medical Center in New York City, he was flown to Honolulu on a United Airlines flight. He was then put on board a small private plane flying to Kipahulu, Maui, Hawaii, where he owned an A-frame cottage. He died on August 26, aged 72. The cause of death was cancer of the lymphatic system. When he knew he would not recover, he wished to return to spend his last days at his vacation home in Hawaii.

On August 27, dressed in simple work clothing, his body was placed in a coffin, made by cowboys from the town of Hana, Maui. He was buried three hours later in the cemetery of the Kipahulu church. A simple memorial service was held on August 28 at Hana. Kipahulu Congregational Churchyard, Kipahulu, Maui, Hawaii 96761.

# *Lodge, Henry Cabot*

Henry Cabot Lodge, the Republican senator who successfully opposed U.S. participation in the League of Nations, was born on May 12, 1850, in Boston, Massachusetts. In 1886 he was elected to the House of Representatives where he helped draft the Sherman Anti-Trust act of 1890. As a Republican conservative, he called for support of the U.S. war effort in World War I. In 1918 he became both

*Henry Cabot Lodge's tomb.*

(Photo: Sammy Edward Baker)

Republican floor leader and chairman of the Foreign Relations Committee. He was thus in a strong position to organize Senate opposition to adoption of the Treaty of Versailles (1919), including the League of Nations Covenant. He was thus the architect of the policy of U.S. isolationism, which was to prevail until Pearl Harbor (1941).

On November 5, 1924 he suffered a severe stroke. He died at 11:14 p.m. on

November 9 at the Charlesgate Hospital, Cambridge, Massachusetts. A simple Episcopal funeral service was held on November 12 at Christ Church in Cambridge. Floral wreaths were received from Great Britain, Cuba, and China. Following the reading of the Episcopal service, the choir sang the hymn: "The Strife is O'er, The Battle Done." Burial was in the Lodge family vault, between two tall elm trees on the shore of a lake. Mt. Auburn Cemetery, 580 Mt. Auburn Street, Cambridge, Massachusetts 02138.

# Lombardo, Guy

Guy Albert Lombardo, the bandleader, was born June 19, 1902, in London, Ontario, Canada. He formed a band called the Royal Canadians consisting of nine members, two of whom were his brothers. In 1924, he came to the U.S., and he became a citizen in 1937. The band played regularly at the Roosevelt Hotel in New York City. Every New Year's Eve it made a broadcast appearance at the Waldorf-Astoria Hotel. In the big band era of the 1930s and 40s his band was probably the most popular, although criticized for its sentimentality by hot jazz afficionados. Lombardo claimed he played "the sweetest music this side of heaven."

In September 1977 he was admitted to Methodist Hospital in Houston, Texas, for open heart surgery. He was re-admitted on October 27, and died on November 5, aged 75, from what was termed "respiratory, kidney and heart failure."

A funeral service was held at Our Holy Redeemer Roman Catholic Church on South Ocean Avenue, Freeport, Long Island, on November 9. The eulogy was delivered by Robert Moses, a former New York state park commissioner, who had been a friend of Lombardo's. He said: "There was only one Guy at midnight on New Year's Eve." Lombardo's body lay in a closed mahogany coffin which was draped in white and gold brocade. Following a private graveside ceremony, burial took place the same day at Pinelawn Memorial Park, Pinelawn Road, Farmingdale, New York 11735.

# London, Jack

Jack London, the author, was born John Griffith London on January 12, 1876, in San Francisco. Between 1893 and 1897 he was first a sailor, and then a hobo, traveling across the United States. He was jailed for vagrancy in New York City, and in 1894 became a Marxist socialist. In 1897-98 he sought his fortune in the Klondike Gold Rush. Back in California, he became a writer. His novels *The Call of the Wild* (1903), *White Fang* (1906), and *Martin Eden* (1909)—stories of struggles for survival—brought him fame and wealth. In later years he became an alcoholic.

At 7:00 a.m. on November 22, 1916, he was found in the bedroom of his Glen Ellen, California, ranch home in a state of narcosis. There were two prescription bottles on the floor. One was labeled "Morphine Sulfate" and the other "Atriphine Sulfate." On the night table there was a pad of paper on which lethal dosage calculations had been made for each drug. A doctor and his assistant washed out his stomach, gave him stimulants, massaged his limbs, and prepared an antidote. Only once did he respond. His eyes slowly opened and he muttered what sounded like "Hello." He died a little after 7:00 p.m. that evening.

*Jack London's gravesite.*
(Photo: California Department of Parks and Recreation)

His body was taken to Oakland, California, and cremated. The ashes were buried on a hill at his estate on November 26, 1916. The site is marked with a stone in scribed: "The Stone the Builders Rejected." Jack London Ranch, Glen Ellen, California 95442.

# Longfellow, Henry Wadsworth

Henry Wadsworth Longfellow, the most renowned American poet of the 19th century, was born on February 27, 1807, in Portland, Maine. After studying in France, Spain, Italy and Germany, he settled down at Harvard in 1836, as professor of modern languages. He began to publish prose and poetry. Some of his works, including his poems "The Wreck of the Hesperus" (1841), "The Song of Hiawatha" (1855), and "The Courtship of Miles Standish" (1858), brought him national and international fame. His *Tales of a Wayside Inn* (1863), which included "Paul Revere's Ride," became nationally popular.

*Longfellow's tomb in Cambridge, Massachusetts.*

(Photo: Sammy Edward Baker)

On March 18, 1882 he caught a chill and was put to bed with a rapid pulse. He began to have what were described as "violent pains" and a doctor was sent for. The doctor diagnosed the illness as peritonitis. On March 21, his sister arrived from Portland, Maine. He looked at her and said: "Now I know that I must be very ill, since you have been sent for." Shortly afterwards he fell into unconsciousness and died at 3:10 p.m. on March 24.

A funeral service was held at Mt. Auburn Cemetery in Cambridge, Massachusetts, on March 26. Essayist Ralph Waldo Emerson *(q.v.)*, who was in attendance, turned to another mourner and said: "I cannot recall the name of my friend, but he was a good man." Later, a memorial to him was unveiled in the Poet's Corner, at Westminster Abbey, London, England.

Mt. Auburn Cemetery, 580 Mt. Auburn Street, Cambridge, Massachusetts 02138.

# Lowell, James Russell

James Russell Lowell, poet, critic, and diplomat, was born on February 22, 1819 in Cambridge, Massachusetts. He was known as one of America's leading men of letters in the 19th century. After graduation from Harvard Law School in 1840 his first volume of poetry was published in 1841. He published works by Edgar Allan Poe, Nathaniel Hawthorne *(q.q.v.)*, and others in *The Pioneer* (1843). He succeeded Henry Wadsworth Longfellow *(q.v.)* as professor of modern languages at Harvard in 1855 and held the position for 20 years. He helped found the *Atlantic Monthly* in 1857, and himself wrote a number of books and essays. He served as U.S. minister to Spain (1877-80) and ambassador to the United Kingdom (1880-85).

By the summer of 1891 he was dying of cancer. Malignancy had started in his kidneys and spread through his liver and lungs. In a letter to his brother Henry James *(q.v.)*, William James *(q.v.)* wrote that Lowell was "ready to talk and be talked to, alluding to his illness with a sort of apologetic and whimsical plaintiveness that had no querulousness in it, though he coughed incessantly, and last time... was strongly narcotized by opium..." By mid-July his doctors began to administer opium on a regular basis and he passed in and out of consciousness. He died on August 12, 1891.

*James Russell Lowell's headstone.*
(Photo: Sammy Edward Baker)

His funeral service was held in the Chapel at Harvard. Pallbearers included among others Oliver Wendell Holmes, the elder *(q.v.)*. He was buried in a family plot in Mt.

Auburn. He has no monument and his grave has a small tombstone. Mt. Auburn
Cemetery, 580 Mt. Auburn Street, Cambridge, Massachusetts 02138.

# *Luce, Henry*

Henry Robinson Luce, co-founder, editor and publisher of the news magazine
*Time*, was born April 3, 1898, in Tengchow, now P'eng-lai, Shantung province,
China. After studying at Yale and Oxford, he was a reporter for the *Chicago Daily
News* and the *Baltimore News*. In 1923 he and Briton Hadden, a Yale classmate, put
together the weekly news magazine *Time*. The magazine sold well, and became pro-
fitable by 1927. After Hadden's death in 1929, Luce became head of Time, Inc. He
later founded further magazines—*Fortune* (1930), *Life* (1936), and *Sports Illustrated*
(1954).

In November 1966 he went to his winter home in the Biltmore estates section of
Phoenix, Arizona, and spent time playing golf. On February 27, 1967 he was admit-
ted to St. Joseph's hospital for tests. At 10:30 p.m. he told his wife, Clare Boothe
Luce, former congresswoman (1943-47) and ambassador to Italy (1953-56), that he
was feeling better. He collapsed and died of a heart attack, however, at 5:00 a.m. on
February 28.

Eight hundred persons attended a 40-minute memorial service at the Madison
Avenue Presbyterian Church on East 73rd Street in New York City on March 3.
About 700 persons left their desks at the Time-Life Building on the Avenue of the
Americas to gather in a reception lounge and an auditorium where the service was
relayed to them through a private broadcast hookup. The officiating minister said:
"Few men holding no official position exercised greater influence." The organist
played Bach's chorale, *God's Time is Best*. The mourners included Governor Nelson
Rockefeller *(q.v.)*, and former Senator Barry Goldwater.

*Henry Luce's
gravesite.*
(Photo: A Brother
at Mepkin Abbey)

Luce had donated a cemetery and the grounds of an abbey in South Carolina, and
his body was taken here. A private burial service was held at 1:00 p.m. on March 4.
Our Lady of Mepkin Trappist Abbey, Moncks Corner, South Carolina 29461.

# *Lugosi, Bela*

Bela Lugosi, stage and screen actor, was born Bela Lugosi Blasko on October 20, 1882, in Lugos, Hungary. He emigrated to the United States in 1921. He is best known for his portrayal of Count Dracula in *Dracula* (1931), the prototype of later vampire movies. He appeared in numerous other horror movies including *The Black Cat* (1934), and *The Ghost of Frankenstein* (1943).

On August 16, 1956, his wife, Hope, returned from shopping and noticed a stillness in their Los Angeles apartment. She called out to him but there was no answer. She went into the bedroom and found him lying motionless on the bed. Shortly afterwards she said: "He didn't answer when I spoke, so I went to him. I could feel no pulse. Apparently he must have died a very short time before I arrived. He was just terrified of death. Towards the end he was very weary, but he was still afraid of death. Three nights before he died he was sitting on the edge of the bed. I asked him if he was still afraid to die. He told me that he was. I did my best to com-

*Bela Lugosi's grave.*
(Photo: Mary Ellen Hunt)

fort him."

According to his expressed wish, he was laid out in his tuxedo and Dracula cape at Utter McKinley Mortuary, where a short simple service was held. After mourners had left, a woman dragged a screaming boy down the aisle of the chapel to the coffin. As the terrified boy stood in front of the coffin she screamed at him: "I'll show you that he is dead. He won't come back anymore to frighten you. Because he was just a man like your father. Go ahead and touch him." The terrified boy pulled away from the woman and ran out of the chapel.

The coffin was buried in the Grotto section of Holy Cross Cemetery, 5835 West Slauson Avenue, Los Angeles, California 90056.

# *MacArthur, Douglas*

Douglas MacArthur, the general in command of U.S. troops in the Southwest Pacific during World War II, who administered the postwar occupation of Japan, and who was in command of United States forces from 1950-51 during the Korean War, was born on January 26, 1880 in Little Rock, Arkansas.

After graduation from West Point in 1903, he subsequently served in the Philippines, in Mexico, and in combat in World War I. He was superintendent of West Point from 1919 to 1922. After helping form a Filipino defense force, he retired in 1937. Recalled to service in the Philippines in 1941, he and his men retreated before invading Japanese forces. He later began a counter offensive from New Guinea, using "island hopping" strategy, and regaining control of the Philippines in July 1945. On September 2, 1945, he accepted Japan's surrender aboard the battleship *Missouri*. He was appointed commander of the Allied Occupation forces in Japan and oversaw the re-organization of the government. On the outbreak of the Korean war he was made supreme commander of UN forces. After the entry of China into the war, he was disinclined to accept presidential directives to fight a limited war, and was relieved of his command in April 1951 by President Harry Truman (q.v.). Returning to the U.S., he received a hero's welcome before retiring to private life.

By March 1964 he was suffering from headaches and other complaints, including jaundice. President Lyndon Johnson (q.v.) sent an Air Force transport plane to New York to fly him to the Walter Reed Medical Center in Washington, D.C., for exploratory surgery, performed on March 6. No malignancy was found, but there was liver damage, and his gall bladder was removed. Afterwards he felt weak, and blood transfusions were begun. Two more major operations were performed; one to remove an intestinal obstruction, and the other to relieve bleeding. On April 3, he sank into a coma. He died at 2:39 p.m. on April 5. The cause of death was acute kidney and liver failure.

General
MacArthur's
grave in Norfolk
Courthouse,
Virginia.

(Photo: City of Norfolk)

His coffin was taken to Manhattan's Seventh Regiment Armory at Park Avenue and 66th St. President Johnson ordered 19-gun salutes fired at American military posts around the world, and flags to be flown half-mast until the burial. According to his own instructions, he lay in state in a plain gray steel government-issue casket, dressed in his most faded suntans.

The funeral service was held on April 7, after which the cortege went down Park Avenue to Pennsylvania Station. In the procession there was a riderless horse with reversed boots in the stirrups—since the time of Genghis Khan, the symbol of a fallen leader.

His body lay in state in the rotunda of the Capitol in Washington, D.C., and was then flown to Norfolk, Virginia, where it also lay in state. After a service on April 11 at St. Paul's Episcopal Church, the body was entombed in the 114-year-old Norfolk Courthouse. MacArthur Memorial, Norfolk Courthouse, MacArthur Square, City Hall Avenue, Norfolk, Virginia 23510.

# *MacDonald, Jeanette*

Jeanette MacDonald, actress and singer, who with singer Nelson Eddy formed a widely acclaimed singing team, was born on June 18, 1901, in Philadelphia. After working as a Broadway chorus girl in the 1920s, and starring in musicals, she teamed up with Eddy. In the 1930s they gained fame as "America's Sweethearts." Her films included *The Merry Widow* (1934), *The Girl of the Golden West* (1938) and others.

Having undergone abdominal surgery for adhesions in 1964 in Los Angeles, she was sent to Houston Methodist Hospital on January 11, 1965, for open heart surgery. Because of her weakened state, however, the surgery could not be performed. On January 14, at 4:00 p.m., she complained that her feet were cold. Her husband Gene Raymond, who was at her bedside, began to massage her feet and she looked over and smiled at him. A few minutes later she whispered: "I love you" and he whispered back "I love you too." She then closed her eyes and died at 4:32 p.m.

Her body was flown back to Hollywood on January 15. The movie-making community was shocked at the news of her death. Nelson Eddy said: "Jeanette MacDonald. You just can't accept it. I'll never get over it."

Burial place of Jeanette MacDonald, Forest Lawn Memorial Park, Glendale, California.
(Photo: Mary Ellen Hunt)

The funeral service was conducted on January 18, at the Church of the Recessional at Forest Lawn Memorial Park. Among the 350 mourners were Senator Barry Goldwater, actor Maurice Chevalier, film director Alfred Hitchcock, and Nelson Eddy. Jeanette lay in a bronze casket that was half opened and covered with a blanket of pink roses. She held a pink satin prayer book, which had been used at her marriage. The service was held at 2:00 p.m. Afterwards, recordings of Jeannette's voice singing "Ave Maria," and "Ah Sweet Mystery of Life" were played. She was buried in the Sanctuary Heritage Crypts, Forest Lawn Memorial Park, 6300 Forest Lawn Drive, Los Angeles, California 90068.

# MacFadden, Bernard

Bernard MacFadden, the magazine publisher, was born August 16, 1868, near Mill Spring, Missouri. In 1898 he began publishing *Physical Culture*, a magazine dealing with natural foods and fasting. In the 1920s he acquired or established several quasi-sexually-oriented magazines, including *True Story, True Romances*, and *True Detective Mystery Magazine*. He later acquired *Photoplay, Movie Mirror*, and others. In his later years he performed various stunts to demonstrate the good effects of his exercise regimes. These stunts included a 2,500-foot parachute jump into the Hudson River on his 83rd birthday, and a jump into Paris on his 84th birthday.

He died on October 12, 1955, aged 87, at the Medical Center in Jersey City, New Jersey. The cause of death was said to be an attack of jaundice aggravated by a three-day fast.

The funeral service was held on October 15 at Frank Campbell's Funeral Chapel on Madison Avenue at 81st Street, New York City. The service was conducted by the minister of the Presbyterian Church of Teaneck, New Jersey. MacFadden was eulogized by his old friend Rabbi Max Felshin of the Radio City Synagogue. Felshin said he was "an apostle of good health, good clean American living." Burial was in Woodlawn Cemetery, Jerome and Bainbridge Avenues, the Bronx, New York 10470.

# Machen, John Gresham

John Gresham Machen, the Presbyterian theologian, was born July 28, 1881, in Baltimore, Maryland. He was ordained a Presbyterian minister in 1914. In the theological controversy between fundamentalists and modernists in the Presbyterian Church, he became a spokesman for the conservatives. He was suspended from the ministry in 1933 for opposing a liberal revision of the 17th century Presbyterian creed. In 1936 he organized the Presbyterian Church of America, later known as the Orthodox Presbyterian Church. His publications included *Christianity and Liberalism* (1923).

While on a speaking tour in late December 1936, he was stricken with pneumonia. He died in Philadelphia, at 7:30 p.m. on January 1, 1937, of lobar pneumonia. An interdenominational funeral service was held on January 5, in Philadelphia at the Spruce Street Baptist Church. Burial was in Green Mount Cemetery, Greenmount Avenue at Oliver Street, Baltimore, Maryland 21202.

# Mack, Connie

Connie Mack, the professional baseball player and manager, was born Cornelius Alexander McGillicuddy on December 23, 1862, in East Brookfield, Massachusetts.

He played, mostly as catcher, in 700 major league games between 1886-96. He shortened his name to "Mack" so it would fit on a baseball scoreboard. When the American League was formed he became part owner of the Philadelphia Athletics, which he managed from 1901-50, during which time they won five world series. He was known as a discoverer of young baseball players. His bust in the Baseball Hall of Fame in Cooperstown, New York, was inscribed: "Mr. Baseball."

On October 1, 1955 he fell out of bed and broke his right hip. The hip was set, but on February 8, 1956 his condition took a turn for the worse, and a Catholic priest administered the last rites. He died peacefully at 3:20 p.m. at his daughter's home in Philadelphia.

The funeral service was held on February 11 in Philadelphia. The cortege slowly moved through mid-city Philadelphia and up to East Falls, to St. Bridget's Roman Catholic Church, where a requiem mass was held. About 1,200 mourners attended, including many of his former players, such as outfielders Bing Miller and Elmer Valo. Some 200 family members and friends braved the rainy day and crowded under canvas for the burial, at Holy Sepulchre Cemetery, Cheltenham Avenue and Easton Road, Philadelphia, Pennsylvania 19105.

# *McCarthy, Joseph*

Joseph Raymond McCarthy, a Republican U.S. senator from Wisconsin whose demagogic resort to character assassination in the earlier 1950s generated the term "McCarthyism," was born on November 14, 1908, in Grand Chute, near Appleton, Wisconsin. An attorney, who served in the U.S. Marines in World War II, he won a Senate seat from Robert M. LaFollette, Jr. in 1946. He was re-elected in 1952. In 1950 he claimed to know of 205 Communists employed by the Department of State, but, when called to testify before a Senate subcommittee, was unable to provide proof. Because of the then current Cold War fears, he was able to continue attacking public officials, and, sometimes to cause them to lose their jobs, although he never presented satisfactory legal evidence to substantiate his accusations. In 1954 nationally televised 36-day hearings concerning his charges led to the decline of his popular power. Subsequently, he was formally condemned by the Senate on two counts, one of which was his "abuse of fellow senators."

He died of a liver ailment, aged 47, at 6:02 p.m. on May 2, in Washington, D.C. Vice-President Richard M. Nixon issued a statement saying: "Years will pass before the results of his work can be objectively evaluated."

About 8,000 persons viewed his body on May 3 and 4 at Gawler's Funeral Home in Washington. Two thousand mourners attended a mass on May 6 at St. Mathew's Roman Catholic Cathedral, where Monsignor John J. Cartwright said that McCarthy's role in warning against communism "will be more and more honored as history unfolds its record." A service was then held in a Senate chamber, attended by 32 of the 49 Democrats and 38 of the 46 Republicans. His body was then flown to Green Bay, Wisconsin, on May 7. Burial was in St. Mary's Cemetery, 317 East College Street, Appleton, Wisconsin 54911.

# McCormick, Robert

Robert Rutherford McCormick, newspaper editor and publisher, was born on July 30, 1880, in Chicago, Illinois. Popularly known as "Colonel" McCormick, he became editor of the *Chicago Tribune* in 1910, and president of the Tribune Company in 1911. He and his cousin Joseph Medill Patterson shared the editorial and publishing functions at the *Tribune* from 1914-25. In World War I he served with the American Expeditionary Force in France. A staunch Republican, he staged aggressive political campaigns in the pages of the *Tribune* in which he espoused a number of causes, including freedom of the press and of big business, while denouncing labor unions, Prohibition, Russian Bolshevism, the New Deal, and U.S. entry into both World Wars. At the time of his death the *Tribune* empire included not only newspapers but also paper mills, forest lands, and radio and television stations.

In 1953 he had pneumonia, from which he never completely recovered. He underwent surgery in January 1955 to correct adhesions, and also bladder and liver conditions. After spending some weeks in Florida, he returned to Chicago on March 10. His condition worsened throughout the month of March and he died at his farm home in Wheaton, Illinois, at 2:47 a.m. on April 1, aged 74.

A private funeral service was held at his home on April 4, attended by about 350 persons. He was buried in his World War I uniform. The pastor of the First Presbyterian Church of Wheaton read the sermon and eulogized McCormick. Burial was on the grounds of his home, Cantigny, 1 South, 151 Winfield Road, Wheaton, Illinois 60187.

# McGraw, John Joseph

John Joseph McGraw, baseball player, nicknamed "Little Napoleon" because of his short height, shrewdness, and blunt manner, was born on April 7, 1873, in Truxton, New York. During the 1890s he played with the Baltimore Orioles and other National League clubs. He was appointed manager of the New York Giants in 1902 and under his 33-year direction the Giants won ten National League championships and three World Series titles. He retired as manager of the Giants in 1932. He wrote several books including: *How to Play Baseball* (1914), and *My Thirty Years in Baseball* (1923).

In early February 1934 he complained of a sore throat, and was hospitalized on February 16. His condition worsened, and he fell into a coma on February 24. He died at 11:50 a.m. on February 25, aged 61. The cause of death was said to be an internal hemorrhage caused by uremia.

A requiem mass was celebrated at St. Patrick's Cathedral on Fifth Avenue in New York City on February 28. The officiating priest read part of the gospel of St. John: "He is not dead, but sleeps." His plain mahogany coffin was shipped to Baltimore for burial at New Cathedral Cemetery, 512 Cathedral Street, Baltimore, Maryland 21201.

# McKinley, William

William McKinley, 25th president of the United States (term of office 1897-1901), was born on January 29, 1843, in Niles, Ohio. In the Civil War he served in the Union Army as an aide to Colonel (later President) Rutherford B. Hayes *(q.v.)*. He was elected to the House of Representatives in 1876 where, except for one term, he remained until 1891. He was elected governor of Ohio in 1891 and re-elected in 1893. He contested the 1896 presidential election on the Republican ticket against William Jennings Bryan *(q.v.)*, and won the election. The Spanish American War of 1898 occurred during his administration, as a result of which the Philippines became a U.S. dependency. Through his secretary of state, John Hay, *(q.v.)* he supported the Open Door Policy toward China (1899-1900), which American troops upheld by helping contain the Boxer Rebellion of 1900.

McKinley was shot by Leon Czolgosz, an anarchist, while visiting the Pan-American Exposition in Buffalo, New York, on September 6, 1901. After the shooting, crowds pinned Czolgosz to the floor, but the president, who had been led to a chair, said: "Don't let them hurt him." In the week that followed, he recovered consciousness and could talk and smile at the doctors. He complained of being lonely in his sick-room. By the end of the week, however, he had developed general infection and gangrene. His fever rose and he was unable to take nourishment except by enema. On September 13 he rallied from his comatose state and said: "It is useless, gentlemen. I think we ought to have prayer." He died in Buffalo on September 14.

*President William McKinley's tomb in Canton, Ohio.*

(Photo: State County Historical Society)

The body was taken to Washington, D.C., where it lay in state first in the East Room of the White House, and then in the Capitol. It was then taken by train to Canton, Ohio, where national dignitaries gathered for the final rites at the Methodist Church. Burial was adjacent to Westlawn Cemetery, 1919 7th, N.W., Canton, Ohio 44708.

# Madison, Dolley

Dolley Payne Madison, the famous Washington hostess who was the wife of President James Madison *(q.v.)*, was born Dolley Payne Todd on May 20, 1768, in

Guilford County, North Carolina. (She spelled her name "Dolley," and not "Dolly," as it is often given today.) Born a Quaker, she was beautiful and vivacious. In 1794 she married James Madison, and was consequently expelled from the Society of Friends [the Quakers] because her husband was not a Quaker. When the British captured Washington in the War of 1812, she saved many papers, as well as a portrait of George Washington, (q.v.) when she fled the city. She is best remembered for her charm and tact, as well as for her social gifts.

By July 1849 she had fallen very ill, and was confined to bed. By July 10, she was only intermittently conscious. She died while praying with her pastor on July 12.

The funeral service was held on July 16 at St. John's Episcopal Church in Washington, D.C. The burial service, held the same day, was attended by many federal officials, and took place at the Congressional Cemetery.

On February 10, 1852, her body was transferred to the privately-owned vault of a friend of her niece. On January 12, 1858, it was moved again, this time to the Madison family vault, next to the body of her husband, at Montpelier Plantation in Orange County, Virginia. Her grave is marked by a white marble shaft, on which her death date is incorrectly given as July 8, instead of July 12, 1849. The Cemetery, Montpelier Plantation, Montpelier, Virginia 23192.

# *Madison, James*

James Madison, fourth president of the United States, (term of office 1809-17), was born on March 16, 1751, in what is now Port Conway, Virginia. In 1776 he was elected to Virginia's revolutionary convention. He was elected to the Continental Congress in 1780, and from 1784 to 1786 was a member of the Virginia legislature. Because of his influential work at the Federal Constitutional Convention of 1787, he is often called the "Father of the Constitution." After serving as secretary of state in the administration of President Thomas Jefferson (q.v.), he was elected to the presidency in 1808, and was re-elected in 1812. As U.S. commander-in-chief during the War of 1812 (1812-15), he kept the country together during the difficult months of the British occupation of Washington, D.C., and piloted it through the worst of the financial crisis which followed. He later served as rector of the University of Virginia which he had helped Jefferson found.

During his last years he lived at his Montpelier estate, but was bedridden. He nevertheless maintained voluminous correspondence. By 1836 he was so weak that he had to be carried on a couch from his bedroom to a sitting room. On June 28, 1836 he had difficulty swallowing. His niece asked him: "What is the matter uncle James?" He answered: "Nothing more than a change of mind, my dear"—and died. He was buried at the family cemetery in Montpelier. A memorial service was held in August, One speaker said: "None could forget how it pierced our souls when the body of our Madison was lowered into the grave." The Cemetery, Montpelier Plantation, Virginia 23192.

# Magnes, Judah Leon

Judah Leon Magnes, the rabbi and religious leader, was born July 5, 1877, in San Francisco. After graduating from Hebrew Union College in Cincinnatti, and receiving his doctorate from the University of Heidelberg in Germany in 1902, he served as rabbi at temples in Brooklyn and Manhattan until 1912. A pacifist and a Zionist, from 1912 to 1920 he was head of the Society for the Advancement of Judaism. In 1922 he went to Palestine and was the prime founder of Hebrew University in Jerusalem (1925). He was its chancellor (1925 to 1935), and then served as its president until his death.

He died on October 27, 1948, in his suite at the Mayflower Hotel, on Central Park West in New York City, of a heart condition. He was aged 71. With him at the time of his death were his wife and the hotel doctor. About 500 persons attended a simple outdoor funeral service at the Jewish Theological Seminary of America on Broadway and 122nd Street, on October 28. Scriptural references read in Hebrew were the 15th and 121st Psalms, and the 23rd Psalm. Following the service, burial was in Shearith Israel Cemetery, at Cypress Hills Cemetery, 833 Jamaica Avenue, Brooklyn, New York 11208.

# Malcolm X

Malcolm X, the black militant leader, prominent in the early 1960s, was born Malcolm Little on May 19, 1925, in Omaha, Nebraska. While imprisoned for robbery between 1946-1952 he studied the teachings of Elijah Muhammad, leader of the "Nation of Islam" (Black Muslims). Upon his release in 1952, he went to Muslim headquarters in Chicago, to join the sect and devote himself to religious and social work. Abandoning his "slave" name," Little," he took the Muslim name El-Haji Malik El-Shabazz. He became the sect's first "national minister" in 1963. In 1964 he publicly broke with Elijah Muhammad and formed the Organization of Afro-American Unity. He also made a pilgrimage to Mecca. In October 1964 he confirmed his conversion to orthodox Islamism.

In an interview on November 18, 1964, he said: "I'm a marked man. It doesn't frighten me for myself, as long as I felt they would not hurt my family. No one can get out without trouble. This thing with me will be resolved by death and violence." In February, 1965, his home in Queens, New York, was fire-bombed, and he held the Black Muslims responsible.

While addressing a rally at the Audubon Ballroom at 166th St. and Broadway in Washington Heights, New York City, on February 21, he was shot to death by 22-year old Thomas Hagan. FBI fingerprint data later proved that Hagan's real name was Talmadge Hayer. The autopsy report showed the cause of death to be "multiple shotgun slugs and bullet wounds of the chest, heart and aorta." The medical examiner said there were also wounds in the arms, legs, and a slight wound on the chin. His body was put on view on February 23 at the Unity Funeral Home, West 126th Street, New York City. During the first day of viewing, several bomb threats were made. About 22,000 persons viewed the body. On February 27 the bronze coffin was taken to Faith Temple Church of God in Christ, 147th and Amsterdam Avenue, New York City. His body had been wrapped in white, and could be seen through a glass lid in the coffin. Black actor and playwright Ossie Davis eulogized him, saying: "Malcolm was our manhood, our living black manhood. In honoring him we honor the best in ourselves." After the eulogy, Muslim prayers were offered. Mourners then filed past the coffin.

The body was then taken to Ferncliff Cemetery in Hartsdale where 250 mourners

Malcolm X's
grave marker,
Hartsdale,
New York.

(Photo: Eric Mautner)

heard Muslim prayers at the graveside as six of Malcolm's followers shoveled black earth onto the coffin.

Later in 1965, *The Autobiography of Malcolm X* was posthumously published. The work made him a folk hero, especially among black youth.

Ferncliff Cemetery, Hartsdale, New York 10530.

# *Marciano, "Rocky"*

"Rocky" Marciano was born Rocco Francis Marchegiano, on September 1, 1924, in Brockton, Massachusetts. In 1947, before turning professional, he won 27 out of 30 amateur fights put on by New York City boxing promoters. As a professional, by 1951 he was an established contender for the heavyweight title. In October 1951, in a match with former heavyweight champion Joe Louis, he scored a knock-out in the 8th round, becoming the second person to knock Louis out. He won the world championship in a match against "Jersey" Joe Walcott in 1952. Before his retirement in 1956 he successfully defended the title six times. At the time of his death he had 49 consecutive victories, 43 of which had been knock-outs.

On August 31, 1969 he was traveling with some friends in a single-engine plane. On the approach to Newton Airport in Des Moines, Iowa, the plane crashed in a wooded area, about two miles southeast of the airport.

About 2,000 people attended a funeral service at St. Colman's Roman Catholic Church in Brockton, Massachusetts, on September 4. In the eulogy, Marciano was praised for having worked with children in the parish's Catholic Youth Organization. In addition to many fans, world heavyweight champion Willy Pepp and former middleweight champions Tony Zale and Paul Zender also attended.

The flag-covered coffin was flown to Fort Lauderdale for burial. A requiem mass was held at St. Pius Catholic Church in Fort Lauderdale, on September 6, attended by hundreds of mourners. A military escort from Palm Beach Military Academy accompanied the procession to the cemetery, where taps were played during the burial. Lauderdale Memorial Gardens, 400 N.W. 27th Avenue, Fort Lauderdale, Florida 33310.

# *Marquette, Jacques*

Jacques Marquette, the French Jesuit missionary and explorer, was born on June 1, 1637 in Laon, France. Arriving in Quebec, Canada, in 1666, he established a Catholic mission at Sault Ste. Marie, in what is now Michigan, in 1668. In 1671 he established another mission at St. Ignace, also in what is now Michigan. From there, in 1673, he left on a voyage of exploration, accompanying Louis Jolliet who had been commissioned to find the course and mouth of the Mississippi River. Traveling to Green Bay, now in Wisconsin, they descended the Wisconsin River to the Mississippi, which they followed south as far as the Arkansas River. Finding that the territory ahead of them was in hostile Spanish hands, they returned to Green Bay, via the Illinois River. In the winter of 1674-75 he, with two companions, camped near the present site of Chicago, before reaching the Illinois Indians in the spring. Falling ill, he sought to return to St. Ignace, but died on May 18, 1675, on the eastern shore of Lake Michigan, at the mouth of a river.

Marquette's superior in Quebec later reported that, the evening before his death,"He announced that he was going to die, and gave instructions concerning his burial, and how his hands and feet should be arranged, and that a cross should be erected over his grave." At the moment of his death, Marquette repeated the words "Jesus Mary," spoken by one of his companions, and then died without a struggle.

Ludington, Michigan, formerly called Marquette, claims to be the site of his death. The exact spot is marked by a boulder on a knoll, in Pere Marquette Park, near the harbor. This is known as his first grave. Frankfort, Michigan, to the north, has also claimed to be the site. In 1677, a band of Ottawa Indians, returning from a winter hunt, took Marquette's remains back to St. Ignace, to which he had asked that his body be returned. As was their custom, the Ottawa stripped away the flesh, and brought back only the bones, which they had dried. These were buried a second time, beneath the floor of the mission's log building. After the mission was burned in 1706, the location of the grave remained unknown until 1877, when it was accidentally unearthed. A marble statue was erected on the site, in Marquette Park, St. Ignace, and some of the bones were sent to Marquette College in Milwaukee, Wisconsin. Marquette Park, St. Ignace, Michigan 49781.

*An artist's conception of the death of Father Marquette.*
(Photo Courtesy of James M. Babcock)

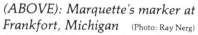

*(ABOVE): Marquette's marker at Frankfort, Michigan* (Photo: Ray Nerg)
*(RIGHT): Marquette's marker at Ludington, Michigan.*
(Photo: The Rose Hawley Museum, Ludington, Michigan)

# *Marx, Groucho*

Groucho Marx, a member of the Marx brothers, a slapstick comedy team of stage and screen, was born Julius Henry Marx on October 2, 1895 in New York City. Making his stage debut in 1904, he performed with his brothers in a group called "Six Musical Mascots." Together with his brothers—Arthur (Harpo), Herbert (Zeppo), and Leonard (Chico)—he made a series of comedy movies in the 1920s and 1930s. Another brother, Milton (Gummo), had left the act earlier. The team disbanded in 1949.

He was hospitalized in Los Angeles on June 22, 1977, for a respiratory ailment, and stayed in the hospital until his death on August 19. He was aged 86. Death was attributed to pneumonia. Other famous comedians paid him tributes. One of his contemporaries, George Jessel, said: "He made people laugh. He was one of our great talents, one of our great wits. We're all going to miss him but what he said will live forever." Comedian Red Skelton called him "one of the greatest clowns; he'll really be missed." Comedienne Lucille Ball called his death both a "tragedy and a blessing"—pointing out that he had been in ill health.

His body was cremated. Instead of a religious service, a private gathering was held at the California home of his son, Arthur. Among those present were Harpo Marx's widow, and a number of people who had known Groucho in his early career.

Comedians George Jessel and George Burns were displeased that Hollywood did not pay the final respects that they felt Marx deserved. Burial was in the Jewish Cemetery at Eden Memorial Park. His grave is marked by a square bronze plaque, bearing his vital statistics, and a star of David. Eden Memorial Park, 11500 Sepulveda Boulevard, San Fernando, California 91345.

# *Masters, Edgar Lee*

Edgar Lee Masters, poet, renowned as the author of the *Spoon River Anthology* (1915), was born August 23, 1869, in Garnett, Kansas. After growing up in New Salem, Illinois, he was admitted to the Illinois bar in 1891, and was for a short while in practice with Clarence Darrow. He built a successful law practice in Chicago. He began to publish poems in 1898, some under the pseudonym of Webster Ford. He also published several novels. The success of the *Spoon River Anthology* led Masters to give up his law practice and move to New York City. His later works never achieved the quality of the *Spoon River Anthology*. He also wrote biographies of Abraham Lincoln, Walt Whitman, and Mark Twain (*q.q.v.*).

He died on March 5, 1950, in a convalescent home in Melrose Park, a suburb of Philadelphia. After a private funeral service on March 10, he was buried in the cemetery at Petersburg, Illinois, overlooking the Spoon River. Oakland Cemetery, Petersburg, Illinois 62675.

# Masterson, Bat

William Barclay Masterson, frontier gunfighter, nicknamed "Bat," was born November 24, 1853, in Iroquois County, Illinois. After hunting buffalo, fighting Indians, and serving as an army scout, he became deputy marshall of Dodge City, Kansas in 1883. He was also an associate of Wyatt Earp (q.v.) in Tombstone, Arizona. Nationally known for upholding law and order in Kansas, he later went to New York City in 1902, where he worked as a sports writer on the *New York Morning Telegraph.*

On October 25, 1921, he was sitting at his desk, writing a column, and trying to catch up on his work after being out sick with a bad cold. A fellow worker asked him how he was feeling, and he answered: "All right." Those were his last words. A few minutes later he was found dead in his office.

On October 27, 1921, a funeral service was held at the Campbell Funeral Home in New York City, conducted by the clergyman from St. Steven's Protestant Episcopal Church. Hundreds of his friends and admirers came for the service. An ex-boxing commissioner for the state of New York eulogized him, saying that he "had never known Bat Masterson to do a dishonorable deed, never to betray a friend, ... never to fear an enemy." Burial was in Woodlawn Cemetery, 233rd Street and Webster Avenue, the Bronx, New York 10470.

# Mather, Cotton

Cotton Mather, Puritan clergyman, author, and scholar, was born on February 12, 1663 in Boston. He was the son of Increase Mather (q.v.). He was ordained a minister in 1685 and joined his father at Boston's Second Church. He had an intense interest in the mystic and occult sciences. He published more than 400 titles in a variety of fields, from botany to ecclesiastical music. His most famous work was *Magnalia Christi Americana* (1702), which was a comprehensive history of New England. He incurred unpopularity by being a pioneering advocate of smallpox inoculation. At the time of his death he was one of the most famous men in America.

By December of 1727 he had fallen ill. He wrote to one of his doctors: "My last enemy is come; I would say, my best friend." At the time of his death, his son Richard was at his bedside, and asked him for a word of inspiration which could be remembered. He firmly replied: "Fructuosus" [Fruitful]. He died on February 13, 1728. The funeral service was held on February 19.

Burial was in Copps Hill Burial Ground, Charter and Hull Streets, Boston, Massachusetts 02113.

# Mather, Increase

Increase Mather, Puritan leader, diplomat, and educator, was born on June 21, 1639, in Dorchester, Massachusetts. After graduating from Harvard in 1656, he took a degree at Trinity College in Dublin in 1658, returning to Massachusetts in 1661. He occupied the pulpit at Boston's Second Church from 1664 to the time of his death. From 1685-1701 he was president of Harvard. In 1691 he obtained a new charter for Massachusetts from James II, but this proved unpopular with the colonists. A prolific writer, he wrote many volumes including his *Case of Conscience Concerning Evil Spirits Personating Men* (1693), relating to the hysteria of the Salem witch trials of 1692.

By late 1722 he was in a state of mental disorientation, and called out continuously to have the Seventy-first Psalm read to him. On August 23, 1723 he was in an extreme amount of pain. His son, Cotton Mather *(q.v.)*, came to him and asked: "This day thou shalt be in paradise, do you believe it sir? And rejoice in the views and hopes of it?" With obvious pain and difficulty the old man embraced his son and with his last breath said: "I do, I do, I do." He then died.

The funeral service was held on August 29 at Boston's Second Church. Other ministers preached funeral services in churches throughout New England. His service was attended by many notables of Boston. Burial was at Copps Hill Burying Ground, Charter and Hull Streets, Boston, Massachusetts 02113.

# *Mayo, Charles Horace*

Charles Horace Mayo, physician who introduced modern procedures in goiter surgery and neurosurgery, was born on July 19, 1865, in Rochester, Minnesota. After graduation from the Chicago Medical College, (now part of Northwestern University), he and his brother, William James Mayo *(q.v.)*, staffed St. Mary's Hospital in Rochester in 1889. As their reputations increased, other physicians were drawn to Rochester to what became known as the Mayo Clinic, which itself became renowned for group medicine. In 1915 Charles and William also founded the Mayo Foundation for Medical Education and Research, which later became part of the graduate school of the University of Minnesota. Meanwhile the Mayo Clinic's size and reputation grew, as patients came to it from all over the world.

*The Mayo family plot in Rochester, Minnesota. (Charles Mayo's grave is to the left of the man in the foreground).*

(Photo: Mayo Clinic)

While on a business trip to Chicago in May 1939, Charles became ill and was admitted to Mercy Hospital. There he died at 5:55 p.m. on May 26, aged 74. The cause of death was pneumonia.

Private and public funeral services were held on May 29 in Rochester. The private services were held in the Mayo country home, with family members and his close friends attending. Public services were in Calvary Episcopal Church, with the Bishop Coadjudtor of the Minnesota Episcopal Diocese officiating. As the procession passed St. Mary's hospital, 250 uniformed nurses stood in front of the hospital as an honor guard. Burial was in Oak Wood Cemetery, 217 South Broadway, Rochester, Minnesota 55901.

# *Mayo, William James*

William James Mayo, the physician specializing in surgery of the abdomen, pelvis, and kidney, was born in Le Sueur, Minnesota, on June 29, 1861. After graduation from the University of Michigan Medical School in 1883, he and his brother Charles Horace Mayo (*q.v.*) were the sole surgical staff at St. Mary's Hospital, Rochester, Minnesota, from 1889 to 1905. By keeping informed of surgical advances and techniques, they increased their skills and reputations. Other doctors were drawn to Rochester to cooperate in a voluntary association that became known as the Mayo Clinic. William and his brother also established the Mayo Foundation for Medical Education and Research.

After returning to Minnesota from a winter vacation in the southwestern United States, Dr. Will, as he was known in Rochester, underwent abdominal surgery in April 1939 at the Mayo Clinic, but never fully recovered. He grieved constantly after the death of his brother, Dr. Charles Mayo, on May 26. William died in his sleep in the early morning hours of July 28. Death was from an ailment that he had specialized in treating—a sub-acute perforating ulcer.

A brief service was held at the Mayo Foundation House in Rochester, on July 30. The clergyman of the Congregational Church of Rochester eulogized William as "a surgeon, scholar, soldier and lover of his fellow man." Burial was next to his brother. Oak Wood Cemetery, 217 South Broadway, Rochester, Minnesota 55901.

# *Melville, Herman*

Herman Melville, author of *Moby Dick* and other works, was born on August 1, 1819 in New York City. Failing to find other work, he first went to sea at the age of 19. Having voyaged to the South Seas in the early 1840s, he wrote of these experiences in his book *Typee* (1846). It was followed by *Omoo* (1847). In 1850, after having bought a farm in Massachusetts, he wrote *Moby Dick* (1851). A classic of American literature, it was not to be recognized as such for many years, and brought him in his lifetime neither fame nor fortune. His last completed work, *Billy Budd*, was completed in 1891 but was not published until 1924.

By 1890 he complained of illness. He died in New York City at 12:30 a.m. on September 28, 1891 of what his death certificate described as "cardiac dilitation [sic], mitral regurgitation... contributory asthenia."

Not realizing his place in literature, the *New York Daily Tribune*, at the time of his death, commented: "He won considerable fame as an author by the publication of a book in 1847 entitled *Typee* ... This was his best work although he has since written a number of other stories which were published more for private than for public circulation."

The funeral service was on September 30, and burial was in Woodlawn Cemetery in the Bronx. The grave, which has become a place of pilgrimage for scholars from all over the world, lies beneath a large oak tree. The gravestone has an unrolled scroll and a quill pen carved on it. In the 1930s the grave was the site of a dramatic nocturnal meeting. Dr. John F. ("Jafsie") Cordon, who acted as an intermediary in the Lindbergh kidnapping case, met there in 1932 with a man later suspected to be Bruno R. Hauptmann, (subsequently executed after a controversial trial), in an unsuccessful effort to recover the kidnaped child. Woodlawn Cemetery, 233rd Street and Webster Avenue, the Bronx, New York 10470.

# Miller, Henry

Henry Valentine Miller, the author whose novels were pioneering works in the field of sexual candor, was born on December 26, 1891 in New York City. Raised in Brooklyn, he worked for Western Union Telegraph Company in New York City and, after writing his first book but failing to find a publisher, he went to France in 1924. Here he wrote *Tropic of Capricorn* (1934), *Tropic of Cancer* (1939), and other books. Some critics have judged his *Colossus of Maroussi* (1941), a travel book about Greece, his best work. His books were the subject of a 1964 Supreme Court ruling, dealing with obscenity, that was in his favor.

He died on June 7, 1980, "peacefully," in the arms of his housekeeper, Bill Pickerel, at his Pacific Pallisades, California, home. The cause of death was said to be circulatory failure. A private memorial service was held, attended only by the family. He was cremated, and his ashes scattered off the coast at Big Sur, California, not far from where he used to live.

# Mitchell, Margaret

Margaret Mitchell, author of *Gone With The Wind*, was born on November 8, 1900, in Atlanta, Georgia. She was a reporter and feature writer for the *Atlanta Journal* from 1922 to 1926. Because of an injury she gave up reporting and spent the next ten years writing a novel, which was published in 1936 as *Gone With The Wind*. It won the Pulitzer Prize for fiction in 1937, sold more than ten million copies, and was translated into more than 30 languages. The movie version, made in 1939, was one of the longest and most popular films ever made. Margaret Mitchell's *Gone With The Wind Letters* were published in 1976.

On August 11, 1949, Mitchell and her husband, John Marsh, were crossing Peachtree Street in Atlanta when she saw an oncoming speeding car, driven by off-duty taxi driver Hugh D. Gravett. She jerked away from her husband, panicked, and tried to escape. Gravett went into a skid, leaving marks later measured as 67 feet long. The car hit Mitchell, and she was thrown to the ground. She was taken to Grady Memorial Hospital where her condition was said to be critical, and where she was found to have cerebral concussion and a possible skull fracture. By August 15 she developed a fever of 102° F. and her pulse dropped below normal. She died at 11:59 a.m. on August 16.

A nine-minute Protestant Episcopal service was held at Spring Hill, a funeral home at 10th and Spring in Atlanta, on August 18, attended only by close friends and family. Her body lay in a silver finish metal coffin covered by a heavy glass plate; she wore two orchids on her gown. Organ music included, Bach's "Come Sweetly Death," and the hymn "The Strife is Over." Burial was at Oakland Cemetery, 248 Oakland Avenue, S.E., Atlanta, Georgia 30312.

# *Monroe, James*

James Monroe, fifth president of the United States, (in office 1817-24), was born on April 28, 1758 in Westmoreland County, Virginia. He was elected to the Virginia legislature, served in Congress from 1783-86, and was elected to the Senate in 1790. He held diplomatic posts in France from 1794-96, and in France, Britain and Spain from 1803-07. Between these posts, he served as governor of Virginia from

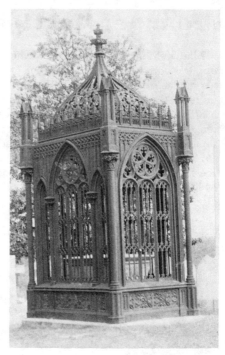

*President James Monroe's grave in Hollywood Cemetery, Richmond, Virginia.* (Photo: Theresa Breschel)

1799-1802, and later was again governor in 1811. From 1811-17 he was U.S. secretary of state.

In 1816 he was elected to the presidency on the Democratic-Republican ticket, and was re-elected in 1820. On leaving the presidency, he retired to his home in Leesburg,

Virginia. During his administration, the U.S. acquired the Floridas from Spain, and the Monroe Doctrine (1823)—according to which the U.S. opposed European intervention in the affairs of American states—was enunciated. This doctrine has since been a fundamental tenet of U.S. foreign policy.

Monroe died, apparently of tuberculosis, while visiting his daughter in New York City, on July 4, 1831. He was the third president to die on July 4—the anniversary of the signing of the Declaration of Independence—the other two being John Adams and Thomas Jefferson, (q.q.v.). The funeral service was held at St. Paul's Episcopal Church in New York City, and he was eulogized by the president of Columbia University. Church bells tolled throughout the city, and guns were fired at Fort Columbus in New York Harbor. The cortege moved up Broadway to the Marble Cemetery on Second Street, where he was buried. Three volleys were fired over his grave by an honor guard.

On July 2, 1858, in the centennial year of his birth, his remains were placed on board the steamer *Jamestown,* and escorted by the Seventh New York Regiment to Richmond, Virginia. There he was re-buried in the Hollywood Cemetery, 412 South Cherry Street, Richmond, Virginia 23220.

# *Monroe, Marilyn*

Marilyn Monroe, the film actress who became America's most renowned sex symbol, was born Norma Jean Mortenson on June 1, 1926, in Los Angeles. She later took her mother's name, Baker. After modeling, she appeared in movies for the first time in 1948. (Earlier, in 1946, when signing a contract, she had taken the name of Marilyn Monroe.) Her appearance in the movie *All About Eve* (1950) gained her a long-term contract with Twentieth-Century-Fox, and her name soon became a household word. Her other movies included *Let's Make It Legal* (1951), *Gentlemen Prefer Blondes* (1953), and *Some Like It Hot* (1959). In 1954 she married baseball star Joe DiMaggio, whom she later divorced. In 1956 she married playwright Arthur Miller, and for a short while retired. Her final role was in the 1961 movie *The*

*Marilyn Monroe's grave in West Los Angeles.*

(Photo: Mary Ellen Hunt)

*Misfits.*

On August 5, 1962, she was found dead in the bedroom of her Brentwood Section, Los Angeles, home, aged 36. Beside the bed was an empty bottle of sleeping pills, as well as 14 other bottles of medicines and tablets, many of which were barbiturates. After an autopsy the Los Angeles coroner said that her death "was not a natural death," and that it was drug related.

A brief and simple funeral service was held on August 8, and was attended neither by Hollywood stars nor by the press. The 60 policemen who had been assigned to the funeral found little to do. Her body lay in state at the Westwood Village Mortuary in Hollywood. She was wearing a green jersey dress and no jewelry. The service was conducted by the pastor of the nondenominational Village Church of Westwood. He read the 23rd Psalm, and John 14. Classical music was played, as well as the hit tune "Over The Rainbow."

Just before the coffin was closed and placed in a crypt, her second husband, Joe DiMaggio, bent over and kissed her, saying: "I love you" several times.

Following her funeral there was a rash of suicides in New York City, and the president of the National Save-a-Life League suggested that the suicides could have been influenced by Monroe's death. A New York psychologist commented: "Many individuals identify with a movie king or queen, and the death of one so prominent disturbs a little bit of every one of us." Joe DiMaggio made arrangements for red roses, constantly replaced with fresh ones, to be set on her monument three times a week. By the mid-1980s, this practice had been continued unbroken since the time of her death. Westwood Cemetery, 1218 Glendon Avenue, West Los Angeles, California 90024.

# *Morton, Jelly Roll*

"Jelly Roll" Morton, the pioneer jazz pianist and composer, was born Ferdinand Joseph La Menthe Morton on September 20, 1885, in New Orleans. At an early age he participated in the development, in New Orleans, of the music that became known as "jazz," and that swept throughout the world. Outstanding and talented, he later claimed that he invented jazz in 1901, and he certainly could lay claim to introducing several of its characteristic features. After playing with several groups in a number of states, including those on the West Coast, he organized Jelly Roll Morton's Red Hot Peppers in 1926. The group recorded a series of records which brought him national attention. During the 1930s his fame was eclipsed by big band artists, although he continued to play professionally and to record. His vanity offended many colleagues, and lost him many opportunities for success. As a composer, he is known for a number of pieces, especially *King Porter Stomp.* In 1938 he made a series of recordings for the Archives of American Folk Songs at the Library of Congress, in which he played many of his compositions and narrated his life story.

In a letter he wrote on February 22, 1941, he said: "My breath has been very short lately and I had to go to the hospital and had been spitting blood and many other symptoms too numerous to mention." He died at Los Angeles County hospital on July 10, of heart trouble and asthma.

According to his common-law wife, Anita Gonzalez, Morton had been sacrificed to Satan as a child by his godmother, Eulalie Echo, who was, she said, a voodoo witch. This meant that when Eulalie Echo died, Morton would die too, and be "taken down" with her. Eulalie died two months before Morton did. "He died in my arms," said Anita, "begging me to keep anointing his lips with oil that had been blessed by a bishop in New York."

A requiem high mass was held at St. Patrick's Church in Los Angeles, and about 150 persons, were present. His pallbearers were four of his former bandmembers—old-time jazz stars Kid Ory, Mutt Carey, Ed Garland, and Fred Washington. His old song-writing partner Reb Spikes had no car, and almost did not make it to the cemetery. Paradoxically, the thousand-dollar diamond that Morton had had inlaid into one of his front teeth—as an insurance policy for hard times—was missing. He had often said: "I've always lived with diamonds and I want to be buried with them." But the diamond was gone, and there was only a hole in his tooth where it should have been. Burial was at Calvary Cemetery, 42001 Whittier Boulevard, Los Angeles, California 90023.

# *Morton, William Thomas Green*

William Thomas Green Morton, the pioneer anesthetist, was born August 9, 1819, in Charlton, Massachusetts. A dentist, he experimented with the use of nitrous oxide while performing oral surgery. In September 1846 he used ether during a tooth extraction. In October of that year he again used ether, at Massachusetts General Hospital, during surgery to remove a neck tumor. His discovery was recorded in a

*Monument marking the grave of William T.G. Morton in Cambridge, Massachusetts.* (Photo: Kevin Gleason)

medical journal and he applied for a patent for the drug under the name of "Letheon."

During a heat wave in New York City on July 15, 1868 he expressed difficulty in breathing, and said that he had "considerable leg pain." He got out of bed saying that his sheets were like fire. After dressing, he hired a carriage for a ride through

Central Park with his wife. During the ride he stopped the carriage, got out, and staggered across the grass toward the lake at the other end of the park. His wife ran after him and found him kneeling on the ground trying to thrust his hands into the lake. He was taken to St. Luke's Hospital where he died on July 15, 1868.

The funeral service was held at Etherton Cottage, Morton's home at West Needham, (now Wellesley), southwest of Boston, on July 18, at 2:00 p.m. Burial was in Mount Auburn, Cambridge.

Although others have been recognized as having priority in discovering anesthesia, he was the first to demonstrate this use of ether. His grave is marked by a marble monument inscribed: "William T.G. Morton, inventor and revealer of anesthetic inhalation by whom pain in surgery was averted and annulled. Before whom in all time, surgery was agony. Since whom, science had control of pain." Mt. Auburn Cemetery, 580 Mt. Auburn Street, Cambridge, Massachusetts 02138.

# Moses, "Grandma"

Anna Mary Robertson Moses, the painter known as "Grandma Moses," was born on September 7, 1860, in Greenwich, New York. In 1905 she and her husband Thomas Moses settled on a farm in Eagle Bridge, New York, where she lived for the rest of her life. In her late seventies she began oil painting as a hobby. Her "career" started when a connoisseur saw some of her paintings in a drug store window, drove to her farm, and bought her entire stock of paintings. Three of them were shown in an exhibit entitled "Contemporary Unknown Painters" in the Museum of Modern Art in New York City. Altogether, she painted more than 2,000 canvases, many of which were reproduced in prints and on Christmas cards.

In August 1961 she had a fall in her home and was admitted as a patient to the Hoosick Falls Health Center, where she died on December 13, aged 101. Her doctor said that she died of hardening of the arteries, but then suggested that the best way to describe the cause of death was that "she just wore out." New York's Governor Nelson Rockefeller (*q.v.*) said: "She painted for the sheer love of painting, and throughout her 101 years she was endeared to all who had the privilege of knowing her."

The funeral service was held at her home on December 16, and was conducted by the rector of St. Mark's Protestant Episcopal Church in Hoosick Falls. He said that she had found "real consolation from the word of God, and real hopefulness from the Scriptures." Burial was in Maple Grove Cemetery, Hill Road at the end of Church and Main, Hoosick Falls, New York 12090.

# Murray, Philip

Philip Murray, the labor leader, was born May 25, 1886, in Scotland. He came to the United States in 1902 and worked as a coal miner. He joined the United Mine Workers of America (UMW) union, and by the age of 26 was on the national board, later serving as vice-president. When the Committee for Industrial Organization

(CIO) was formed, Murray was given the task of reorganizing the steel industry unions, subsequently becoming president of the United Steel Workers of America (USWA). He was also elected vice-president of the independent Congress of Industrial Organizations (CIO).

At 6:30 a.m. on November 9, 1952, he was found dead in his hotel room at the Mark Hopkins Hotel in San Francisco, after he had failed to answer a telephone call. The funeral service was held on November 13 at St. Paul's Cathedral in Pittsburgh, Pennsylvania. Following the Roman Catholic service, burial took place in Pittsburgh. A special requiem mass was held on December 6 in Boston, at which the archbishop of Boston, who officiated, said: "No man in the American chapter of the [trade union's] history had given it more dignity, prestige and potential for good than had Phil Murray." St. Anne's Cemetery, 3936 Willow Avenue, Pittsburgh, Pennsylvania 15234.

# Murrow, Edward R.

Edward Roscoe Murrow, radio journalist, was born April 25, 1908, in Greensboro, North Carolina. He began to work for the Columbia Broadcasting System (CBS) in 1935, and in 1937 became director of the European bureau, training war correspondents, including Eric Sevareid and Howard K. Smith. He did a series of transatlantic wartime broadcasts from London during the blitz (German aerial bombing) in 1940 that brought the war home to Americans as nothing else had to that time. He later broadcast from other wartime locales. Returning to the United States in 1946 he became CBS vice-president of Public Affairs. During the McCarthy era (see McCarthy, Joseph), he courageously presented an exposé of McCarthyism on television in 1954. President John F. Kennedy (q.v.) appointed him head of the U.S. Information Agency (USIA), a post he held from 1961-64.

He began a battle against cancer in October 1963, going in and out of the hospital. He was released from New York Hospital in early April 1965 and died at his home in Pawling, New York, on April 27, aged 57.

The funeral service was held on April 30 at St. James' Episcopal Church, Madison Avenue at 71st Street, New York City, and was attended by 1,200 persons, including (then) Ambassador Adlai Stevenson (q.v.), Senator Robert F. Kennedy (q.v.), and William S. Paley, (chairman of the board of CBS). Musical selections included Bach's "God's Time is Best." Following the service, the body was cremated at Green-Wood Cemetery, Brooklyn, New York 11232.

# Naismith, James

James Naismith, the inventor of basketball, was born on November 6, 1861 in Almonte, Ontario, Canada. While enrolled at the Young Men's Christian Association (YMCA) training school in Springfield Massachusetts, in 1891, he hung up two peach baskets—one at each end of the gymnasium— and made up the rules for "basketball." Since then, the rules have changed very little. When basketball was introduced as an Olympic sport in 1936, Naismith attended the Olympic games in Berlin Germany. He wrote two books—*Basis of Clean Living* (1918), and *Basketball, Its Origin and Development* (1941). He is also given credit for inventing the protective helmet for football players.

He died at the age of 78 in Lawrence, Kansas, on November 28, 1939, of a heart ailment. Cause of death was a cerebral hemorrhage. The funeral service was at the First Presbyterian Church in Lawrence. At the burial Masonic Blue Lodge No. 6 performed the rites. Memorial Park Cemetery, 1517 East 15th Street, Lawrence, Kansas 66044.

# Nash, Ogden

Ogden Nash, the humorous poet, was born August 19, 1902 in Rye, New York. After attending Harvard, he worked during the 1920s at advertising, teaching, and editing. He contributed poems to the *New Yorker* from 1930 on, later joining the editorial staff. He published 20 books of verse, including *Bad Parents' Garden of Verse* (1936), *Musical Zoo* (1947), and *Can't Get There From Here* (1957). One of his poems, entitled "Reflections on ice-breaking," includes the celebrated line: "Candy is dandy but liquor is quicker."

In March 1971 he had abdominal surgery. In April he developed pneumonia, and experienced kidney failure. In early May, while a patient at Johns Hopkins Hospital in Baltimore, he suffered a stroke. He died on May 19. The cause of death was heart failure.

A memorial service was held on May 21 in the Church of the Redeemer in Baltimore. The funeral service was held at 2:00 p.m. on May 23 at St. Andrews Episcopal Church, Rye Beach, New Hampshire, near his summer home in North Hampton. Burial was in Little River Cemetery, North Hampton, New Hampshire 03862.

# Nation, Carry

Carry Amelia Moore Nation, the temperance reformer, whose campaigns were characterized by direct action, was born on November 25, 1846, in Garrard County, Kentucky. After the death of her first husband, Charles Gloyd, an alcoholic, she developed a hatred for liquor and saloons. In the 1890s she began a series of hatchet-swinging trips into bars and saloons—first in Kansas, and then in cities across the country. With hymn-singing supporters she entered saloons and bars, and destroyed the property with hatchets. She was arrested many times for destruction of property and for disturbing the peace. She was able to pay for her fines by selling miniature souvenir hatchets. In the early 1900s she was in great demand as a temperance lecturer, appearing in the garb of a deaconess, holding a hatchet.

On January 13, 1911, while giving a speech in Eureka Springs, Missouri, she stopped speaking and her face showed confusion. As her speaking required more effort, she brought one hand to her face and paused. After a short while she uttered the slowly spaced out and barely audible words: "I—Have—Done—What—I—Could!"

She was taken to Evergreen Hospital in Leavenworth, Kansas, where she died five months later, on June 2. The cause of death was given as paresis, but was probably a stroke. At the time of her death a doctor and a nurse in her room told her that "her time was near." She made no attempt to speak but smiled instead.

The funeral service was held at her niece's home in Kansas City, Kansas, on June 11, attended by a large number of friends. She was buried in the Cemetery in Belton,

*Carry Nation's grave in Belton, Missouri.*

Photo: *The Belton-Raymore Star Herald)*

Missouri. In 1923 friends and supporters solicited funds for the erection of a granite marker which reads: "Faithful to the Cause of Prohibition, She Hath Done What She Could." Belton Cemetery, Cambridge Road, Belton, Missouri 64012.

# *Neumann, John von*

John von Neumann, the mathematician, famous for his theory of games and economic behavior, was born on December 28, 1903 in Budapest, Hungary. After studying mathematics from the University of Budapest, he lectured at the Universities of Berlin and Hamburg. He came to the U.S. in 1931, and was named professor of mathematics at the Institute for Advanced Study at Princeton, in 1933. The inventor of the theory of Rings of Operators—known as the Von Neumann theory of algebra—he wrote, together with Oskar Morgenstern, "The Theory of Games and Economic Behavior" in 1944. His theory of self-reproducing automata, a pioneering work in the field of cybernetics, was published in 1966.

He became ill in the summer of 1955. He died in Washington, D.C., on February 8, 1957, aged 53. The cause of death was cancer. Members of the Atomic Energy Commission mourned his death and issued a statement in tribute to him.

The funeral service was held at 11:00 a.m. on February 11 in the chapel of the Walter Reed Army Hospital, in Washington, D.C. Burial, which was private, was on February 12, at the Princeton University Cemetery, Princeton, New Jersey 02138.

# *Oakley, Annie*

Annie Oakley, the markswoman, was born Phoebe Ann Oakley Mozee on August 13, 1860, in Darke County, Ohio. When she was about 15 years old she won a shooting match against vaudeville shooting ace Frank E. Butler. Later they married and performed in vaudeville circuses as a team. She later joined Buffalo Bill Cody's (*q.v.*) Wild West Show. Her superb marksmanship was well known and she was nicknamed "Little Sure Shot." She was able to split playing cards held at the edge, and dimes that were tossed into the air. As a result of a train accident in Chicago in 1901, one side of her body was almost completely paralyzed. She returned to the stage, however, and continued to amaze audiences for a while longer.

She died of pernicious anemia on November 3, 1926, in Greenville, Ohio, where she spent her last years. Before dying, she had planned her own funeral in detail, specifying that strict privacy was to be observed. She had always been modest, and had specified that she was to have a woman embalmer. The press was told that the funeral service would be held in Greenville on November 6, but in fact was held secretly, one day earlier, to keep the curious away. It took place at the home of her friends, Mr. and Mrs. Fred Grote of Greenville.

She was cremated at a Cincinnati cemetery, after which her ashes were brought to Greenville. There they were placed in a covered silver cup she had been given, and which was inscribed: "To Annie Oakley from the People of France: Exposition Universal, 1889." The cup and the ashes were placed in an oak box and kept in a safe until November 23, Thanksgiving day. Her husband, Frank Butler, had died soon after her, and they were buried together. There are two grave markers, but it is understood that her ashes were buried with her husband's casket. She is buried, ten miles north of Greenville, in Brock Cemetery, Brock, near Versailles, Ohio 45380.

# *Ochs, Adolph Simon*

Adolph Simon Ochs, publisher of the *New York Times* from 1896-1935 was born on March 12, 1858 in Cincinnati, Ohio. He worked on the *Knoxville Chronicle* and the *Chatanooga Dispatch*, which (later became the *Chatanooga Times).* He introduced the masthead slogan—"All the news that's fit to print"—and in 1898 reduced the cost of the paper to one cent, which at the time was economically competitive with other sensationalist New York newspapers. At the same time he retained high standards of integrity, and within a year circulation of the newspaper tripled. He also published the *Philadelphia Ledger*. From 1900 to the time of his death he was a director of the Associated Press.

On April 8, 1935, at 1:45 p.m., while having lunch with some friends in a Chatanooga, Tennessee, restaurant he suffered a cerebral hemorrhage. He was taken to Newell Sanatorium where he died. He was aged 77. New York's Mayor Fiorello La Guardia proclaimed April 12 a day of mourning, and flags on New York City buildings were flown half-mast.

More than 3,000 persons attended Ochs's funeral service at Temple Emanu-El at Fifth Avenue and 65th Street. Burial was at Temple Israel Cemetery at Mount Hope, Hastings-on-Hudson, New York 10706.

# O'Hara, John Henry

John Henry O'Hara, the author, was born January 31, 1905, in Pottsville, Pennsylvania. In 1934 he published his first novel, *Appointment in Samara*. His next book, *Butterfield 8* (1935), further established his reputation.

He died in his sleep at his secluded French manor-style house in Princeton, New Jersey, of a heart attack, early on the morning of April 11, 1970. Although O'Hara was not affiliated with any church, an Episcopal funeral service was held on April 16 at the Princeton University Chapel. He was buried in Princeton Cemetery, Witherspoon and Wiggins Streets, Princeton, New Jersey 08540.

# Oldfield, Barney

Barney Oldfield, the automobile racing driver, was born Berna Eli Oldfield on January 29, 1878, in Wauseon, Ohio. He drove Henry Ford's racing car—the 999—and on June 15, 1903 at Indianapolis, covered five miles in 5 minutes 28 seconds. He was the first man to travel a mile a minute, or 60 miles per hour. During a period of 15 years he won many races and survived many accidents. In 1910 he set a record of 131.724 miles per hour—a record that endured unbeaten until after World War I. The name Barney Oldfield became synonymous with speed, and fast, daredevil drivers were often called "Barney Oldfields."

*Barney Oldfield's grave.*
(Photo: Mary Ellen Hunt)

On October 4, 1946, his wife, Bessie Gooby Oldfield, found him dead in bed at their Beverly Hills, California, home. He was aged 68. The funeral service was held on October 8 in Beverly Hills. Among the pallbearers were his racing rivals—Earl Cooper, Peter de Paola, and Art Klein. Burial was in Holy Cross Cemetery, 5835 West Slauson Avenue, Los Angeles, California 90056.

# Olds, Ransom Eli

Ransom Eli Olds, the automobile manufacturer, was born on June 3, 1864, in Geneva, Ohio. After buying an interest in his father's machine shop in 1885, he produced a horseless carriage. In 1895 he built his first gasoline-powered car. The Olds Motor Vehicle Company was formed in 1896, and in the first year built six cars. In 1899 the company became the Olds Motor Works, which was eventually bought by General Motors. Olds himself became wealthy, and was a benefactor to many universities, including Michigan State College (now Michigan State University).

On August 20, 1950, the newspapers reported that he was ill and close to death. He died on August 26, aged 86, from what were called "complications of old age." His doctor said he put up "a game fight" until the day before he died, when he sank into a coma.

The funeral service was held on August 29 at the Estes Leadley Funeral Home in Lansing, Michigan, and was conducted by the minister from the First Baptist Church. All production at Oldsmobile plants was halted for two minutes at 2:00 p.m., in tribute of the company's founder. Burial was in Mt. Hope Cemetery, 1709 East Mt. Hope, Lansing, Michigan 48910.

# O'Neill, Eugene

Eugene Gladstone O'Neill, the playwright, was born on October 16, 1888, in New York City. The early years of his life were unstable; his father was an actor and Eugene grew up 'on the road,' receiving his education for the most part at boarding schools. He did, however, attend Princeton University for a year. Later he worked as a seaman and a journalist. Because he made a suicide attempt, and also because of alcoholism and tuberculosis, he spent some time in a sanatorium. Later he began to experiment with writing drama, and in 1916 one of his plays, *Bound East for Cardiff,* was staged in New York City. Other works followed, including *Beyond the Horizon* (1920), the first of four Pulitzer Prize winning plays. The other three were *Anna Christie* (1922), *Strange Interlude* (1928), and *Long Day's Journey Into Night* (1941). In 1946 he became the first U.S. playwright to be awarded the Nobel Prize for literature.

By 1953, illness confined him to bed in the Shelton Hotel, Boston. In late November, an infection weakened him further, and he began to sink rapidly. He was given antibiotics, but, according to his doctor, "no longer had a will to live." Shortly before dying he struggled to attain a sitting position. Looking with wild eyes around the room, he yelled: "I knew it! I knew it! Born in a hotel room and God damn it, dying in a hotel room." On November 26, he lost consciousness and sank into a coma, dying on November 27. The desk clerk at the hotel said: "It hurt me, to see this great man, wrapped in a dark blanket and strapped to the undertaker's stretcher, carried out... like anybody else." His autopsy showed that he suffered from a "familial tremor."

The body was taken to J.S. Waterman's Funeral Home in Kenmore Square. Elaborate precautions were taken to prevent the press from finding out the location of his body, and when and where the funeral service was to take place. His body was taken to Forest Hills Cemetery on December 1, where a six-minute ceremony was held. A *Boston Post* reporter wrote: "There were no formal prayers. Even the sounds coming across the cemetery from distant traffic were muted... a funeral director's assistant stepped forward and placed a single spray of white chrysanthemums on the casket (a plain black one). Then the three mourners turned and walked to the automobile. Not a word was spoken, no hymns were sung." Forest Hills Cemetery, 95 Forest Hills Avenue, Jamaica Plain, Boston, Massachusetts 02130.

# Oppenheimer, J. Robert

J. Robert Oppenheimer, the physicist, was born April 22, 1904, in New York City. He studied at Harvard as well at Cambridge, England, and in 1927 received his doctorate from the University of Gottingen, Sweden. Returning to the United States he was on the faculty of the California Institute of Technology and the University of California at Berkeley. He was appointed to the" Manhattan" Project in 1943, and was later hailed as the "father of the atomic bomb." In 1953 he was accused of disloyalty and possible treason. His security clearance was revoked. An investigation by the AEC (Atomic Energy Commission) cleared him of disloyalty charges, but maintained that he was a security risk. In 1963 he was awarded the AEC's highest honor, the Fermi award, by President Lyndon B. Johnson (*q.v.*).

He died at 8:00 p.m. on February 18, 1967 in Princeton, New Jersey, after having been ill for a year with cancer of the throat. The first Japanese scientist to win the Nobel prize, Hideki Yukawa, said that Oppenheimer was "a symbol of the tragedy of the modern nuclear scientist." In Washington, D.C., Dr. Glenn Seaborg, chairman of the AEC, said: "All people, as well as the whole world of science, have suffered a tremendous loss."

A memorial service was held on February 25 at Princeton, New Jersey, attended by, among others, the poet Stephen Spender, the novelist John O'Hara (*q.v.*), and the daughter of Albert Einstein. After the eulogies, members of the Juilliard String Quartet performed the "Adagio in Allegro" of Beethoven's Quartet 14 in C Sharp Minor. After cremation, his ashes were flown to the Virgin Islands and scattered on the waters he had once sailed.

# Oswald, Lee Harvey

Lee Harvey Oswald, the alleged assassin of President John F. Kennedy (*q.v.*), was born on October 18, 1939, in New Orleans, Louisiana. His career was checkered. He lived in the Soviet Union from 1959-1962, and was said to be a sympathizer with the Cuban regime headed by Fidel Castro.

On November 22, 1963, President Kennedy, while on a visit to Dallas, Texas, was mortally wounded by two rifle bullets which were supposedly fired from the sixth floor of the Texas School Book Depository where Oswald was an employee. Oswald was subsequently arrested but never admitted guilt, and did not live to stand trial.

On November 24, Oswald was being transferred by Dallas police from the city jail to the county jail. As he stepped onto a ramp in the basement of the Dallas Municipal Building at 11:20 a.m. (CST), a Dallas night club operator named Jack Ruby (Rubenstein) stepped from the crowd of newsmen and plunged a 38-caliber revolver into Oswald's left side, firing a single shot. As the shot was fired, a Dallas police detective recognized Ruby and said: "Jack, you son of a bitch." The entire scene was witnessed by millions of Americans on national television.

A few reacted with delight, but the overwhelming majority of Americans were mystified and horrified by the act. One New York lawyer said, "It just doesn't seem like America this weekend." Others feared that the motives behind the Kennedy assassination would never be uncovered as a result of Oswald's murder. Oswald was taken to Parkland Hospital in Dallas where he died shortly after arrival. It was the same hospital where President Kennedy had died two days earlier.

The Secret Service contacted undertaker Paul J. Grody at Miller's Funeral Home in Fort Worth, Texas. Oswald's body was placed in a plain cloth-covered wooden coffin. On November 25, his body was taken out of the back door at the Miller Funeral Home and placed in a heavily guarded hearse. It was then taken to Rose Hill Cemetery on the eastern edge of Fort Worth, where a simple funeral service was held under guard, attended only by Oswald's wife, mother, brother, and children, and by security agents. His wife, Marina Oswald, who was dressed in a simple black dress and a beige coat, kissed her husband's body when the coffin was opened for a moment before the service began. The officiating clergyman said: "We are not here to judge, we are here to lay him away before an understanding God." He closed the service with the reading of Psalm 23. The coffin, adorned by a few red and white chrysanthemums, was then lowered into the ground, after which the family was led away by the Secret Service.

The cemetery manager was not happy about the selection of Rose Hill as the burial site for Oswald. He said that it would hurt his business, but that under Texas law he could not refuse burial. In early December authorities at Rose Hill received threats that the grave would be broken into, and that the body would be mutilated or disturbed. The cemetery manager mentioned to reporters the desirability of cremation. He pointed out that the grave, which was being guarded by two Fort Worth policemen, was vulnerable if left untended. He added: "A 2,700 pound vault doesn't mean a thing. One blast of dynamite and the body is mutilated." Oswald's mother, Mrs. Marguerite Oswald, said that she was not inclined to consider cremation unless it was recommended by the manager of Rose Hill.

In the early 1980s, a British writer, Michael Eddowes, theorized that the body in Rose Hill was not Oswald's, but that of a Soviet agent who had assumed Oswald's identity when he had lived in Russia.

On October 4, 1981, as the public and reporters were kept out of the cemetery, the grave was opened and Oswald's remains exhumed. The coffin was covered with a white sheet, put into a hearse, and driven to Baylor University Medical Center in Dallas. There a team of pathologists examined the body. According to Mr. Eddowes's lawyer, the coffin contained "just skeletal remains," and "could not be removed in one piece." The pathologists compared the teeth with Oswald's Marine Corps dental records. A scar from a childhood mastoid operation was also found on the body. Dr. Linda Norton, who headed the team, said: "We, both individually and as a team, have concluded beyond any doubt, and I mean beyond any doubt, that the individual buried under the name Lee Harvey Oswald in Rose Hill Cemetery is Lee Harvey Oswald." The pathologists also said that the rings which Mrs. Oswald had placed on the body just before burial were still in place.

After the autopsy, Oswald's remains, along with pieces from the former coffin, were re-buried in the same plot in a metal coffin, placed in a steel vault.

The exhumation, which was estimated to cost between ten and fifteen thousand dollars, was reportedly paid for by Eddowes. Rose Hill Cemetery, 7301 E. Lancaster, Fort Worth, Texas 76112.

# *Paine, Thomas*

Thomas Paine, whose pamphlet *Common Sense* (1776) convinced many Americans to opt for independence, was born on January 29, 1737, in Thetford, Suffolk, England. He came to the United States in 1774, and worked as the editor of *Pennsylvania Magazine*. In 1776 he published *Common Sense*, which called for the independence of the American colonies from England. He then wrote a series of 16 pamphlets called *The Crisis*. In 1779 he became clerk of the Pennsylvania Assembly. In 1787 he went to England, where he issued the first part of his *Rights of Man*. He was subsequently indicted for treason, but he escaped to Paris, where he was imprisoned for a year during the Reign of Terror, and narrowly escaped being guillotined. He returned to the United States in 1802, and settled in New York City. By 1807 he was an invalid. His illness was then described as "an outgrowth of paralytic affection." By January 1809 he was confined to bed most of the time. His feet and other parts of his body began to swell.

In March 1809, Paine sent a letter to Willet Hicks, son of the famous Quaker preacher Elias Hicks, requesting to be buried in a Quaker cemetery. He said: "I am now in my seventy-third year and do not expect to live long. I wish to be buried in your burying ground. I could be buried in the Episcopal Church, but they are so arrogant; or in the Presbyterian, but they are so hypocritical."

He died on June 8, 1809 at 8:00 a.m., after what was described as "a peaceful night." His housekeeper, Madame de Bonneville, who had placed a rose on his body when he died, wrote: "Death had not disfigured him. Though very thin, his bones were not protuberant. He was not wrinkled, and had lost very little hair." She further wrote: "On the ninth of June, my son and I, and a few of Thomas Paine's friends, set off with the corpse to New Rochelle, a place 22 miles from New York. It was my intention to have him buried in the orchard of his own farm; but the farmer who lived there at the time said that Thomas Paine, walking with him one day, said, pointing to another part of the land, he was desirous of being buried there. 'Then,' said I, 'That shall be the place of his burial.' And, my instructions were accordingly put in execution. The headstone was put up about a week afterwards, with the following inscription: 'Thomas Paine, Author of 'Common Sense,' Died the eighth of June, 1809, Aged, 72 years." A wall 12 feet square was erected around his tomb.

Four trees have been planted outside the wall, two weeping willows and two cypresses." Thomas Paine's Grave, North Avenue and Paine Avenue, New Rochelle, New York 10801.

# *Patton, George*

George Smith Patton, Jr., a U.S. Army tank general who won fame as a tactician in World War II, was born on November 11, 1885 at San Gabriel, California. After

*The limousine in which General Patton met with a fatal accident.*

(Photo: Patton Museum, Fort Knox, Kentucky)

graduating from West Point in 1909, he participated in the Mexican campaign of General John J. Pershing *(q.v.)*. In 1942 he took part in the North African Campaign and in 1943 commanded the U.S. Seventh Army in Sicily. In 1944 in France he wag-

*General Patton's grave.*

(Photo: American Battle Monuments Commission)

ed a brilliant campaign, and participated in the Battle of the Bulge. In 1945, he campaigned in Germany, capturing 100,000 prisoners. His own troops nicknamed him "Old Blood and Guts."

On December 9, 1945, while being driven in a 1938 Cadillac 75 special limousine, near Mannheim, Germany, an accident occurred at 11:45 a.m. He was admitted to a Heidelberg hospital—conscious, but unable to move his arms or legs. While his wife was reading to him on the afternoon of December 20, he sat up and said: "I feel like I can't breathe." X-rays showed that he had an embolism in the right upper lung. He died on December 21, at 5:55 p.m. Death was attributed to pulmonary edema and congestive heart failure.

His body lay in state on December 22 at the Villa Reiner, a mountain house overlooking Heidelberg. On December 23 his casket was closed, and was taken to the Protestant church in Held. The funeral service was attended by delegations from Britain, France, the Soviet Union, Sweden, Belgium, and Luxembourg. His body was then taken by train to the American Military Cemetery in Luxembourg. His grave marker was a white cross inscribed with his name, rank, and serial number. In 1948 his body was removed to a more central place in the cemetery. The five surrounding graves were left vacant to accomodate the many tourists who visit the site. The American Military Cemetery, Luxembourg, Grand Duchy of Luxembourg.

## *Pearson, Drew*

Drew Pearson, the newspaper columnist, was born on December 13, 1897, in Evanston, Illinois. After World War I he worked with the American Friends Service Committee and for the British Red Cross. He was a foreign correspondent until he joined the *Baltimore Sun* in 1929, when he became the newspaper's Washington bureau head. Together with Robert Allen of the *Christian Science Monitor*, he wrote *The Washington Merry-Go-Round*(1931). In 1932 the two men began to write a daily column. Publication of their research resulted in the retirement and jailing of a number of corrupt political figures. By 1969 his column was carried by more than 650 newspapers. After his death the column was continued by his associate, Jack Anderson.

In early August 1969, he was confined to Georgetown University Hospital for what was thought to be a virus. Later in August he was found to have had a serious heart attack, and he was told to avoid exertion and excitement. He was discharged from the hospital on August 28. While on an inspection tour of one of his farms on September 1, 1969, he became excited when a poacher was spotted running in a field. Pearson slumped forward, fighting for breath, and fell unconscious. He was taken to his house and then to Georgetown Hospital, where he was pronounced dead on arrival.

A memorial service was held in the Washington Cathedral. His remains were cremated, and the ashes placed in a bronze urn, which was then inserted in a rock on his farm, overlooking the Potomac River. There is no inscription. Merry-Go-Round Farm, 13130 River Road, Potomac, Maryland 20854.

# *Peary, Robert Edwin*

Robert Edwin Peary, explorer, generally credited with leading the first expedition to reach the North Pole, was born on May 6, 1856, in Cresson, Pennsylvania. He joined the U.S. Navy in 1881, obtaining leaves of absence for exploration. He explored Greenland's interior in 1886. After later explorations from 1893 to 1897, he published *Northward Over the Great Ice,* which was a record of his explorations. After earlier unsuccessful attempts, he reached the North Pole, on April 6, 1909, accompanied by a personal aide and four Eskimos. On his return to the United States, he learned that Dr. Frederick A. Cook, who had been with him on a Greenland trip in 1891, claimed to have reached the North Pole the previous year. Cook's claim was, however, not generally recognized. Peary was awarded the rank of rear admiral by Congress.

By late 1917 he began to feel tired after exertion, and his condition was diagnosed as pernicious anemia. In September he made the following entry in his diary: "Spells of small coughing apparently from stomach. Perspirations. Sudden brief uneasy feelings. Pain across forehead on rising suddenly. Palpitations. Diaphragm spasms preventing sleep until lie on side [sic]." On February 13, 1920 he was given his 35th and final blood transfusion, and his doctors told him that he had only one week to live. During that week he was alert and responsive, was able to talk, and dictated a number of memoranda from his bedside. Around noon on February 19 he became delirious and comatose. He died at 1:20 a.m. on February 20. As news of his death reached the world, the many tributes which poured in included those from British explorer Ernest Shackleton, President Woodrow Wilson *(q.v.),* inventor Alexander Graham Bell *(q.v.),* as well as kings, geographers, and other explorers.

Burial was on February 23 in Arlington National Cemetery. His casket was covered with the flag he had carried with him on all his Arctic trips. At the end of the ceremony, military aircraft flew over the cemetery as a navy bugler sounded taps. Arlington National Cemetery, Fort Myer, Arlington, Virginia 22211.

# *Perry, Mathew*

Mathew Galbraith Perry, the U.S. Naval officer who forced Japan to end two centuries of isolation and to trade with the West, was born on April 10, 1794, in South Kingstown, Rhode Island. He commanded the first U.S. steam warship the *Fulton* (1837-40), served on the anti-slavery patrol in African waters (1843), and commanded U.S. naval forces during the war with Mexico (1846-48). Sent by President Millard Fillmore *(q.v.),* he arrived in Tokyo Bay, Japan, on July 8, 1853, and threatened force in order to obtain a treaty establishing diplomatic relations. He returned in February, 1856, and the treaty was signed on March 31. It led to the opening of relations with other Western powers, and to the modernization of Japan. Perry returned to the United States in 1855.

On February 1858 he caught a severe cold, and developed "rheumatic gout." He died in the early morning hours of March 4.

The funeral service was held in New York City on March 6. His body was taken from his residence at 38 West 32nd Street to St. Mark's Church, accompanied by the Seventh Regiment, 200 militia officers, a contingent of 50 Bluejackets who had taken part in the Japan expedition, and others. Minute guns were fired at the Brooklyn Naval Yard. His coffin as well as his sword were placed in a vault in St. Mark's Churchyard. After the reading of the burial service, three volleys were fired by the Marines. In 1866, his body was re-buried in the cemetery where he had wished to lie—Island Cemetery, 30 Warner Street, Newport, Rhode Island 02840.

# Pershing, John Joseph

John Joseph Pershing, U.S. Army general who commanded the American Expeditionary Force (AEF) in Europe in World War I, was born September 13, 1860, in Laclede, Missouri. After graduation from West Point in 1886, he served in the Sixth Cavalry in several Indian campaigns. He also served in Cuba during the Spanish American War in 1898, in the Philippines from 1906-13, and in Mexico in 1916. In 1917-19 he organized and commanded the AEF in France and contributed to overcoming German resistance in the final months of the war. From 1921 to 1924 he was the Army's chief of staff. In 1931 he published *My Experiences in the World War*, which won him a Pulitzer Prize. From 1941 on he made his residence in a special wing of the Army's Walter Reed Hospital in Washington, D.C., where he charted the progress of World War II on War Department maps pinned to the wall.

On July 15, 1948 he died in his sleep at 3:30 a.m., aged 88. Plans of the arrangements for his funeral had been kept in a Pentagon "Top Secret" file. In accordance with these, his death was announced to President Harry S. Truman (q.v.), after which, at 0930 (9:30 a.m.) hours, the State Department issued a presidential order for a period of national mourning "upon all public buildings and at all forts and military posts and naval stations, and on all vessels of the United States."

An Episcopal funeral service was held on July 19, 1948, in the Memorial Amphitheater in Washington D.C. Burial was in a plot which he had selected himself at Arlington National Cemetery, Fort Myer, Arlington, Virginia 22211.

# Pierce, Franklin

Franklin Pierce, fourteenth president of the United States (in office 1853-57), was born on November 23, 1804, in Hillsborough, New Hampshire. He served in the U.S. House of Representatives (1833-37) and in the Senate (1837-42). Little known nationally, he was nominated as a compromise candidate to break a deadlock at the 1852 Democratic nominating convention. Unexpectedly, Pierce was elected by a wide margin over his opponent, the Whig candidate General Winfield Scott. As president he encouraged the development of transcontinental railroads. Unable to resolve the conflict in Kansas, which opened the way to the struggle over the issue of slavery that was to divide the States, Pierce was not chosen as a candidate for re-election. He retired to Concord where he spent most of the rest of his life.

After the death of his wife on December 2, 1863, and of his closest friend, Nathaniel Hawthorne *(q.v.)*, on May 19, 1864, Pierce experienced a period of illness. In the summer of 1868 he again fell ill, and in September was confined to his room at his Concord home. Just before dawn on October 18, 1869 he died of what was called stomach inflammation.

His body lay in state at the New Hampshire state capitol on October 9 and 10, and the townspeople came to pay him tribute.

A funeral service was held at noon on October 11 at St. Paul's Episcopal Church in Concord. He was buried at the Old North Cemetery, North State Street, near Bouton Street, Concord, New Hampshire 03301.

# *Poe, Edgar Allan*

Edgar Allan Poe, poet and author, famous for macabre themes and mystery stories, was born on January 19, 1809 in Boston, Massachusetts. He entered West Point in 1830 but was dismissed for neglecting his duties. In 1835 he became editor of the *Southern Literary Messenger*, where he became known for his critical writings. He then married his 13-year-old cousin, Virginia Clemm. In 1839 he published his tale of the supernatural, "The Fall of the House of Usher," and in 1841 wrote the first detective story, "The Murders in the Rue Morgue." In the period between 1844 and 1846 he produced other works that were to win him fame—his poem "The Raven" and stories such as "The Pit and the Pendulum," and "The Premature Burial."

Alcohol was a distinctive force in Poe's life. When on an alcoholic binge, he would wander the streets randomly.

On leaving Richmond for Baltimore in September 1849, he had premonitions of his death. In Baltimore, in October, after toasting a lady at her birthday party, he drank heavily. He was picked up unconscious near a rum shop. His clothes and baggage had been stolen. He was taken to Washington Hospital in Baltimore, where he was admitted unconscious on October 3. The wife of the resident physician, Mrs. Moran, said she read him "The fourteenth chapter of St. John's Gospel, gave him a quieting draught, wiped the beads of perspiration from his face, smoothed his pillow and left him." Her husband wrote that Poe was delirious, constantly talking and having "vacant converse with spectral and imaginary objects on the walls." His replies to questions about his residence, relatives, etc., were incoherent and unsatisfactory. At one point Poe said that "the best thing [my] best friend could do would be to blow out [my] brains with a pistol." On October 7, he fell into a violent delirium, so that it took "the efforts of two nurses to keep him in bed." He then "became quiet and seemed to rest for a short time; then gently moving his head he said: 'Lord help my poor soul,' and expired."

He was placed in a mahogany coffin. Records of the time show that his funeral was attended by only the undertaker and two other unidentified people. He was buried in a graveyard which he frequented for inspiration. His epitaph is "Quoth The Raven, Nevermore." The Westminster Presbyterian Churchyard, Fayette and Green Streets, Baltimore, Maryland 21201.

# *Polk, James*

James Knox Polk, eleventh president of the United States (term of office 1845-49), was born on November 2, 1795, in Mecklenburg County, North Carolina. He was elected to the U.S. House of Representatives in 1825, remaining there until 1839. He was then elected as a compromise Democratic candidate, and was elected president in 1844 on the slogan "Fifty-four Forty or Fight"—which referred to the boundary line in dispute with Britain in the Pacific Northwest. During his administration the war with Mexico occurred, as well as the acquisition by the U.S. of territories that were to become the states of California, New Mexico, Oregon, and Texas. Confidence in his administration was, however, eroded by his inability to resolve the slavery issue. After serving his term he retired to Nashville, Tennessee.

Shortly after arriving in Nashville he was plagued by what was then called an intestinal disorder. A cholera epidemic was raging in Nashville, and he may have been a victim of it. He died on June 15, 1849. The funeral service was held in Nashville's Methodist Church. He was buried on the grounds of his home, the Polk House. On the death of his wife in 1891, both their bodies were buried together on the grounds of the State Capitol, Sixth at Charlotte, Nashville, Tennessee 37219.

# *Pontiac*

Pontiac, the Ottawa Indian chief who was the moving spirit of the Ute intertribal uprising of 1763-64 known as Pontiac's War, was born around 1720, near the Maumee River in northern Ohio. By 1755 he had become a chief. He and others were mistrustful of the British because they were often cheated in trading. By 1762 he persuaded many of the tribes of the Midwest region to commit themselves to what was to be known as "Pontiac's Rebellion." Many British forts were overrun, and he himself led an unsuccessful attack upon, and laid siege to Detroit, in May 1763. A peace treaty was later signed in 1766, but Pontiac himself, counting on French support, remained a symbol of Indian resistance.

During the spring of 1769, Pontiac traveled to what is now St. Louis to visit his old French friend, St. Ange. For the trip he dressed in the white and gold uniform of a French officer presented to him earlier by the French general, Montcalm. A few days later, Pontiac attended a meeting of Kaskaskian, Cahokias, and Peorias, in a village across the Mississippi from St. Louis. He found them drinking white man's alcohol, and living in the dilapidated houses of a ruined fort. He spoke to them saying that they could meet all their needs by taking advantage of the forests and rivers, and that they should return to the Indian way of life. He then left the campfire and walked into the woods, but was followed by one of the Peoria, who stabbed him to death. His motives were unclear, but he was possibly sent by an English trader. Pontiac's death led to warfare among the tribes, in which his death was fully avenged. Meanwhile his friend St. Ange sent men to the camp to retrieve his body. It was buried in his white and gold French officer's uniform, near the fort, somewhere on the site of present day St. Louis, Missouri.

# Porter, Cole

Cole Porter, the lyricist and composer, was born on June 9, 1893, in Peru, Indiana. He published his first song at the age of 10. He entered Harvard's Law School, but at the suggestion of the dean transferred to the school of music. By the late 1920s many of his songs were appearing in Broadway plays. He wrote a number of Broadway musicals including *Fifty Million Frenchmen* (1929), *The Gay Divorcee* (1932), and *Anything Goes* (1934). He is known for such songs as "Night and Day," "Begin the Beguine," and "I've Got You Under My Skin."

In early September, 1964, Porter was admitted to St. John's Hospital in Santa Monica, California, for a bowel obstruction. Although this in itself was not serious, his general condition began to deteriorate and he developed pneumonia. X-rays showed that a kidney stone had wedged in the tube that connects the kidney to the bladder, causing a toxic condition to develop. Surgery was performed on October 13, and was considered a success. He died, however, at 11:05 p.m. on October 15.

Two years earlier he had left specific funeral instructions in his will. They were: "I direct my executors to arrange for my burial in Peru, Indiana. I further direct my executors to arrange for no funeral or memorial service, but only for a private burial service to be conducted by the pastor of the First Baptist Church of Peru in the presence of my relatives and dear friends. At such service I request the following quotation from the Bible: 'I am the resurrection and the life; he that believeth in Me, though he were dead, yet shall he live; whosoever liveth and believeth in Me shall never die'—and to follow such quotation with the Lord's Prayer. I request... that neither said pastor nor anyone else deliver any memorial address whatsoever. I particularly direct that there be no service for me of any kind in New York City."

These instructions were followed to the letter, and burial took place on October 18, in Mount Hope Cemetery, West 12th Street, Peru, Indiana 46970.

# Presley, Elvis

Elvis Aron Presley, the rock and roll singer who became a cult figure in the 1950s, was born on January 8, 1935, in Tupelo, Mississippi. He made his first record in 1954 and in that same year he toured the South as "The Hillbilly Cat." After appearing on television, he became a national entertainment phenomenon. He signed a major recording contract in 1955, and a movie contract in 1956. His recordings include: "Hound Dog," "All Shook Up," and "Love Me Tender."

At 2:30 p.m. on August 16, 1977 he was found unconscious in the bedroom of Graceland, his Memphis, Tennessee, mansion. He was taken to Baptist Memorial hospital where doctors worked for an hour trying to revive him. He was then pronounced dead. The cause of death was listed as "cardiac arrhythmia," meaning an irregular and ineffective heartbeat.

His body lay in state on August 17 at his mansion. He was laid out in a cream-colored suit, a light blue shirt, silver tie, diamond cufflinks, and stick pin. He also wore a ring with the initials "TCB," which stood for "Taking Care of Business." The

900-pound seamless copper casket in which he lay had been flown in from Oklahoma City.

A private funeral service was held on August 18 at Graceland, attended by such notables as actress Ann Margret, country guitarist Chet Atkins, Tennessee's Governor Ray Blanton, actor George Hamilton, and singer James Brown. Following the service the body was taken to Forest Hill Memorial Cemetery along with floral arrangements from singer Frank Sinatra, Alabama Governor George C. Wallace, and the Presley fan club of Africa. The funeral cortege consisted of a white Cadillac hearse preceded by 17 Cadillac limousines.

On August 29, four men were arrested outside the cemetery. Police said that they had been plotting to break into the mausoleum, steal his body, and hold it for ran-

*A view of Elvis Presley's grave at Graceland, Memphis, Tennessee.*
(Photo: Edward George Baker)

som. After this, the bodies of Presley and his mother were moved to the grounds of his mansion, and it was announced that visitors would be allowed from 9:00 a.m. to 4:00 p.m. daily in groups of 25. He is buried beneath a bronze tablet with the epitaph "Legend in His Own Time." On the bottom of the tablet is a lightning bolt and the initials" TCB," which formed his insignia. Graceland, 375 Elvis Presley Road, Memphis, Tennessee 38116.

# *Pullman, George M.*

George Mortimer Pullman, industrialist and inventor of the Pullman railroad sleeping car, was born on March 3, 1831, in Brocton, New York. He moved to Chicago in 1855, and it was there that he had the idea of building sleeping cars. Throughout 1858 and 1859 he tested the idea, yet railroads were reluctant to adopt it. In 1865, together with a friend, he was granted a patent for the sleeping car with an upper berth. In 1867 he organized the Pullman Palace Car Company, of which he was president, to build sleeping cars. Plants were located throughout the country. He built the town of Pullman, now incorporated in Chicago, to house his employees. He also owned the Eagle Wireworks in New York, and became president of the Metropolitan Elevated Railroad in New York City.

In mid-October, 1897, Pullman, living in his Chicago home, complained of heat during a hot spell. On October 19, at 4:30 a.m., he called a servant to his bedroom, and asked for a doctor. Before the doctor could come, however, he had died of a heart attack.

The funeral service was held on October 23 at the family home on Prairie Avenue, in Chicago. Several clergymen spoke and musical selections were sung by a quartet. Before being placed in his mausoleum, his steel casket was put in a lead-lined box which was then wrapped in tar paper, covered with an inch of asphalt, and laid on a concrete base. Graceland Cemetery, 4001 North Clark Street, Chicago, Illinois 60613.

# *Rachmaninoff, Sergei*

Sergei Vassilievitch Rachmaninoff, the composer and piano virtuoso, was born on April 1, 1873, in Oneg, Russia, (now in the Russian Soviet Federated Socialist Republic). After studying at the St. Petersburg and Moscow conservatories, he was a conductor at the Bolshoi theater. In 1906 he left Russia with his family, and moved to Dresden, Germany. He later returned but then left Russia permanently in 1917, to settle in the United States. His works include Symphony No. 2 in E Minor, his piano concertos, and his *Rhapsody on a Theme by Paganini*. He played with the Philadelphia Orchestra, the London Philharmonic, the Moscow Philharmonic, and the Boston Symphony Orchestra.

While on a concert tour in 1943, after a presentation in Chicago, he complained of a pain in his side. A Russian doctor was called and the diagnosis was pleurisy and neuralgia. By late February he had become worse, and had to cancel several concerts. On March 2 he arrived at his Los Angeles home but by mid-March it was determined that he was suffering from a rare form of cancer, which was spreading throughout his vital organs. His doctor wrote: "Soon his illness was progressing, not by days, but by hours. An arrested pneumonia developed, the pulse weakened, and three days before death came, Rachmaninoff began to lose consciousness for long periods." In his delirium he often moved his hands as if he were conducting an orchestra, or playing piano. On March 27 a priest was called who administered last rites. He died at 1:30 a.m. on March 28.

The funeral service was held on March 30, at the Russian Orthodox Church in Los Angeles. As the "Requiem of the Ageless Chants" was given, the mourners stood, as according to custom the church had neither pews nor chairs. The women in attendance carried lighted prayer candles. It had been his wish that his remains be buried in Russia at the cemetery of the Novo-Divichy Monastery, built by Duke Vassily III in 1524. His family, however, had his remains buried at Kensico Cemetery, Valhalla, New York 10595.

# *Rathbone, Basil*

Basil Rathbone, the actor, was born Philip St. John Basil Rathbone on June 13, 1892, in Johannesburg, South Africa. He was the star of the Sherlock Holmes film series. He played notable roles in such movies as *Hound of the Baskervilles*, and *The Mark of Zorro*, (both released in 1940), and others.

On July 21, 1967 he was found dead of a heart attack on the floor of his study in his New York City apartment.

The funeral service was held on July 25, at 11:00 a.m., at St. James Episcopal Church, Madison Avenue at 71st Street, New York City, and was attended by 350 people. A friend of the family, the actress and author Cornelia Otis Skinner, read one of Rathbone's favorite poems: "How Do I Love Thee?" by Elizabeth Barrett Browning. Following the service, burial was in Ferncliff Cemetery, Hartsdale, New York 10530.

# *Rayburn, Sam*

Samuel Taliaferro Rayburn, Democratic Party leader in the U.S. House of Representatives, was born January 6, 1882, in Roanne County, Tennessee. After serving in the Texas legislature, he was elected to the U.S. House of Representatives in 1912, and was then re-elected 24 times, serving for the record time of 48 years, 8 months. He was elected Democratic leader in 1937 and Speaker of the House in 1940—holding the latter post until the time of his death, except for two two-year intervals. Through personal influence, he was able to convince many in both parties to support his policies. A powerful speaker, he was known for his honesty, and was a confidant and advisor to presidents from Franklin D. Roosevelt to John F. Kennedy (*q.q.v.*).

*Sam Rayburn's grave,*
*Willow Wild Cemetery,*
*Bonham, Texas.*
(Photo: David A. Ross)

In early 1961 his health began to fail. During the summer he once lost consciousness while in the Speaker's chair, but continued to work. In September he was told that he had cancer. The disease spread through his body and into his brain, causing his respiratory system to fail. Death came painlessly at 7:20 a.m. on November 16, while he was sleeping.

On November 17 his body lay in state 24 hours at the Sam Rayburn Library in Bonham, Texas. A funeral service was held on November 18 at the First Baptist Church in Bonham, attended by former Presidents Harry Truman and Dwight D. Eisenhower *(q.q.v.)* and President John F. Kennedy. Red carnations and an American flag draped the coffin. At the close, the organist played "America The Beautiful." A memorial service was also held the same day at the Washington Cathedral, attended by 300 diplomats and government officials. The body was buried at Willow Wild Cemetery, Bonham, Texas 75418.

# Reed, Walter

Walter Reed, the pathologist and bacteriologist who proved that yellow fever is transmitted by mosquito bite, was born on September 13, 1851, in Gloucester County, Virginia. After receiving an M.D. degree from the University of Virginia and a second one from Bellevue Hospital Medical College in New York, he worked for the New York City and Brooklyn boards of health. In 1875 he joined the U.S. Army Medical Corps and served as a surgeon in New York, Arizona, and Baltimore, and, later, as the curator of the Army Medical Museum in Washington, D.C. In 1898-99 he investigated the spread of typhoid fever, and uncovered new facts. When there was a yellow fever epidemic among U.S. troops in Cuba in 1900, he was sent there to investigate. While there, he demonstrated that yellow fever is spread only by a particular type of mosquito, and instituted a program which wiped out the disease in Havana, Cuba.

He returned to Washington D.C. in 1901. On November 17, 1902 his ruptured appendix was removed. Toxins had already entered his system, however, and he died early on the morning of November 23.

The funeral service was held on November 25 at St. Thomas's Episcopal Church in Washington, D.C. He is buried on top of a grassy knoll at Arlington National Cemetery and his tombstone says: "He gave to man control over that dreadful scourge, yellow fever." Arlington National Cemetery, Fort Myer, Arlington, Virginia 22211.

# Reuther, Walter

Walter Philip Reuther, the labor leader, was born on September 1, 1907, in Wheeling, West Virginia. In the late 1920s and early 1930s he worked in the automobile industry in Detroit while taking night classes at Wayne State University. From 1932-1935 he toured Europe, the Soviet Union, and the Far East by bicycle. In 1935 he formed local 174 of the United Automobile Workers (UAW). From 1939-1946 he was director of the UAW's General Motors department, and after 1946 was president of the international union. Upon the death of Philip Murray *(q.v.),* Reuther became president of the Congress of Industrial Organizations (CIO). He was active in many social, political, and human rights causes.

On May 9, 1970, Reuther was a passenger in a private Lear jet. While making an approach to Pellston airport in Michigan, the plane sheared off the top of a 50-foot elm tree and crashed through a small pine grove. The bodies of Reuther, of his wife, and of the pilots were charred beyond recognition. Positive identification could be made only through dental records. The National Transportation Safety Board (NTSB) later determined that the cause of the crash was a faulty altimeter, part of which had been installed upside down.

The bodies of Reuther and his wife lay in state in oak caskets at the Veteran's Memorial Building in Detroit, Michigan, on May 13 and 14. The funeral service took place on the stage of Ford Auditorium in downtown Detroit.

At the hour that the funeral service began, assembly lines in auto plants around the country stopped for a three-minute tribute. Thousands of truck drivers who belonged to the Teamster's Union also paid a three-minute tribute by pulling over to the side of the road. At the simple service, a recording of "He's Got The Whole World in His Hands" by Marion Anderson was played, and Reuther was eulogized. One of Reuther's favorite ballads, "I Dreamed I Saw Joe Hill Last Night," was also played. Thirteen months after the accident, on June 9, 1971, Walter and May Reuther's ashes were interred on a hillside at the UAW camp in Black Lake, Michigan. An oriental lamp donated by the Trade Unionists of Japan marks the grave. UAW Camp, Black Lake, Onaway, Presque Isle, Michigan 49765.

# *Revere, Paul*

Paul Revere, the revolutionary patriot, famed for his midnight horseback ride to warn Bostonians that the British were coming, was born on January 1, 1735, in Boston, Massachusetts. Revere was active in local patriotic activities and in 1773 himself participated, dressed as an Indian, in the Boston Tea Party protest against British taxes. He also carried the news of the Boston Tea Party to New York City. On April 18, 1775 he made his famous ride to warn John Hancock and John Adams (q.q.v.) that British troops were coming. His ride was celebrated in Longfellow's (q.v.) poem, "Paul Revere's Ride." He was also a well-known silversmith, whose work is highly prized today, and was the engraver of the official seal of the colonies.

Revere died on May 10, 1818. The *Boston Intelligencer*, commenting on his death, said: "A long life, free from the frequent afflictions of diseases, was the consequence of constant bodily exercise and regular habits." The funeral service was held in the New Brick Church on Hanover Street, where he had been christened, and to which he belonged. Burial was in Old Granary Burying Ground, Tremont Street, Boston, Massachusetts 02108.

# *Rickenbacker, Eddie*

Edward Vernon Rickenbacker, nicknamed "Eddie," the World War I U.S. air ace and industrialist, was born on October 8, 1890, in Columbus, Ohio. By the time the U.S. entered World War I he was internationally famous as a speed driver and held a world speed record of 134 miles per hour. After pilot's training he was assigned to the 94th Air Pursuit Squadron where he won 26 victories in aerial combat. He was given many decorations, including the Congressional Medal of Honor. He returned to the United States as a hero. After the war he entered the auto industry, and in 1927 bought a controlling interest in the Indianapolis Speedway. In 1932 he joined American Airways and later worked with North American Aviation (1933), and Eastern Airlines (1935). Flying on a mission in the Pacific in 1942, his plane was forced down, and he and others were adrift for 23 days on rafts before being rescued. After the war he returned to Eastern Airlines until retiring in 1963.

On July 12, 1973, while on a trip to Switzerland, he had a spell of irregular breathing, and was admitted to a Zurich hospital. He was found to be suffering from pneumonia. By July 21 he was unconscious most of the time. He died at 4:15 a.m. on the morning of July 23. The cause of death was heart failure.

Three memorial services were held—one on July 27, at the Presbyterian Church of Key Biscayne, Florida; the second at Marble Collegiate Church, on Fifth Avenue in New York City, on August 7; and the third on August 10 in Columbus, Ohio, where his ashes were interred at Green Lawn Cemetery. At the time of the committal, four Air Force jets passed overhead. When they were directly overhead, the first plane shot straight up while the other three continued on. This maneuver is known as the missing leader formation and is the Air Force equivalent of the riderless horse. Green Lawn Cemetery, 1000 Green Lawn Avenue, Columbus, Ohio 43223.

# Ringling, Charles

Charles Ringling, who headed the Ringling Brothers Circus organization in the early 20th century, was born Charles Rungeling on December 2, 1863, in McGregor, Iowa. His older brothers formed the first Ringling circus in 1884. By 1888 the road show began to expand, and by the 1890s had become famous. After Bailey's death in 1907, they purchased the Barnum and Bailey Circus—the "Greatest Show on Earth." After the death of his brothers, Ringling—known as "Mr. John"—ran the Ringling organization alone for ten years, bringing 11 major circuses under his control.

He died on December 3, 1926 in Sarasota, Florida, of a cerebral hemorrhage. The funeral service was held on December 6 at Sarasota. Burial was at Manasota Memorial Park, Sarasota, Florida 33578.

# Ripley, Robert

Robert Leroy Ripley, cartoonist, and author of the popular newspaper column, "Believe It Or Not," was born on December 25, 1893 in Santa Rosa, California. In 1910 he was hired as a sports cartoonist for the *San Francisco Bulletin,* and later worked for the *San Francisco Chronicle.* In 1913 he went to New York City and joined the staff of the *New York Globe.* In 1918 he started his weekly column, "Believe It Or Not." In 1923 he moved to the *New York Evening Post,* and his column was soon syndicated. He published an illustrated collection of his columns that was so successful that it brought contracts from Warner Brothers and King Features Syndicates. Eventually the column was carried in 326 newspapers in 38 countries. After his death, in 1949, his staff continued the column.

By 1949 he was suffering from hypertension, and having frequent blackouts. On May 24 he entered the Harkness Pavilion at the Columbia Presbyterian Medical Center in New York City. On May 27 he called a friend Buggs Baer, and said: "I'm just in for a check-up, and I'll be out to the farm to see you tomorrow." After hanging up the phone, he fell back on his pillow and died of a heart-attack.

The funeral service was held on May 31 at St. James Protestant Episcopal Church in New York City, and was attended by many notables, including aviator Eddie Rickenbacker *(q.v.)* and boxer Jack Dempsey. He was buried in the Rural Cemetery, Franklin Avenue, Santa Rosa, California 95404.

# *Robeson, Paul*

Paul Bustill Robeson, the internationally famed black American singer who espoused Communism, was born on April 9, 1898, in Princeton, New Jersey. The son of a former slave who became a preacher, he attended Rutgers University before graduating from Columbia Law School in 1923. He began a singing and acting career, in which his characteristic deep bass voice was to make him celebrated. He first became a star with his stage performance in the title role of Eugene O'Neill's *The Emperor Jones,* which he played in New York in 1924 and London in 1925. Movies in which he appeared included *Sanders of the River* (1935), and *Showboat* (1936). His rendition of the song "Old Man River," in *Showboat*, became a best-selling record.

After visiting the Soviet Union in 1934, he became increasingly identified with

*Paul Robeson's grave.*

(Photo: Eric Mautner)

Communism and Communist causes, although he refused to state whether or not he was a member of the Communist Party, and in consequence had his passport withdrawn by the U.S. State Department in 1950. After the U.S. Supreme Court ruled in 1958 that his passport should be restored, he traveled to Europe, where he lived until 1963, when, suffering from ill health, he returned to the United States.

A politically controversial figure, he went into self-imposed privacy on his return, and friends and newsmen found the blinds of his house drawn even in the middle of the day. On December 28, 1975, he was admitted to Presbyterian University Hospital in Philadelphia for treatment of a mild stroke. He was found to be suffering from a cerebral vascular disorder. He died on January 23, 1976.

The funeral service was held on January 29 at the African Methodist Episcopal (AME) Church in Harlem, New York. The eulogy was spoken by his son, Paul Robeson, Jr. Reciting a poem which a friend of his had written the day before, he said: "I may keep memories of him, but not his essence, for that will pour forth tomorrow."

Burial was in Hartsdale, New York. The inscription on his plaque reads: "The artist must elect to fight for freedom or for slavery. I have made my choice. I had no alternative." These were the words that he had spoken in June 1937, when supporting the Loyalist cause at the time of the Spanish Civil War (1936-39). Ferncliff Cemetery, Hartsdale, New York 10530.

# Rockefeller, John D.

John Davison Rockefeller, the millionaire industrialist and philanthropist, was born on July 8, 1839, in Richford, Tioga County, New York. In the 1860s, realizing the potential of oil wells, he and his associates built several oil refineries in Cleveland, Ohio, which after reorganization in 1870 became the Standard Oil Company of Ohio, of which he was president. Standard Oil bought other oil companies and by 1877 was pre-eminent in the oil industry. In 1890 the company controlled about 95 percent of the petroleum industry in the United States—a factor in the passage of the Sherman Anti-Trust Act of that year, aimed at discouraging industrial monopolies. After the company was dissolved, by court order in 1892, the intent of the act was evaded by the formation of a holding company— the Standard Oil Company of New Jersey. From the 1890s onwards, Rockefeller began donating millions to philanthropy. A grant made possible the founding of the University of Chicago in 1891. From 1897 on, Rockefeller devoted all his time to philanthropy. Together with his son, John D. Rockefeller, Jr., he founded the Rockefeller Institute for Medical Research (1901), and the Rockefeller Foundation (1913). In his lifetime he donated more than $500 million dollars to philanthropy.

He died on May 23, 1937 at his Ormond Beach, Florida, winter home, aged 97. His death was so sudden that none of his immediate family was with him at the time. The cause of death was listed as sclerotic myocarditis. His body was shipped by train to his Pocantico Hills, New York home, where it lay in state in a mahogany coffin in the central hall.

A half-hour non-denominational funeral service which consisted of prayer, Bible readings and organ music was held on May 26 at his home. The music included Handel's "Largo." The body was then taken by a special train to Cleveland, Ohio for burial which took place at 10:00 a.m. on May 27. Lake View Cemetery, 12316 Euclid Avenue, Cleveland, Ohio 44106.

# Rockefeller, John D., Jr.

John Davison Rockefeller, Jr., the millionaire businessman and philanthropist, was born January 29, 1874, in Cleveland, Ohio. After graduation from Brown

University in 1897, he followed in the footsteps of his father, John D. Rockefeller *(q.v.)*, in business and philanthropy. Among his achievements were the restoration of colonial Williamsburg, Virginia; the establishment of the United Services Organization (USO) during World War II; and the donation of the site for the United Nations headquarters in New York City.

In December 1959, Rockefeller was admitted to the Tucson Medical Center in Tucson, Arizona. He stayed there until late April, 1960 then he was discharged. His condition took a turn for the worse on May 9, however, when he was readmitted to the hospital, and family members were notified. He died on May 11 from pneumonia and heart strain.

His body was immediately cremated, and was then flown to Westchester County Airport, near White Plains, New York, where it arrived on May 12, accompanied by two of his sons, Governor Nelson A. Rockefeller *(q.v.)* of New York, and Laurance S. Rockefeller.

A private funeral service was held on May 15 at Sleepy Hollow Cemetery in Tarrytown, New York. On the same day a public memorial service was held at the Union Church in Pocantico Hills, New York. Another memorial service, attended by 1,500 people, was held on June 8, 1960 at the Riverside Church, Riverside Drive at 122nd Street, in New York City. He was buried on May 15, at the Rockefeller estate, Pocantico Hills, Tarrytown, New York 10591.

# *Rockefeller, Nelson Aldrich*

Nelson Aldrich Rockefeller, millionaire and governor of New York State from 1958-79, was born on July 8, 1908 in Bar Harbor, Maine. He was the grandson of John D. Rockefeller *(q.v.)*. After graduation from Dartmouth College in 1930 he worked in his family business. Under President Dwight D. Eisenhower, he was appointed chairman of the President's Advisory Committee on Government Organization (1952), and undersecretary of Health Education and Welfare (1953). Elected governor of New York in 1958, he was re-elected three times. He served as appointed vice-president under President Gerald Ford from 1974-76, and thereafter gave up politics and devoted considerable time to collecting art.

On January 26, 1979, while in a town house at 13 West 54th Street in New York City, he was stricken by a heart attack and died instantly. A staff assistant called the police, paramedics were called, and he was taken to Lenox Hill Hospital on East 77th Street, where he was pronounced dead. He was cremated on January 28.

A private funeral service was held on the grounds of his Pocantico Hills, New York, home on January 29. During the rites, his son Nelson Jr., said: "Dad, we knew how much you loved us, and we want you to know how much we love you and how much we are going to miss you." The late governor's 68-year-old brother, Laurance Rockefeller, then said to his nephew: "Nelson, you've spoken for all of us." At the conclusion of the ceremony, the 60 family members present stood next to the burial plot and together recited the 23rd Psalm. The small bronze urn containing the ashes was then lowered into the grave, and each family member threw some dirt on top of it. A memorial service was held on February 2 at Riverside Church in New York City attended by President Jimmy Carter, the Rev. Martin Luther King, Sr., and former Secretary of State Henry A. Kissinger. Pocantico Hills, Tarrytown, New York 10591.

# Rockne, Knute

Knute Kenneth Rockne, the football coach who made the team of the University of Notre Dame in Indiana a major force in U.S. college football, was born on March 4, 1888, in Voss, Norway. After emigrating to the United States when he was five, he grew up in Chicago. He entered the University of Notre Dame in Indiana, where he starred on the football team. In 1913 he, together with "Gus" Dorais, popularized the forward pass and brought their team victory. In 1918 he became Notre Dame's head coach. In the 13 years that followed, the team had an overall record of 105 wins, 12 losses and 5 ties. He was well known for emphasizing offensive play and for pep talks. His team's success as well as his own charismatic personality gained him a national following. He published a number of books, including *Coaching, The Way of the Winner* (1925).

On March 31, 1931, Rockne was on Transcontinental Western Flight No. 599 which left Kansas City, Missouri en route to Los Angeles. The plane, with tail numbers "NC-999," crashed near Cottonwood Falls, Kansas, and Rockne was killed. An inquest into the accident surmised that the cause of the crash was ice formation on the wings. On April 2, at 7:45 a.m., his body arrived at Dearborn Station, Chicago, in a gray coffin.

A committee of prominent Notre Dame alumni accompanied the body from Chicago to South Bend, Indiana. Messages of sympathy poured in from the nation's famous as well as from his fans. Every legislature in the country passed resolutions of condolence. President Herbert Hoover *(q.v.)* sent a telegram to Rockne's wife, Bonnie, which read: "I know that every American grieves with you. Mr. Rockne so contributed to a cleanliness and a high purpose in sportsmanship and athletics that his passing is a national loss." Condolence messages also came from General Douglas MacArthur, aviator Charles Lindbergh, comedian Will Rogers *(q.q.v.)*, and King Haakon of Norway; as well as from every governor, senator, and congressman, and every famous football coach in the country. Sermons regretting his passing were prepared and delivered not only in Catholic churches but in hundreds of Protestant churches as well as Jewish synagogues and temples.

His body lay in state in a bronze casket at the Rockne home at 1417 East Wayne Street, in the Sunnymede section of South Bend, Indiana on April 2. The funeral service was held on April 4 at Sacred Heart Church—a replica of a 13th-century Gothic cathedral—on Notre Dame's campus. More than 100,000 people lined the route to the church. The choir opened the services with the chant of "Miserere." Burial followed the services at Highland Cemetery, 2257 Portage Avenue, South Bend, Indiana 46616.

# Rogers, Will

William Penn Adair Rogers—famous and widely loved as the movie actor and folksy humorist, Will Rogers— was born on November 4, 1879 near Oologah, Indian Territory (now Oklahoma). His witty and incisive sayings were still being quoted with relish half a century after his death. After working as a rope artist in wild West and vaudeville shows, he appeared on Broadway in some musical reviews including the Ziegfeld Follies. His humor, combined with "down home" honesty and a satirical viewpoint, made him a national figure. He wrote a national syndicated column for the *New York Times*, as well as a number of books including: *Rogerisms—the Cowboy Philosopher On Probation* (1919), and *There's Not a Bathing Suit in Russia* (1927). He appeared in several films, including *Connecticut Yankee* (1931), and *State Fair* (1933).

In 1935 Rogers went on a trip to northern Canada and Alaska with the famous aviator Wiley Post. They were traveling in a plane that was dangerous because of alterations made by Post who had incorporated parts from two previously damaged planes. The craft was a Lockheed Orion with a Pratt and Whitney Wasp engine, to which had been added wings from a Lockheed Explorer. Post had also added pontoons, which made the plane heavy. On August 15, while flying blindly after losing his way in a storm in Alaska, Post spotted a break in the clouds and landed on Walakpa Lagoon. There he talked to some Eskimos and inquired how far it was to Barrow. When told that it was about 10 minutes away, he taxied to the other end of the lagoon for take-off. Watching from the shoreline the Eskimos saw the plane lift off, start to climb, bank to the right, and turn towards Barrow. Then the engine misfired, sputtered and stopped. The plane became noseheavy and crashed into the lagoon, spewing up a geyser of gravel and water. There was then an explosion and a fire. Both Rogers and Post were killed. The official conclusion was that "the probable cause of the accident was loss of control of the aircraft at a low altitude, after sudden engine failure, due to the extreme noseheaviness of the aircraft." In a 1963 book Charles Browner, who had been in Alaska at the time, said that his son Dave had found, after the bodies had been removed from the plane, "that none of the tanks contained a drop of gas." From this and other evidence, including the sudden sputtering and dying of the motor, he concluded that the plane had probably run out of gas when it landed on the lagoon the first time.

After the accident, aviator Charles Lindbergh *(q.v.)* called the family and said that he would take charge of bringing the bodies home, using the facilities of Pan American airways for which he worked. The linen-wrapped bodies were picked up on August 15, and on August 19 arrived in Burbank, California.

Last rites were held on August 22 at Wee Kirk O' The Heather in Los Angeles. Roger's casket lay in state at Forest Lawn Memorial Park, where 50,000 people had passed the coffin. Burial was in Forest Lawn Memorial Park, Los Angeles.

In 1938 Will's wife, Betty Rogers, donated 20 acres of land to Claremore, Oklahoma, for a memorial to her late husband. In 1944 his remains were transferred there from California. The memorial consists of a simple marble tomb, and a bronze statue which bears the epitaph that he wrote for himself: "I never met a man I didn't like." Will Rogers Memorial, Claremore, Oklahoma 74017.

# *Roosevelt, Eleanor*

Anna Eleanor Roosevelt, wife of President Franklin D. Roosevelt *(q.v.)*, diplomat and humanitarian, was born on October 11, 1884, in New York City. After atten-

# ROOSEVELT

ding school in England, she married her cousin, Franklin Delano Roosevelt, in 1905. When Roosevelt became president in 1933, she made the position of first lady one of influence as she advocated liberal causes and participated in public affairs. She wrote a syndicated newspaper column, and during World War II visited troops on almost every war front. After her husband's death in 1945, President Harry S. Truman *(q.v.)* named her as delegate to the United Nations, where she was influential in the drafting and signing of the Universal Declaration of Human Rights in 1948. After leaving that post in 1953, she traveled widely, promoting the work of the UN. She also wrote a series of books, including *"The Autobiography of Eleanor Roosevelt* (1961). President John F. Kennedy *(q.v.)* re-appointed her to the U.S. delegation to the UN in 1961.

She became feverish in the summer of 1962, and was then in the hospital twice. She returned home on October 18. On October 25, her illness was diagnosed as a rare form of bone marrow tuberculosis. By late November she was determined to die on her own, and rejected pills, clenching her teeth together to keep the hospital staff from administering them.

She died on November 7, 1962. Her remains were placed in an unmarked hearse and taken to Columbia Presbyterian Medical Center for an autopsy. The results showed that she had suffered from sub-acute hemic (blood borne) tuberculosis.

A private funeral service was held on November 10 at St. James Protestant Episcopal Church in New York City, attended by former presidents Harry S. Truman, Dwight D. Eisenhower and John F. Kennedy *(q.q.v.)* as well as then Vice-President Lyndon B. Johnson *(q.v.)*. The hymns "Abide With Me," "Rock of Ages" and "Now the Day is Over" were sung. The rector of the church in his eulogy, said: "The entire world becomes one family orphaned by her passing." Burial was next to her husband at the Roosevelt Home, 259 Albany Post Road, Hyde Park, New York 12538.

# *Roosevelt, Franklin Delano*

Franklin Delano Roosevelt, 32nd president of the United States, (in office 1933-44), was born on January 30, 1882, in Hyde Park, New York. He studied at Groton, Harvard, and Columbia University School of Law. He was elected to the New York State Senate in 1910. President Woodrow Wilson *(q.v.)* appointed him assistant secretary of the Navy in 1913. In 1920 he served as vice-president of the Democratic National Convention. He was stricken with polio in 1921 and thereafter had very little use of his legs. He was elected governor of New York in 1928 and re-elected in 1930. As the Democratic presidential candidate, he won a decisive victory over President Herbert Hoover *(q.v.)* in 1932. On taking office during the Great Depression he introduced a radical program of economic reform known as the New Deal. New federal agencies came into being to provide jobs, relief, and loans. Re-elected in 1936 and 1940, he found the U.S. policy of neutrality increasingly challenged by Japanese aggression in China, and the expansionist policy of Nazi Germany in Europe. After the Japanese attack on Pearl Harbor on December 7, 1941, when the United States declared war on Japan, Germany, and Italy, he became the wartime leader of the country, exercising unparalleled presidential influence. In 1944 he was re-elected for a fourth term. At the time of his death, he was working arduously to establish the Charter of the United Nations.

On April 12, 1945 he was posing for a portrait while signing some official papers at his Warm Springs, Georgia, retreat. He looked at his watch, noticed that it was 1:00 p.m., and said to the artist: "We've got just 15 minutes more." He then lit a cigarette and began to study his papers. Raising his left hand to his temple, he suddenly dropped it but raised it again and pressed it behind his neck, saying: "I have a terrific

*FDR's funeral cortege in Washington, D.C.*

(Photo: National Archives)

headache." His arm dropped a second time, his head fell and his body went limp. A doctor was called and found his breathing to be very irregular. Roosevelt's clothes were sheared away, and amyl nitrate was injected into his heart. The doctor worked on the dying president for almost two hours. When his breathing stopped, adrenalin was injected into the heart muscle. There was no response and the president was pronounced dead at 3:55 p.m. The news reached British Prime Minister Winston Churchill in his study at 10 Downing Street just before midnight, Greenwich (London) Time. Churchill sat silent for a long time, as if he had been struck by a physical blow. In Moscow, the Soviet leader Stalin, upon hearing the news, seemed both "moved and preoccupied." In Chungking, China, Generalissimo Chiang Kai-shek was eating breakfast, but on hearing the news stopped eating, and went into mourning in private. Radio Tokyo read a death bulletin and, although Japan was at war with the U.S., without explanation followed it with special music "in honor of the passing of a great man." In Berlin, Germany, Joseph P. Goebbels the Nazi minister of propaganda, called for champagne and telephoned Hitler saying: "My Führer, I congratulate you. Roosevelt is dead... It is the turning point." Meanwhile, from towns and cities throughout the free world came reports of men and women weeping in the streets on hearing the news.

On the morning of April 13, Roosevelt's body was placed on a funeral train which passed through the cotton fields of Georgia. The train arrived in Washington, D.C.

on April 14, 80 years to the day after Lincoln was shot. The coffin was taken to the White House on a black draped caisson pulled by six white horses. The coffin was taken to the East Room of the White House. Eleanor Roosevelt *(q.v.)* his widow, had the casket opened, placed some flowers inside and then ordered it sealed permanently. Later that evening, a cortege returned the casket to Union Station where it was put on a train en route to Hyde Park, New York, along the same route that Lincoln's funeral train had taken. Six hundred West Point cadets stood in formation at Roosevelt's Hyde Park home on April 15, as a simple Episcopal funeral service was held. As the body was being lowered into the grave, the rector of the St. James Episcopal Church of Hyde Park prayed: "Now the laborer's task is o'er, Now the battle day is passed, Now upon the farther shore, Lands the voyager at last." Three volleys were then fired, and a bugler played taps. The Roosevelt Home, 259 Albany Post Road, Hyde Park, New York 12538.

# *Roosevelt, Theodore*

Theodore Roosevelt, generally referred to as "Teddy" Roosevelt, 26th president of the United States, (term of office 1901-09), was born on October 27, 1858, in New York City. He was a member of the New York legislature from 1882-84, but, having a taste for the rough and rugged life, lived on a ranch in North Dakota from 1884-86. He was assistant secretary of the Navy during the administration of President William McKinley *(q.v.)*, but on the outbreak of the Spanish-American War in 1898, he organized a volunteer cavalry regiment, known as the "Rough Riders," and took them to fight in Cuba. During his campaign, his charge up San Juan Hill, at the head of the Rough Riders, caught the national imagination. He was elected governor of New York in 1899, and vice-president in 1901. When President McKinley, the Republican incumbent, was assassinated that year, Roosevelt became president. After serving out the term, he was elected president in 1904. During his term of of-

*President Theodore
Roosevelt's grave,
Oyster Bay, Long Island.*
(Photo: National Park Service)

fice, the presidency was strengthened. Domestically, he paved the way for a greater governmental role with his "Square Deal" policies, in which government intervened in relations between business and labor. He also pursued a "trust-busting" policy that met with popular approval. In international affairs, with the slogan "Walk softly and carry a big stick," he asserted American power, and built a strong Navy. He encouraged the secession of Panama from Colombia, negotiated the establishment of the Panama Canal Zone under American control, and embarked on the building of the Panama Canal. On leaving office in 1909, he went big game hunting in East Africa, and traveled elsewhere abroad. He also wrote several books, including his autobiography.

Throughout 1917 he was weakened by an illness that he had caught in 1914 while exploring in South America. In 1918 he was twice in the hospital, suffering from leg and ear abcesses, and from "inflammatory rheumatism," but returned home for Christmas. News of the death of a son, in a plane crash in July, 1918, had been a heavy blow. On January 5, 1919, around midnight, he called to his chief butler, a black man named James Amos, and said: "Please put out that light, James." The butler did so. At 4:00 a.m. while Amos was sitting at the foot of the bed, he noticed that Roosevelt's breathing had changed. He hurried to another room to summon a nurse, but by the time he returned Roosevelt's breathing had stopped.

A simple funeral service attended by about 500 persons was held at Christ Episcopal Church in Oyster Bay, Long Island. The rector read the hymn "How Firm a Foundation," which had been one of Roosevelt's favorites. Only close friends and family attended the graveside service at Young's Memorial Cemetery, Cove Road, off East Main, Oyster Bay, Long Island, New York 11771.

# *Russell, Rosalind*

Rosalind Russell, the movie actress, who was a popular star from the 1940s to the 1960s, was born on June 4, 1912, in Waterbury, Connecticut. Known for her portrayals of sophisticated career women, she appeared in dozens of motion pictures including *His Girl Friday* (1940), *Picnic* (1956), and *Gypsy* (1963). She earned four Academy Award nominations, and also appeared in Broadway shows.

*Rosalind Russell's grave.*
*Forest Lawn Memorial*
*Park, Glendale, California.*
(Photo: Mary Ellen Hunt)

She died of cancer on November 28, 1976 at her Beverly Hills, California, home.

A requiem mass was held at the Church of The Good Shepherd in Beverly Hills, California, on December 2. It was attended by other movie stars, including James Stewart, Kirk Douglas, Jack Lemmon, and Frank Sinatra. Sinatra said: "I have a feeling [that] God woke up Sunday and said: 'You'd better send for Roz, she's suffered enough,' " Burial was at Forest Lawn Memorial Park, 1712 South Glendale Avenue, Glendale, California 91205.

# *Ruth, Babe*

George Herman Ruth, the popular and record-breaking baseball player, nicknamed "Babe," was born on February 6, 1895, in Baltimore, Maryland. He joined the Baltimore Orioles in 1914, and later that same year was sold to the Boston Red Sox. By 1919 he was known as the best left-handed pitcher in the American League. He established a record of pitching 29 2/3 consecutive scoreless innings during the 1916 and 1918 World Series. In 1920 he was sold to the New York Yankees, with whom he stayed until 1934. When Yankee Stadium was opened in 1923 it was known as "the house that Ruth Built." His $80,000.00 annual salary made him the highest paid baseball player of the time. In 1935 he joined the Boston Braves, and by the end of his career held 54 records.

*Babe Ruth's grave,*
*Hawthorn, New York.*
(Photo: Wendy Bassett).

In late 1946 he complained of pain over his left eye, which was thought to be a sinus headache. An examination at the French Hospital in New York City revealed, however, that he had a malignant growth on the left side of his neck, which encircled the left cartoid artery. Part of the growth was removed surgically and he was given radiation treatments to control the malignancy. During the next three months, however, he was unable to eat, and was fed intravenously, causing him to lose 80 lbs. He was discharged from the hospital in February 1947, but during the spring what was left of the tumor continued to grow. As he had not been told exactly what was wrong with him, he believed that his teeth were infected, and from time to time he would say: "These damn teeth." Last rites of the Catholic Church were administered on July 21 but he rallied after that and on July 26 was able to leave the hospital for the premier of the movie, *The Babe Ruth Story* . When baseball manager Connie Mack *(q.v.)* visited him at Memorial Hospital in New York City, he said: "Hello Mr. Mack, the termites have got me." He died in his sleep at 8:00 p.m. on August 16, 1948 at the hospital.

His body lay in state on August 17 and 18 in the lobby of Yankee Stadium where more than 40,000 people passed the open bier. A two-foot crucifix stood in front of the mahogany coffin. A high requiem mass was celebrated at St. Patrick's Cathedral in New York City on August 19. Seventy-five thousand people lined the streets along Fifth Avenue from 46th to 57th streets; and 6,000 more were able to enter the cathedral. About 100,000 persons lined the 30-mile funeral route to the cemetery in Hawthorn, New York. Gate of Heaven Cemetery, Stevens Avenue, Hawthorn, New York 10532.

# *Sandburg, Carl*

Carl Sandburg, poet and folklorist who was seen as spokesman for the American common man, was born on January 6, 1878 in Galesburg, Illinois. After fighting in the Spanish-American War of 1898, he graduated from college in 1902, and then traveled throughout the U.S., taking on a number of odd jobs. His first book, *Chicago Poems* (1916), was extremely successful, and invited comparisons to the style of Walt Whitman *(q.v.)*. He followed that with *Cornhuskers* (1918), for which

*Remembrance Rock:*
*Carl Sandburg's*
*grave, in*
*Galesburg, Illinois.*

(Photo: S.B. Pratt, The Holcomb Studio)

he won a Pulitzer Prize, and after several other volumes of poetry he won another Pulitzer Prize in 1940 for the last tome of his 6-volume biography of Abraham Lincoln. (q.v.). He also gave recitals of folksongs, and authored several children's books. His *Complete Poems* (1950) won him a third Pulitzer Prize.

In June 1967 he suffered a heart attack and was confined to bed for six weeks at his Flat Rock, North Carolina, home. He had a second heart attack in mid-July, and died on July 22. His widow, Lillian Sandburg, said: "I thought it was a wonderful way of going. He had a beautiful passing."

A simple 13-minute funeral service was held at St. John In The Wilderness

Episcopal Church in Flat Rock. The service was attended by the family and a small gathering including Sandburg's friend Ralph McGill, publisher of the *Atlanta Constitution*. The organ prelude was "John Brown's Body," which had been one of Sandburg's favorites. The officiating clergyman quoted a line from "Finish,"one of Sandburg's poems:—"Death comes once, let it be easy." His body was cremated, and the ashes were placed under Remembrance Rock, at the Carl Sandburg Birthplace, 331 East Third, Galesburg, Illinois 61401.

# Sherman, William Tecumseh

William Tecumseh Sherman, the Civil War general, who led Union troops on a famous "March through Georgia" in 1864, was born on February 8, 1820, in Lancaster, Ohio. After leading a brigade in the first Battle of Bull Run (Manassas) in July 1861, he became a general, taking part in the battles of Shiloh and Corinth and in the capture of Vicksburg. In 1864 he led his famous "march to the sea" through Georgia, leaving Atlanta on September 2, and entering Savannah on December 21. After the war, in 1869, he succeeded Grant as general and commander of the army. He retired in 1884, and moved to New York City in 1886.

In 1890 he told a friend: "I feel it coming sometimes when I get home from an entertainment or banquet, especially these winter nights. I feel death reaching out for me, as it were. I suppose I'll take cold some night, and go to bed never to get up again."

On February 5, 1891 he developed a severe chill which was complicated by asthma. He died of pneumonia on February 14.

He was given a military funeral which began at his home in New York City, and continued by train to St. Louis, Missouri. Along the funeral route, Civil War veterans held up tattered battle flags and fired salutes with old army muskets. Burial was at Calvary Cemetery in St. Louis. An honor guard fired three rifle volleys, and taps were played. Calvary Cemetery, 5239 West Florissant Avenue, St. Louis, Missouri 63115.

# Sinclair, Upton

Upton Beall Sinclair, author and crusader for socialism, was born on September 20, 1878 in Baltimore, Maryland. After graduating from City College of New York (CCNY) in 1897, he began to write. His sixth novel, *The Jungle* (1906), was very successful. Its description of conditions in Chicago stockyards led to the passage of the Meat Inspection Act of 1906. Altogether he wrote 80 books, including *King Coal* (1917), *Oil* (1927), and *Boston* (1928). Between 1906 and 1930 he several times ran for public office in California, and narrowly missed winning the governorship in 1934.

He died in his sleep on November 25, 1968 at the Somerset Valley Nursing Home in Bound Brook, New Jersey, aged 90. A memorial service was held on November 30 at St. Paul's Episcopal Church in Bound Brook. His remains had been cremated before the service at Rosehill Cemetery, Linden, New Jersey. They were then sent to

Washington, D.C. for burial. Rock Creek Cemetery, Rock Creek Church Road and Webster Street, N.W., Washington, D.C. 20011.

# *Sousa, John Philip*

John Philip Sousa, bandmaster and composer of military marches, was born on November 6, 1854 in Washington, D.C. A trombonist and violinist, he became conductor of the U.S. Marine Band in 1880. He wrote about 140 marches, including "Semper Fidelis" (1888), "The Washington Post," (1889), and "The Stars and Stripes Forever" (1897). During the Spanish-American War he was music director for the Sixth Army Corps, and during World War I he was the director of all Navy bands. He also wrote a number of comic operas including *El Capitan* (1896), as well as three novels, dissertations on the trumpet and violin, and his autobiography, *Marching Along* (1928).

On March 6, 1932, while on a trip to Reading, Pennsylvania, he had a fatal heart attack, dying at 1:30 a.m.

His body was sent to Washington, D.C. where it lay in state in a copper coffin at the Marine barracks, attended by a Marine honor guard. Arrangements of palms and flowers from the botanical gardens were piled on top of the casket. Two Episcopal ministers performed the funeral service. Eight white horses pulled his hearse through the snow-covered Washington streets as the Marine band played the theme from *El Capitan* and "Semper Fidelis." Marines and sailors lined the sides of the grave at the Congressional Cemetery. Freemasons placed an apron and a symbolic sprig of evergreen on the coffin, and sailors fired three volleys. Taps were sounded as the coffin was lowered into the frozen earth. The Congressional Cemetery, 1801 East Street, S.E., Washington, D.C. 20003.

# *Steinbeck, John*

John Ernst Steinbeck, author of *The Grapes of Wrath*, a powerful novel that to many symbolized the bitterness of the Great Depression of the 1930s, was born on February 27, 1902, in Salinas, California. After working at odd jobs, he wrote *Tortilla Flat* (1935), which became a bestseller. His *Of Mice and Men* (1937) won the New York Drama Critics' Circle Award. The *Grapes of Wrath* (1939) won a Pulitzer Prize in 1940 and was made into a motion picture, as also was *East of Eden* (1952). In 1962 he won the Nobel Prize for Literature.

In June 1968 his health became poor, and he moved to Manhattan from his Sag Harbor, Long Island, home. He died on December 20, 1968, at his 72nd Street home in New York City, of valvular heart disease. He was aged 66. More than 300 people attended the simple 20-minute service on December 23 at St. James Episcopal Church on Madison Avenue in New York City. Psalm 46 and Psalm 121 were read, and motion picture actor Henry Fonda, who had starred in the movie *The Grapes of Wrath*, read several poems that had been Steinbeck's favorites, including "Petrarch's Sonnets to Laura," by J.M. Synge; Tennyson's "Ulysses;" and "Songs of Travel and other verses," by R.L. Stevenson. Cremation followed the service, and burial was in Salinas, California. Gardens of Memories Memorial Park, 768 Abbot Street, Salinas, California 93901.

# Stevenson, Adlai

Adlai Ewing Stevenson, twice an unsuccessful Democratic candidate for the presidency in the 1950s, and U.S. ambassador to the United Nations, was born on February 5, 1900 in Los Angeles, California. He began to practice law in Chicago in 1926. He was legal assistant to the secretary of the navy in 1941, and from 1946-47 was a senior advisor to the American delegation to the United Nations General Assembly. He was elected governor of Illinois in 1948. In 1952 he was drafted as Democratic candidate for the presidency but lost to Dwight D. Eisenhower (q.v.). He ran again in 1956, but again lost to Eisenhower. President John F. Kennedy (q.v.) appointed him as U.S. ambassador to the UN in 1961.

On July 14, 1965, while taking an evening walk in London, England, he began to stagger and leaned against a pole to steady himself. He then collapsed on the sidewalk in front of the International Sportsman's Club. A doctor and an ambulance were called. The doctor administered artificial respiration, a series of injections and a heart massage. The ambulance took him to St. George's Hospital, but he was dead on arrival from a heart attack.

His body lay in state on July 15 in a plain wooden coffin covered by an American flag at the American Embassy in London. An honor guard which stood vigil was composed of representatives from each branch of the American and British military. Flags on all American embassies and navy vessels at sea flew at half-mast. His remains were flown back to the United States the same day. His coffin then lay in state in Washington Cathedral. Throughout the night, thousands of people filed past the coffin.

The funeral service was held at the National Cathedral on July 16, attended by President Lyndon Johnson (q.v.) and other government officials. His body was then flown to Springfield, Illinois. En route to the state capitol it was taken through Oak Ridge Cemetery to pass the tomb of Abraham Lincoln (q.v.). His remains lay in state at the state capitol on the same walnut table that had held Lincoln's remains. A private funeral service was held in Bloomington, Illinois, on July 19, attended by President and Mrs. Lyndon Johnson, Vice-President Hubert Humphrey (q.v.), and Supreme Court Justices Earl Warren and Arthur Goldberg. At the same time a memorial service was held in the General Assembly room at the United Nations in New York, where UN Secretary General U Thant gave the eulogy. Burial was in Evergreen Cemetery, 302 East Miller Street, Bloomington, Illinois 61701.

# Stowe, Harriet Beecher

Harriet Elizabeth Beecher Stowe, author of *Uncle Tom's Cabin*, which helped mobilize northern public opinion in favor of Abolition before the Civil War of

1861-65, was born on June 14, 1811, in Litchfield, Connecticut. In 1836 she married Calvin E. Stowe. She then began to write and publish a number of short stories and essays. In 1852 she published *Uncle Tom's Cabin*. Within the first year after publication the book sold 300,000 copies. Popular opinion in the northern states was aroused by it to such an extent that, on meeting with her in 1863, President Abraham Lincoln *(q.v.)* said: "So you're the little woman who wrote the book that made this great war." After the war she continued to write, and traveled widely. Her husband died in 1886, and she then spent the rest of her life in Hartford, Connecticut.

During her last days she said to one of her nurses that she had been waiting a long time to meet her Maker. Her last words were to her Irish nurse: "I love you." She died in her sleep on July 1, 1896, aged 85.

The funeral service was on July 3, at the Chapel Cemetery, Phillips Academy, Andover, Massachusetts. She was buried next to her husband. On July 1, 1897, on the first anniversary of her death, a newspaperman saw her black cook putting flowers on her grave and asked for permission to take a picture. She refused and said: "This is strictly between Mrs. Stowe, me—and her other friends." The Chapel Cemetery, Phillips Academy, North Main, Route 28, Andover, Massachusetts 01810.

# Sullivan, Ed

Edward Vincent Sullivan, journalist, entertainer, and television show host, was born on September 28, 1902, in New York City. After working as a newspaper reporter and sportswriter, he became a Broadway gossip columnist for the *New York Daily News* in 1932. In the same year he began a radio show in New York City, and later a weekly radio show for CBS called "Ed Sullivan Entertains." In 1948 he contracted to do a Sunday night television variety show which was first called "Toast of the Town," and later "The Ed Sullivan Show." At the time it went off the air at the end of the 1970-71 television season, it was the longest running, television show on record. Many celebrities appeared on the show, as well as many little-known people of talent whom Sullivan brought to national attention.

On September 6, 1974, Sullivan entered Lenox Hill Hospital in New York City for treatment of cancer of the esophagus. He died on October 13, aged 73. The funeral service was held at St. Patrick's Cathedral in New York City on October 16, attended by 2,000 people, including the mayor of New York and various celebrities. Burial was in Ferncliff Cemetery, Hartsdale, New York 10530.

# Taft, William

William Howard Taft, 27th president of the United States (in office 1909-13) and a chief justice of the Supreme Court, was born on September 15, 1857, in Cincinatti, Ohio. In 1880 he began a career of law as well as public service. From 1900-04 he was president of the Philippine Commission, responsible for establishing civil government in the islands, and he became civil governor of the Philippines in 1901. In 1904 he became secretary of war. He was elected to the presidency on the Republican ticket in 1908. His administration was undramatic, and despite its honesty, is memorable for Taft's failure to heal the split between conservatives and progressives in his party. In 1913 he left the White House to become professor of constitutional law at Yale University. In 1921 he was appointed chief justice of the Supreme Court.

In February 1930 he was admitted to Washington's Garfield Hospital, where it was found that he had hardening of the arteries. He spent this time in the hospital reading detective stories, and then he went to Asheville, North Carolina to recuperate. After his return to Washington, D.C. he died in his sleep on March 8. President Herbert Hoover (*q.v.*) issued a proclamation calling for 30 days of mourning. The Supreme Court and both houses of Congress adjourned until after the funeral, as did many state legislatures. The New York Stock Exchange and many commodity markets were closed and special services were held in churches and universities across the United States, as well as in foreign capitals, including London, Paris, Berlin, and Tokyo.

*President Taft's grave in Arlington National Cemetery.*

(Photo: U.S. Army)

His body lay in state in the Capitol rotunda for two hours on March 11, on the same catafalque which had supported the bodies of Lincoln, Garfield, McKinley, and Harding (*q.q.v.*). At noon the Marine Corps band played as the coffin was taken down the Capitol's steps and put on a caisson led by eight gray horses and military units of soldiers, sailors and marines. The cortege then moved to All Souls' Unitarian Church where a simple service was held, attended by President Hoover. According to Taft's request, there was no eulogy nor any sermon. The service was conducted by the Rev. Ulysses G. Pierce, a friend of Taft's. Burial was at Arlington National Cemetery, where, at the graveside, three shots were fired, and a bugler played taps. Arlington National Cemetery, Fort Myer, Arlington, Virginia 22211.

# *Taylor, Zachary*

Zachary Taylor, 12th president of the United States, (in office 1849-50), was born on November 24, 1784, in Orange County, Virginia. He grew up on the Kentucky frontier, and in 1808 joined the army. He fought in the Northwest Indian campaign, the War of 1812, the Blackhawk campaign of 1832, and the second Seminole War (1835-42). Nicknamed "Old Rough and Ready," he participated in the Mexican campaigns of 1846-47, winning a decisive victory over the Mexican general Santa Anna. Because of his military reputation he was nominated as presidential candidate at the Whig convention and won the 1848 election. He soon was at odds with Southern representatives because he favored the admission to the Union of the former Mexican territories of California and New Mexico, both of which prohibited slavery.

On July 4, 1850, he participated in ceremonies at the laying of the cornerstone of the Washington Monument. The day was oppressively hot and he drank large amounts of water. When he returned to the White House he said that he felt "very hungry." He ate large quantities of cherries and wild berries, which he washed down with iced milk and water. Within an hour he began to have stomach cramps, and these continued for several days. At one point he said to his doctor: "I should not be surprised if this were to terminate in my death." The public was not informed of his condition until five days later, when, on July 9, a bulletin announced that he had a bilious remittent fever, following an attack of what was then called "cholera morbus."

On July 9 crowds of people gathered at the White House, which precipitated rumors that he had already died. When, at 3:30 p.m., it was announced that he was out of immediate danger, bells rang throughout the city, and boys in the street lit bonfires. Around 9:00 p.m., however, his condition worsened, and at 10:35 his family was called to his bedside. He was asked if he was comfortable. "Very," he replied, "But the storm in passing, has swept away the trunk." He then added what were to be his last words "I have endeavored to do my duty, I am prepared to die. My only regret is in leaving behind me the friends I love." He then died without a struggle.

As soon as his death was announced, several of the bells in the city were tolled; the ringing continued throughout the night and the following day. On July 10 all public offices were closed and many buildings, including the White House, were draped in black crepe. His body was placed in a metallic coffin and lay in state in the East Room of the White House. A contemporary observer reported that: "the body is greatly emaciated, but the lineaments of the face are preserved tolerably perfect."

The funeral service was held on July 13 at the White House, with a clergyman from St. John's Episcopal Church officiating. Burial was at the Congressional Cemetery in Washington, D.C. There his body remained until the fall, when it was taken to the Taylor family plot in Springfield, Kentucky.

On May 6, 1926 the remains of Taylor and his wife were again transferred, this time to a new mausoleum of classic Roman design, erected by the U.S. government. A dedication service was held on May 31, 1926. Zachary Taylor National Cemetery, 4701 Brownsboro Road, Louisville, Kentucky 40207.

# *Tecumseh*

Tecumseh, (meaning "The Panther Passing Across"), the Shawnee chief who sought to oppose American expansion into the Ohio valley, was born in 1768, at Old Piqua (now Oldtown), Ohio. He was given his name because when he was born a shooting star, called "The Panther," appeared.

The murder of his father by frontiersmen made Tecumseh the enemy of white settlers in the Ohio valley, and he quickly became a leader of his people in frontier warfare. A man of great bravery, he also had many other qualities. and opposed the traditional practice of torturing prisoners. In 1791 he participated in the defeat of General St. Clair's army that had been sent to crush the Indian forces, and also fought against General Anthony Wayne *(q.v.)* at the Battle of Fallen Timbers in 1794. In the years that followed he sought to bring into being a great Indian nation that would have halted the westward expansion of white settlers. His plan received a set-back when William Henry Harrison *(q.v.)* overran his headquarters, in his absence, at the battle of Tippecanoe.

In the War of 1812, Tecumseh allied himself with the British, and was killed by Harrison's forces at the battle of the Thames, in Ontario, on October 5, 1813. Armed with a war club, Tecumseh was killed in close combat with Colonel Richard M. Johnson, (who was later vice-president from 1837-41 in President Van Buren's administration), who shot him in the chest with his pistol. After the battle, the Shawnees buried Tecumseh in a secret place on a bank beside a creek, distant from the battlefield. Some years later, they returned, intending to exhume the body and take it to Oklahoma for a burial suitable for one of his importance. But the creek had often overflowed, obliterating evidence as to the exact spot of burial. Rather than make an extended search at that time, the Indians left the spot. In September 1941, however, his bones were disinterred, re-assembled, and placed in a cairn of stones on the bank of the St. Clair River, on Walpole Island Indian Reserve, Ontario. It remains a Shawnee tradition that Tecumseh will one day return and that at that time all Indian tribes will be united. The Tecumseh Cairn, Walpole Island Indian Reserve, Ontario, Canada.

# *Teilhard de Chardin, Pierre*

Pierre Teilhard de Chardin, the paleontologist who advanced a philosophy which blended science and Christianity, was born on May 1, 1881, in Sarcenat, France. After serving as a stretcher-bearer in World War I, and being decorated for gallantry, he received a doctorate from the Sorbonne. He then undertook a series of paleontological missions to China, between 1923 and 1945, and was one of the discoverers of the fossilized skull of "Peking Man." He wrote several books, of which the most fundamental is *Le Phenomene Humain* (1938-40). In his last years he worked at the Wenner-Gren Foundation in New York City.

On April 9, 1955 he made a confession to a Jesuit priest, who was his friend, Father de Breuvery. A short time before, he had remarked to his cousin, Jean de Lagarde, that it was his wish to die on the day of the Resurrection. On Easter Sunday, April 10, he said Mass and then attended a pontifical high mass in St. Patrick's Cathedral in New York City. That afternoon he took a walk in Central Park, and then attended a concert. Later, while having a cup of tea, he fell suddenly to the floor and it was thought that he had fainted. A cushion was put under his head and he opened his eyes, saying: "But where am I? What's happened?" He was told that he had had a heart attack and he replied: "I can't remember anything... this time I feel it's terrible." By the time a doctor arrived, he had already died.

*Teilhard de Chardin's grave, near Poughkeepsie, New York.*

(Photo: Julie Maserjian)

His body lay in state in a chapel on Park Avenue, dressed in his vestments. A crucifix and a rosary were placed in his hands. A funeral service was held on April 12, at which Father de Breuvery officiated. Few people attended the service, but one of them was the French ambassador to the United Nations. One of those in attendance later wrote: "My heart was so heavy that I could hardly pay attention. It seemed too incredible and too sudden to be real." His body was sent to the Jesuit Novitiate of St. Andrews near Poughkeepsie, on the Hudson River, where it was placed in a vault until the frozen ground thawed. Burial subsequently took place in the grounds of the Novitiate. The Novitiate is now on the grounds of the Culinary Institute of America, North Road, (U.S. route 9), Hyde Park, New York 12538.

# *Thoreau, Henry*

Henry David Thoreau, naturalist and Transcendental philosopher who expounded his ideas in his book *Walden* (1854), was born on July 12, 1817, in Concord, Massachusetts. After attempting to become a teacher, he made a canoe trip, which led him to develop his own philosophy of nature. He was a friend of Ralph Waldo Emerson (*q.v.*) and other Transcendentalists, and his early writings appeared in the Transcendentalist journal, *The Dial*. In 1845 he moved for a time to the shores of Walden Pond, not far from Concord, and began to keep a journal. Excerpts from this were published in 1854 as *Walden, or Life in the Woods*—his most famous work.

In 1849 he published his essay "Civil Disobedience," which contained the statement: "Under a government which imprisons any unjustly, the true place for a just man is also a prison." In the 20th century, Thoreau's philosophy was to inspire Mahatma Gandhi to develop his own concept of passive resistance to unjust laws. After Thoreau's death, his journal was published in 14 volumes in 1906. In the last years of his short life, spent in Concord, he developed tuberculosis. A fervent Abolitionist, he admired John Brown, and the shock of Brown's execution in December 1859 may have contributed to his decline. In early 1862, a friend, Bronson Alcott, father of Louisa May Alcott (q.v.), wrote: "He grows feebler day by day and is evidently failing and fading from our sight." His aunt Louisa, at about this time, asked him if he had made his peace with God and he replied: "I did not know we had ever quarreled." When another friend told him: "You seem so near the brink of the Dead River that I almost wonder how the opposite shore may appear to you." Thoreau answered: "One world at a time."

On May 6, 1862, at 7:00 p.m., he became restless and wanted to be moved. A friend then arrived with some hyacinths which Thoreau smelled and said that he liked. His last sentence was unintelligible but contained the words "moose" and "Indian." Around 9:00 p.m., as his mother, sister, and aunt Louisa watched, his breathing grew fainter and fainter and he died without a struggle. His sister, Sophia, said: "I feel as if something very beautiful had happened—not death."

The funeral service was held on May 9 at Concord's First Parish Church. Louisa May Alcott commented that while he was not much considered while living, he was honored in death. His coffin was covered by wild flowers and a wreath of andromeda. Selections from the Bible were read. Six friends carried his coffin to Sleepy Hollow Cemetery. As Emerson turned away from the grave he said: "He had a beautiful soul." Louisa May Alcott later wrote: "Perhaps we should know a closer relationship now than even while he lived." Sleepy Hollow Cemetery, Bedford Street, Concord, Massachusetts 01742.

# *Thumb, Tom*

Charles Sherwood Stratton, the midget and circus performer known as "Tom Thumb," was born on January 4, 1838, in Bridgeport, Connecticut. While his family was of normal height, Stratton stopped growing at six months of age and remained 25 inches tall. He weighed only 15 lbs. After puberty, however, Stratton grew to a height of 40 inches, and his weight increased to 70 lbs. Circus impressario P.T. Barnum (q.v.) hired him and promoted him as "General Tom Thumb," an "11-year-old dwarf from England." Another midget in Barnum's circus, Mercy Lavinia Warren Bumpus, married Stratton in an elaborate ceremony at Grace Episcopal Church in New York City in 1863. The stage act of "Tom Thumb" and his wife enabled Barnum to regain his fortune, after the burning of Barnum's New York Museum in 1868.

On the morning of July 15, 1883 he got out of bed at his home in Middleboro, Massachusetts. After being left alone by his brother-in-law, he fell to the floor. When his brother-in-law returned, he found him dead on the floor. The cause of death was apoplexy. He was 45 years old.

His body lay in state in Middleboro on July 18, from 8:00 to 9:00 p.m. It was then sent to Bridgeport, Connecticut, where it lay in state at St. John's Episcopal Church from 10:00 till noon on July 19. The casket was three feet ten inches long, and was covered by black broadcloth with silver trimmings and masonic emblems. His body was dressed in a suit, and on the left lapel was a 32nd degree masonic pin.

The funeral service was held at the church at 2:00 p.m. on July 19. The largest floral arrangement was sent by P.T. Barnum, and was in the shape of an anchor and cross. Later, Barnum erected a column at the gravesite, in memory of Stratton. Mountain Grove Cemetery, 2675 North Avenue, Bridgeport, Connecticut 06604.

# *Tracy, Spencer*

Spencer Tracy, the motion picture actor, was born on April 5, in Milwaukee, Wisconsin. After studying at Ripon College in Wisconsin, he went to New York City where, while appearing in the play "The Last Mile" (1930), he was spotted by movie director John Ford, after which his movie career began. He won an Academy Award

*Spencer Tracy's grave :
Forest Lawn Memorial
Park, Glendale, California.*
(Photo: Mary Ellen Hunt)

in 1937 for his performance in the movie *Captains Courageous*, and in 1938 he won another Oscar for the role of Father Edward Joseph Flanagan *(q.v.)* in *Boys' Town*. He and Katherine Hepburn played unforgettable roles in such movies as *State Of The Union* (1948), *Adam's Rib* (1949), and *Guess Who's Coming to Dinner?* (1967).

On June 10, 1967, at 6:00 a.m., he suffered a heart attack and died, at his Beverly Hills, California, home. He was aged 67.

A requiem mass was held on June 12 at Immaculate Heart of Mary Roman Catholic Church in Hollywood. Monsignor John O'Donnell, who had acted as technical adviser for the movie *Boys Town*, officiated. Among those attending were singer Frank Sinatra, director John Ford, and actors James Stewart, Edward G. Robinson, and Gregory Peck, Katherine Hepburn, his long-time friend and frequent co-star, did not attend. Burial was at Forest Lawn Memorial Park, 1712 South Glendale Avenue, Glendale, California 91205.

# Truman, Harry S.

Harry S. Truman, 33rd president of the United States, (term of office 1945-53), was born on May 8, 1884, in Lamar, Missouri. After a varied early career as bank clerk, farmer, and small businessman, he saw action as a captain in World War I. After the war he ran a clothing store in Kansas City, but it failed during the Depression of the 1930s. In 1934 he was elected to the U.S. Senate and was re-elected in 1940. In 1944 he was elected to the vice-presidency. He unexpectedly became president on the death of Franklin D. Roosevelt (q.v.), on April 12, 1945. He had not previously known about the atomic bomb, but after learning of its existence decided to use the weapon against Japan in 1945 to end World War II, and this was done. He was re-elected in 1948, and firmly opposed Communist expansion in Europe and Asia, at a time when the Cold War between the Soviet Union and the West was at its height. His administration was memorable for the Truman Doctrine (1947), the Marshall Plan (1948), and the Berlin Airlift (1948-49). In 1950 he ordered U.S. forces into action in the Korean War. Upon leaving the presidency in 1953, he retired to Independence, Missouri, where he lived until his death in 1972.

He was hospitalized in early December at the Research Hospital and Medical Center in Kansas City, Missouri. He was placed on the critical list after his lungs filled with fluid and it was noted that his heart had weakened. He received telephone calls and messages from former President Lyndon B. Johnson (q.v.), Senator Hubert H. Humphrey (q.v.), Senator Edward M. Kennedy, and the Shah of Iran. President Richard M. Nixon sent flowers.

By the middle of the month he was semi-conscious, and he continued to lose ground against lung congestion, heart irregularity, and partial kidney failure. He died on December 26.

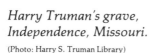

*Harry Truman's grave,*
*Independence, Missouri.*
(Photo: Harry S. Truman Library)

President Nixon declared December 28 a national day of mourning and ordered all American flags to be flown at half-mast for 30 days. On December 27 his body was taken to the Harry S. Truman Library in Independence, Missouri where the first mourners to pay their respects were President Nixon and former President Johnson.

A simple funeral service was held on December 28 at the library, attended by Truman's hometown friends rather than Washington dignitaries. Burial was on the grounds of the library. A memorial service was also held on January 5 at Washington National Cathedral, attended by many notables. The Harry S. Truman Memorial Library, 24 Highway and Delaware, Independence, Missouri 64050.

# *Twain, Mark*

"Mark Twain," Samuel Langhorne Clemens, the author and humorist, was born on November 30, 1835 in Florida, Missouri. He had a limited education, and worked as printer, apprentice steamboat captain, prospector, and miner. After going west, and working as a feature writer for several newspapers, he settled in Hartford, Connecticut, where he authored such American literary classics as *The Adventures of Tom Sawyer* (1876), *The Adventures of Huckleberry Finn* (1884), and others. Becoming bankrupt as a result of bad investments in the early 1890s, he undertook an international lecture tour to pay off his debts. A few years later he was once more

(Photo: Mark Twain Memorial, Hartford, Connecticut)

*Mark Twain's coffin is placed in the hearse, as his funeral cortege is formed.*

solvent. His last years were clouded by sorrow following the death of his wife in 1904.

Throughout his life he had predicted that as he had "come in" with Halley's Comet, which had appeared in 1835, the year of his birth, he would leave with it when it returned, in 1910. In fact he died two days before the comet reached its height.

On December 23, 1909 he told the Associated Press: "I hear the newspapers say I am dying. The charge is not true. I would do no such thing at my time of life. I am behaving as good as I can. Merry Christmas to everybody." He sailed for Bermuda on January 6, 1910, but—plagued by crushing chest pains caused by angina pectoris—he was forced to return to the United States. During most of his return trip he was under heavy sedation from injections of morphine. He arrived home in April, after which his thoughts and speech became incoherent. On April 21, he wrote several notes. One asked for his glasses and a glass pitcher. Another, written to his daughter Clara, said: "Dear, you didn't tell me, but I have found out that you. Well, I …" He was unable to finish this note, but it is possible that he wished to convey his knowledge of the fact that Clara was at that time five months pregnant. The same day he became weaker and lapsed into unconsciousness. He died, without a struggle, on April 21, 1910, at his home, Stormfield, in Redding, Connecticut. His last words, recorded by his doctor and Clara, although not the ones mentioned in the newspaper accounts at that time, were to Clara: "Goodbye, dear, if we meet…"

His body was dressed in a white cashmere suit and put in his downstairs living room. A wreath of laurel leaves was placed on the coffin, which bore a copper plate that said: "Samuel Langhorne Clemens, Mark Twain, 1910." All businesses and stores in the Hartford suburb of Redding were closed.

*Mark Twain's grave,*
*Elmira, New York.*
(Photo: Elizabeth Thomas)

The coffin was taken to the Brick Presbyterian Church in New York City on April 23. Four hundred people were invited to attend. During the 20-minute service, the music played included Chopin's "Funeral March." The coffin was then opened, and 3,000 persons filed past it. Among the notables present were Andrew Carnegie and the writer O. Henry (Sydney Porter) *(q.q.v.)*.

His remains were then shipped to Elmira, New York, where last rites were held at the home of his brother-in-law, General Charles J. Langdon, at 3:30 p.m. on April 24. The service was held in the same room as the one in which he had gotten married 40 years earlier. Some of the same friends who had been at his wedding were in attendance. Just before the simple service began, a card arrived from "500 boys of Louisville (Kentucky) Male High School." It read: "In remembrance of Samuel E. Clemens, who has brightened their lives with innocent laughter and taught them squareness and grit and compassion."

His burial, at Woodland Cemetery, took place during a heavy downpour of rain. Woodland Cemetery, 1200 Walnut Street, Elmira, New York 14905.

# *Tyler, John*

John Tyler, 10th president of the United States, (term of office 1841-45), was born on March 29, 1790, in Charles County, Virginia. After studying law he was elected to the Virginia legislature and later served as a U.S. congressman from 1817-21. He

*President John Tyler's grave,*
*Hollywood Cemetery,*
*Richmond, Virginia.*
(Photo: Theresa Breschel)

was governor of Virginia from 1825-27, and a U.S. senator from 1827-36. He became vice-president in 1841, and upon the death of President William Henry Harrison (*q.v.*) on April 4, 1841, became president. Elected as a Whig, Tyler showed independence, and was thus repudiated by Whigs and Democrats alike. During his administration the U.S. Navy was reorganized, the U.S. Weather Bureau was established, and Texas annexed (1844). In 1861 he headed the Washington Peace Conference—which unsuccessfully attempted to resolve sectional differences on the eve of the Civil War. He was elected to the Confederate House of Representatives in Richmond, Virginia, a few days before his death.

On January 12, 1862, he rose early at his Richmond home, but became nauseated. After drinking some tea, he fell to the ground unconscious. In the next few days he had severe headaches and a cough. Just after midnight on the morning of January 18 his wife Julia awoke and found him gasping for air. When a doctor who had been called the day before, arrived at his bedside, Tyler told him: "Doctor, I am going." The doctor replied: "I hope not sir." Tyler then added: "Perhaps it is best." He died at 12:15 a.m.

His body lay in state on January 20 in the hall of the Confederate Congress in Richmond; the coffin was covered by the stars and bars of the Confederate flag, and by evergreens and white roses. Thousands of mourners filed past his casket.

The funeral service was held on January 21 at St. Paul's Episcopal Church. A cortege of 150 carriages then accompanied the body to Hollywood Cemetery; where he was buried next to the tomb of President James Monroe *(q.v.)*. Hollywood Cemetery, 415 South Cherry Street, Richmond, Virginia 23220.

# *Typhoid Mary*

Mary Mallon, nicknamed "Typhoid Mary," was born, probably in the United States, in or around 1870.

In a 1904 typhoid epidemic, she was recognized as the carrier of the bacteria. By the time the disease was traced to her, she had already left the house where she had worked as a cook. She continued moving from household to household but was eventually found and institutionalized at Riverside Hospital, on North Brother Island, in New York City. She was finally released when she promised that she would find other employment besides cooking.

During a later epidemic in 1914, she was again found to be working as a cook, and was again detained on the island. Although she herself was immune to the disease, her system was so full of typhoid bacteria that some doctors referred to her as "the human culture tube."

She died of a stroke on November 11, 1938, aged 68. A requiem mass was held for her at St. Luke's Roman Catholic Church in the Bronx, on the morning of November 12, and was attended by three men, three women, and three children, all of whom refused to be identified. She was buried in St. Raymond's Cemetery, 1201 Balcom Avenue, the Bronx, New York 10465.

# *Valentino, Rudolph*

Rudolph Valentino, the motion picture actor, famed as the "Great Lover" on cinema screens of the 1920s, was born Rodolpho Alfonzo Raffaelo Pierre Filibert Guglielmi de Valentina d'Antonguolla, in Castellaneta, Italy, on May 6, 1895. He came to the United States in 1913, where he worked as a dishwasher, gardener, and at odd jobs. He also worked as a vaudeville singer and dancer. In 1918 he went to Hollywood, where he played some minor roles in movies before obtaining a major role in the 1921 movie *The Four Horsemen of the Apocalypse,* which catapulted him to stardom. He also starred in *The Sheik* (1921), *Blood and Sand* (1922), and *The Son of the Sheik* (1926). By this time he had a huge following, especially among female movie goers. While at the height of his career, however, he developed pneumonia and peritonitis.

On August 14, 1926 he was in his suite at the Hotel Ambassador in New York. He became ill, clutched at his stomach, and fell to the floor in agony. The following day he was rushed to Polyclinic Hospital, where he underwent surgery for a gastric ulcer. He was found to have peritonitis from a ruptured appendix. For six days he fought death, and hourly radio bulletins were given on his condition. The urgency and anxiety in the announcer's voice generated emotional responses that were close to hysteria. Newspapers in New York, and around the country, attempting to compete with radio, outdid each other in generating "scoops." One newspaper went so far as to fake a photograph of Valentino in the operating room. In the media, the condition of the fallen star took on the dimensions of a national catastrophe. On August 22 he worsened, and on the morning of August 23, when in a delirium in which he rambled incoherently in French and Italian, he received extreme unction. He died shortly after noon on August 23.

*Rudolph Valentino's grave in Hollywood, California.*

(Photo: Mary Ellen Hunt)

His managers planned to publicize his funeral, but the publicity got out of control, generating a mass hysteria that was manifest not only in New York but in other parts of the world. To boost circulation, one newspaper even ran a "photograph" of the star arriving in heaven and being greeted by Enrico Caruso, the Italian operatic tenor. On the afternoon and evening of August 24, excited crowds stretched for eleven blocks around as Valentino's body lay in state in a half-opened casket covered with cloth of gold, at Frank E. Campbell's Funeral Home then on Broadway at 66th Street, in New York City. Tens of thousands of men, women, and children packed the streets outside, milling around in the rain. Despite the use of clubs, the police lost control, and hundreds were trampled by the excited crowds, or by police horses. Shop-windows were smashed, and cars overturned, as the crowds plundered the funeral home, fighting over mementos. Traffic was held up, and the mounted police, after repeated charges, eventually cleared the crowds off Broadway. Ambulances took away fainting women, police collected groups of lost children, and a truckload of abandoned umbrellas was picked up from the streets and pavements. More rioting occurred when the Fascists sent a guard of honor and came into conflict with the anti-Fascists. Finally the public was barred from the funeral chapel, but hundreds of women, claiming to be former dancing partners, ex-lovers, filmstars, or relatives, nevertheless succeeded in getting in to view the body. It took two days for the police to restore enough order for floral arrangements from Hollywood to be brought in. Meanwhile, several people committed suicide at the news of his death, including a woman in London, England.

The funeral service was held on August 30, at St. Malachi's Roman Catholic Church at 239 West 49th Street. Peace was preserved, after police barred the public for four blocks around the church. Two Italian operatic singers, one from the Chicago Civic Opera Company, and the other from the San Carlo Opera Company, were soloists at the mass, singing the "Miserere," "Ave Maria," and other selections. Many notables were present, including a veiled woman filmstar, who fainted and was taken back to the Hotel Ambassador after she had told reporters she was Valentino's intended. Chopin's "Funeral March" was played as the coffin left the church.

On September 2, his body left New York, bound for California, in the train "Lakeshore Limited." The body was placed in two coffins, the inner one of silver-bronze, the outer of gold-bronze. The outer, which was inscribed with his real name, his stage name, and his vital statistics, was covered with a blanket of gold silk, which in turn was covered with an arrangement of snapdragons, larkspur, gladioli, and roses. The doors of the baggage compartment containing the coffin were closed and sealed. When the train arrived in Chicago, several people were hurt attempting to view the coffin. By the time the train reached Hollywood on September 6, however, interest had waned, and the *New York Times* was satisfied with reporting its arrival on page 23. The body, nevertheless, was removed at a suburban Los Angeles station to avoid any risk of further disorderly scenes. A private funeral service was held at 10 p.m. that evening at the Church of the Good Shepherd in Beverly Hills. Movie studios throughout Southern California ceased activity at the hour of the service. A heavy police guard was assigned to the church to keep the curious away. Burial was in a private mausoleum of imported Italian marble in Hollywood Cemetery.

Following his burial, an editorial appeared in the *Catholic News of New York*, explaning while Valentino, who had been divorced and re-married, was allowed the Catholic Mass. It said: "Was Valentino Ever Validly Married?—In the eyes of God and the church, no. Since 1908 Catholics, when they marry among themselves or with non-Catholics, are validly married only when they contract before a duly authorized priest and before two witnesses. Exception to this rule is allowed only in danger of death and when an authorized priest cannot be reached for a lengthy period. The pastor of St. Malachi's Church, Church of the Catholic Actors, was called to the bedside of Valentino. What did he find? A public sinner bound neither in the eyes of the church nor the state by a previous marriage. Valentino made his confession, and the priest, guided by canon 886, administered the sacraments. Since

Valentino died as a Catholic, he was entitled to a Catholic burial. The church gave him what she gives all her children, simply this and nothing more."

For years after his death a mysterious "Lady in Black"—sometimes several "Ladies in Black"— arrived at his burial crypt on the anniversary of his death, bearing red roses. Hollywood Cemetery, 6000 Santa Monica Boulevard, Hollywood, California 90038.

# Van Buren, Martin

Martin Van Buren, the eighth president of the United States, (term of office 1837-41), and one of the founders of the Democratic Party, was born on December 5, 1782 in Kinderhook, New York. He served two terms in the New York Senate (1812-20), and was elected to the U.S. Senate in 1821, but resigned in 1827 to become the governor of New York. After three months he gave up the governorship to become secretary of state in the administration of President Andrew Jackson (q.v.). He resigned in 1831, and for a short time served as minister to Great Britain. After serving as Jackson's vice-president, he himself was elected president in 1836. He took office at the time of the panic of 1837, and he subsequently called for an independent treasury—a measure that was finally adopted in 1840. On the slavery question Van Buren tried to stay in the middle. He supported slavery in the South but opposed its extension into other territories. He lost popularity during the second Seminole War in Florida, and his popularity further declined because of his refusal to annex Texas. He was renominated in 1840 and 1848 but lost both elections.

Following his defeat he retired to Kinderhook, New York where he remained an interested non-participant in the politics of his day.

By 1862 Van Buren was suffering from frequent and debilitating attacks of asthma. By June of that year he was spending all of his time in his room on the second floor of his Kinderhook home. On days when he was not too weak, he was allowed to sit upright in a chair. He died, after an asthmatic attack, at 9:00 a.m. on July 24. His last words were: "There is but one reliance."

He lay in state for three days in a large hall at his home, while friends and neighbors filed past his simple rosewood coffin. On the coffin was a small silver plate engraved: "Martin Van Buren. Died July 24, 1862, aged 79 years, 7 months, 19 days."

On July 27 Van Buren's fellow townsmen, acting as pallbearers, carried his coffin to the village hearse, which was parked outside the porch of his home. Eighty-one carriages composed the cortege, which made its way to the local church. The governor of New York was a passenger in one of the first carriages. Representatives of the cities of Troy, Albany, Hudson, and New York were also present, while hundreds more followed on foot.

In accordance with Van Buren's wishes there was no ringing of bells, and the only hymn sung was "O God Our Help in Ages Past." The Episcopal Bishop of Pennsylvania, an old friend of Van Buren's, conducted the simple service. The coffin, now draped with the Stars and Stripes, was borne to the Kinderhook Cemetery by red-shirted members of the Kinderhook Fire Engine Company. At the cemetery, the bishops read the burial service of the Episcopal Church, as cannons thundered throughout the land. Kinderhook Cemetery, Kinderhook, New York 12106.

# Von Braun, Wernher

Wernher von Braun, a pioneer in rocketry and space craft engineering, was born in Wirsitz, Germany (now Wyrzysk, Poland), on March 23, 1912.

He studied engineering in Zurich and Berlin. Under Adolph Hitler's Nazi regime in Germany, he was instrumental in the development of the V-2 rocket, which was used against England towards the end of World War II. In 1945, after surrendering to the United States, he worked—and later was made technical director—of the U.S. Army's proving grounds at White Sands, New Mexico. He also became director of the missile research center in Huntsville, Alabama. Von Braun became a U.S. citizen in 1955. His works include *First Men to the Moon* (1960) and *Space Frontier* (1967). After serving as deputy administrator for the National Aeronautics and Space Administration (NASA) from 1970-1972, he left to work for private industry.

While acting as vice-president for research and engineering at Fairchild Industries, (an aircraft manufacturer), in Germantown, Maryland, von Braun began cancer treatment in May 1976. At that time he was said to be weak but in good spirits. He died on June 16, 1977, of cancer, at an Alexandria, Virginia, hospital.

He was buried later on the same day, and no announcement of his death was made until Friday, June 17, 1977. At the request of the National Space Institute, a Werhner von Braun memorial fund was established to promote space activities. The family has requested that the details of his death and funeral not be revealed. He was buried in a unnamed cemetery in Alexandria, Virginia.

# Washington, Booker T.

Booker Taliaferro Washington, educator, founder of Tuskegee Institute, and spokesman for black people, was born in a slave hut, on April 5, 1856, in Franklin County, Virginia. After emancipation, he worked in a coal mine, then attended Hampton Institute in Virginia, where he later taught on the staff. In 1881 he was chosen to become the first principal of Tuskegee Institute in Alabama, a school for blacks. Both he and the institute subsequently gained a high reputation. After his historic speech at Atlanta, Georgia, in 1893, in which he advocated industrial, economic, and educational, instead of political, advancement for blacks, a new chapter opened in black-white relations in the United States. Although criticized by black radicals for his new approach, he became the most influential black man in the country. He also wrote a dozen books including his autobiography, *Up From Slavery* (1901).

In early November 1915 he was admitted in St. Luke's Hospital in New York City for what was termed "overwork." Realizing that his end was near, he decided to make the journey to Tuskegee, Alabama. He had many times said: "I was born in the

South, I've lived all of my life in the South, and [I] expect to die and be buried in the South." He left New York City on November 11 at 4:00 p.m., and arrived in Tuskegee just after midnight, on the morning of November 14. He died at 4:40 a.m. on that same day. The cause of death was given as "hardening of the arteries."

A simple Protestant Episcopal funeral service was held at the chapel of the Tuskegee Institute on November 17. During the service, a number of old plantation songs were sung. Burial was on the grounds of the Institute. Tuskegee Institute, Tuskegee, Alabama 36088.

# *Washington, George*

George Washington, first president of the United States, was born into a family of wealthy Virginia farmers, on February 22, 1732, in Westmoreland County, Virginia. His first military campaigns were in the French and Indian Wars of 1754-63. After the wars he managed his estate until 1775, when he became commander of the American army during the Revolutionary War. After five years of fighting, he was present at the British surrender at Yorktown in 1781 which brought the war to a victorious conclusion. He was chosen president of the first Constitutional Convention in 1787, and was then elected the first president of the United States, in 1789, being re-elected in 1792. He established numerous precedents and had an indelible influence on the office of the presidency. His farewell address in 1796 contained advice to the nation, including a warning against "entangling alliances."

On December 13, 1779, while living at his Mount Vernon estate, he went riding in cold and snow for several hours. Late the next day he had acute laryngitis, (then called "quinsy"). He was bled four times, gargled with molasses, vinegar, and butter, and had a poultice of cantharides (dried beetles) put on his throat. His feet were soaked in warm water, and a steaming kettle of vinegar and water was brought to his bedside for him to inhale. In the late afternoon of December 14, he said: "I find that I am going. My breath cannot continue long. I believed from the first attack it would be fatal... I thank you for your attention. You'd better not take any more trouble about me; but let me go off quietly, I cannot last long." That evening he gave burial instructions to his secretary, saying: "Have me decently buried, but do not let my body be put into a vault in less than two days after I am dead." His last words were: "'Tis well." He died at 10:00 p.m.

A mahogany coffin was made, and arrived at his mansion on December 17. The head of the casket had the inscription: *Surge Ad Judicium* ["Fly To Justice"] and in the middle the words *Gloria Deo* ["Glory Be to God"]. On a silver plate was inscribed: "General/George Washington/departed this life on the 14th of December/1799, aged 68." Before he was placed in the coffin, a lock of his hair was cut for his wife Martha to keep.

The funeral service was held on December 18 and the order of the burial of the dead from the Episcopal Prayer Book was read. He was buried on the grounds of his Mount Vernon estate. A grand master of the Alexandria Lodge of Free and Accepted Masons conducted full masonic rites.

The nation was plunged into mourning by his death. A resolution was adopted by the U.S. House of Representatives, honoring him as "First in war, first in peace, and first in the hearts of his countrymen." Abroad, the British Royal Navy's fleet in the English Channel, as well as Napoleon's armies, paid tribute to his memory.

The Cemetery, Mount Vernon, Virginia 22121.

*A drawing of George and Martha Washington's tomb, Mount Vernon, Virginia.*

(Courtesy: The Free Library of Philadelphia)

# *Washington, Martha*

Martha Washington, wife of George Washington (*q.v.*), the republic's First Lady, was born Martha Dandridge, on June 2, 1732 near Williamsburg, Virginia. In 1749 she married Daniel Parke Custis, a wealthy Virginia planter. Following his death in 1757, she married Washington in 1759. Apart from her considerable fortune, she also brought her second husband four children by her first marriage. She was distinguished by common sense, charm, and a gracious manner.

Following the death of her husband in 1799, she moved to an attic room above their bedroom, as it was the custom to close off any room where someone had died for a period of two years. Because of a clause in George's will that freed all of the estate slaves upon Martha's death, she began to believe that the slaves were in collusion to try to hurry her death by letting the fire in her room go out, causing her to catch cold, or even to poison her. This preyed on her mind to such an extent that she would sit for long periods in her bolted attic room, even refusing to eat.

In May 1802 she had an attack of bilious fever. She died on May 22, 1802. The following day her grandson-in-law wrote that "from the beginning she prepared for death, gave advice to her grandchildren, sent for the Clergyman and took the sacrament, and at last directed a white gown to be brought which she had previously laid by for her last dress." A notice in the *Washington Federalist* said: "Died, at Mt. Vernon, on Saturday evening, the 22nd ultimo, Mrs. Martha Washington, widow of the late illustrious general George Washington. To those amiable and Christian virtues, which adorn the female character, she added dignity of manners, [and] superiority of understanding... The silence of respectful grief is our best eulogy."

She lay in state at her Mount Vernon home between the time of her death and her burial three days later, primarily to assure that she was indeed dead. She was wearing her favorite blue dress, with a miniature sculpture of George Washington placed on her breast. Newspapers of the time did not carry an account of her funeral, and none is known to exist. She was buried at the family mausoleum at Mount Vernon beside her husband. Mount Vernon, Virginia 22121.

# *Wayne, Anthony*

Anthony Wayne, a brigadier general in the Revolutionary War, and later commander in chief of the U.S. Army, was born on January 1, 1745, at Waynesboro, near Paoli, Pennsylvania. As a result of the complaint of a deserter, he was nicknamed "Mad Anthony Wayne."

In January 1776 Wayne was commissioned a colonel in the Continental Army, and was promoted to brigadier general the following year. He played a role in the battles of Brandywine, and Germantown, Pennsylvania. After being defeated at Paoli, he wintered at Valley Forge in 1777-78. His most famous exploit was the storming of Stony Point, New York, in July 1779. In 1781 he and one thousand other men united with the Franco-American units in the siege of Yorktown, Virginia, which ended the war. He then served with the Continental Army in the South, after which, in 1790, Georgia elected him to the U.S. House of Representatives. In 1791 President George Washington *(q.v.)* appointed him commander in chief of the United States Army. In 1794 he defeated hostile Indians at the Battle of Fallen Timbers. He then negotiated the treaty of Greenville (1795), by which the Northwest Territory was opened to American settlement.

In early December 1796, while serving in what is now Erie, Pennsylvania, he had an attack of gout, accompanied by violent stomach pains. He was bled twice a day. While this appeared to comfort him, it also weakened him and made him prone to sleep. As a stimulant he was given whiskey. His last words were: "I am dying. Bury me on the hill, at the foot of the flagpole." Death came early in the morning of December 15, 1796. He was buried as he had wished, at the foot of the flagpole on a site known as Garrison Hill.

On July 7, 1807, an admirer of Wayne, Christian Schultz, from New York state, visited his hero's grave. He was shocked to find the fence around the grave rotting away, and the only marker an oddly-shaped stone with the initials "A.W." scratched on it. At first Schultz wept, then, angry at finding the grave so ill-tended, he took his knife and carved, beneath the initials, "Shame on my country."

In 1809 the Society of Cincinnati , wishing to honor him, decided to have him reburied at St. David's Churchyard in Radnor, Pennsylvania. His son Isaac Wayne, accompanied by Dr. J.G. Wallace, drove through the mountains with one horse in order to get the body. When the grave was opened, the body was found in an almost perfect state of preservation. On the advice of Dr. Wallace, Isaac Wayne, in order to facilitate the trip back across the mountains, and also to prevent decay during the journey, decided to separate the flesh from the bones. They did this by boiling the body in a large kettle used for scalding pigs. The flesh, the viscera and the knives that had been used to strip the flesh from the bones were replaced in the coffin and restored to their former resting place. The bones then were taken to Radnor where a funeral service was held on July 4, 1809.

The service was attended by large numbers of people from Philadelphia and other surrounding towns. After this, his bones were buried. Wayne is the only notable American known to have two gravesites simultaneously within the continental United States.

The first (1796) gravesite is near a blockhouse behind the Soldiers' and Sailors' home. In 1876 the blockhouse was rebuilt, and Wayne's gravesite was excavated. One of Wayne's boots was found and fell into the possession of a local bartender, who sometimes wore it in his bar. The leather cover of the coffin was also uncovered at that time, and may still be seen. The Soldiers' and Saliors' Home, 560 Third Street, Erie, Pennsylvania 19013.

The second gravesite is St. David's Churchyard, Radnor, Pennsylvania 19087.

# *Wayne, John*

John Wayne, the motion picture actor, was born Marion Michael Morrison in Winterset, Iowa, on May 26, 1907. He grew up in Southern California, and attended the University of Southern California for two years on a football scholarship. He took a summer job working as a prop man at Fox movie studios, and in 1929 was given a part in the Western *The Big Trail*. He went on to become the biggest box-office attraction in Hollywood history. He starred in more than 200 outdoor action films, mostly Westerns, including: *Stagecoach* (1940), *She Wore a Yellow Ribbon* (1949), and *True Grit* (1970)—winning an Academy Award in the latter for a role which was a parody of himself as the rugged conservative American folk-hero.

In 1964, a malignant tumor was removed from his lungs, and from then on he referred to his battle with "the big C." On January 12, 1979, doctors in Los Angeles removed his cancerous stomach, and cautioned that the cancer would probably spread. After surgery, well-wishers sent him more than 100,000 get-well cards and telegrams. On April 9, Wayne attended the Academy Awards presentation in Hollywood, and presented an award. Although he appeared thin and hoarse, he said that the Oscars "first came to the Hollywood scene in 1928, and so did I. We're both a little weatherbeaten, but we're still here and plan to be around for a whole lot longer."

He was re-hospitalized on May 2 at the University of California Medical Center in Los Angeles and it was reported that more cancer was in his body. On a May 5 visit to the hospital, President Jimmy Carter said that "he had the love, affection and prayers of not only everybody in our own nation, but of millions of persons around the world." He died at the UCLA Medical Center at 5:35 p.m. on June 11, with his seven sons and daughters at his bedside. The cause of death was listed as "complications of cancer."

Tributes poured in from around the world. Former President Richard M. Nixon said that his friend "will inspire Americans for generations to come." Ronald Reagan, the actor and future president, said: "I always wanted to be in a film with him and will always regret not having done so." In France, three national television networks announced that a tribute to the actor was being planned.

Wayne had converted to Catholicism on his deathbed, and a secret Catholic funeral service, attended only by the family, was held before dawn on July 15, at Our Lady Queen of Angels Catholic Church in Corona del Mar, California. Music from many of Wayne's movies was played on the organ. The service ended before 6:00 a.m.

Burial was on a hill overlooking the ocean at Pacific View Mortuary in Newport Beach, California. His body was sealed in a concrete vault and buried in an unmarked grave to thwart possible body-snatchers. Reportedly, when his grave was dug, additional graves were also dug, to confuse curious outsiders trying to establish its exact location. Before his death he had publicly said that he would like his epitaph to be the Spanish words: "Feo, Fuerte y Formal," ("Ugly, Tough, and Dignified"), but in the event his grave, being unmarked, has no epitaph. Ronald Mowry, general manager of the cemetery, said: "The location of Wayne's grave is secret. There is no marker whatsoever and now it merely looks like a patch of grass... All I can say is that John Wayne lies on a hill overlooking the Pacific Ocean. On a clear day you can see his home from the site." Pacific View Memorial Park and Mortuary, 35000 Pacific View Drive, Newport Beach. California 92660.

# *Whitman, Walt*

Walter (Walt) Whitman, the poet, whose *Leaves of Grass* was a milestone in American literature, was born on May 31, 1819, in West Hills, Long Island, New York.

After leaving school at 11 years of age he held a series of odd jobs, living in Brooklyn, New York City, Washington, D.C., and finally Camden, New Jersey. His *Leaves of Grass* first appeared in 1855. During the Civil War he gave up his Bohemian way of life, and thereafter was known as "The Good Gray Poet." Subsequent editions of *Leaves of Grass* were much enlarged and rearranged. One of his most famous poems, for example—"Out of the Cradle, Endlessly Rocking"—first appeared in the third (1859) edition. After the Civil War he received a bureaucratic government post in Washington, D.C., but was discharged for being the author of a "notorious" book. He was hired by the then attorney-general's office, a job he kept until he was stricken with paralysis in 1873.

During his last years, in addition to paralysis, he suffered from tuberculosis, frequent debilitating headaches, and abdominal distress. He died in Camden, New Jersey, on March 26, 1892.

On March 30 friends and admirers gathered at his Mickle Street home in Camden for a final look at his remains, which rested in a polished oak coffin. At 2:00 p.m. the

*Whitman's tomb in Camden, New Jersey—An illustration by Vicki Manos.*

crowds followed a cortege to Harleigh Cemetery to hear his funeral service. The agnostic Robert Ingersoll *(q.v.)* eulogized him, saying: "Death is less terrible than it was before. Thousands and millions will walk into the dark valley of the shadow holding Walt Whitman by the hand." The service closed with readings from Confucius, Buddha, Plato, the Koran, the Bible, and Whitman's *Leaves of Grass.*

He was buried in Harleigh Cemetery in Camden in a tomb which he himself had designed. The tomb is said to resemble the walls of King Solomon's temple. It was made from granite quarried in Quincy, Massachusetts, and some of the stones are said to weigh 10 tons. The front of the structure weighs 70 tons; the door of the vault is made of granite six inches thick and swings on brass pivots. Inside the tomb there are eight crypts which contain the remains of members of Whitman's family. Inside the tomb, in addition to the remains of Whitman are those of his mother, father, two brothers, a sister, and a sister-in-law. Harleigh Cemetery, 1640 Haddon Avenue, Camden, New Jersey 08103.

# *Wilson, Woodrow*

Thomas Woodrow Wilson, 28th president of the United States, (term of office 1913-21), was born on December 28, 1856, in Staunton, Virginia. He led the U.S. into World War I, and later was a prime mover in the establishment of the League of Nations. After graduating at Princeton University in 1879, he took his doctorate at Johns Hopkins University, and in 1890 became a professor of jurisprudence and political economy at Princeton. In 1902 he became president of Princeton, and in 1910 he was elected governor of New Jersey. In 1912 he was elected president of the United States on the Democratic ticket. He was re-elected in 1916, using the slogan "He kept us out of war." After Germany waged unrestricted warfare against Atlantic shipping, resulting in the loss of American lives, however, Wilson led the U.S. into World War I on the Allied side in April 1917.

In January 1918, Wilson proclaimed U.S. war aims, which were summarized in his "Fourteen Points," which called for an end to secret diplomacy, and the formation of what was to become the League of Nations. At the end of the war Wilson enjoyed unequaled international prestige, and visited Europe, where adoring crowds in Britain and France granted him unprecedented honors. He used his prestige to promote the League of Nations and other concepts. On returning to the U.S., however, he found his policies challenged in the U.S. Senate, and despite an exhausting nation-wide speaking tour, was unable to overcome Senate opposition to the U.S. joining the League. On October 2, 1919, he suffered a thrombosis that affected control of the left side of his body. A broken man, he remained in seclusion in the White House for the rest of his term of office, nursed by his second wife.

On leaving office, Wilson moved into a house on S Street in Washington, D.C. He then went into a physical decline, with his eyesight failing, and other ailments developing. On January 31, 1924 his digestive and renal functions failed. At one point he said to his doctor: "The machinery is worn out. I am ready." He remained conscious for 12 hours before dying at 11:15 a.m. on February 3, 1924, without a struggle.

At the funeral of President Warren Harding (q.v.), Wilson had said that he wanted a private funeral for himself. On another occasion, while driving through Arlington National Cemetery with his wife, he had said that he did not think he could "rest easily" in Arlington. In accordance with his wishes, a simple funeral service was held at the National Cathedral in Washington, D.C. on February 6. After the service, the body was entombed in a vault at the National Cathedral. Tennyson's "Crossing the Bar" was read during the committal. The National Cathedral, Massachusetts and Wisconsin Avenues, Washington D.C. 20016.

# *Wolfe, Thomas*

Thomas Clayton Wolfe, author of autobiographical novels concerned with time and memory, was born on October 3, 1900, in Asheville, North Carolina. After graduating from the University of North Carolina in 1920, and studying at Harvard, he settled in New York City in 1923, teaching at New York University. With the help of Maxwell Perkins, an editor with whom he established a close working relationship, he published a long autobiographical novel, *Look Homeward Angel* (1929). Its success enabled him to become a full-time writer. His later books included *Of Time and the River* (1935), and *You Can't Go Home Again* (1940)—the latter published posthumously.

On a trip to the West coast of North America in July 1938, he began to have chills and fever in Vancouver, British Columbia. He was diagnosed as having pneumonia, and infections of the kidneys and of the muscles around the heart. Despite his ex-

*Thomas Wolfe's grave:*
*Asheville, North Carolina.*

(Photo: Russ Johnson)

treme fear of hospitals, in early August he was taken to Providence Hospital in Seattle, Washington, for X-rays, and tests. At first he was believed to have tuberculosis, but in September he began to have frequent headaches, and was diagnosed as having a brain tumor. He was taken by train to Baltimore, where he was admitted to Johns Hopkins Hospital. He was scheduled for surgery on September 12, but—according to a doctor—when his skull was opened up, the doctor took one look inside, and laid his scalpel down. The doctor said: "He has tuberculosis of the brain. His brain is simply covered with tubercles. There must be millions of them there." After surgery, Wolfe lay in a coma with his head in bandages. He died peacefully on September 15.

He was very tall—six feet seven inches—and a coffin large enough to accommodate his body could not be found in Baltimore. One was therefore made in New York and sent to Baltimore where, after embalming and the fitting of a toupee to cover the surgical incisions, his body was placed in the coffin and sent to his home in Asheville, North Carolina.

The funeral service was held in the Presbyterian Church in Asheville. Burial was on September 18 at Riverside Cemetery, Birch Street, Asheville, North Carolina 28802.

# Wright, Frank Lloyd

Frank Lloyd Wright, the most creative architectural talent America has as yet produced, was born on June 8, 1867, in Richland Center, Wisconsin. After studying at the University of Wisconsin he went to Chicago where, from 1888-93, he worked with and was influenced by the architect Louis Sullivan. In 1893 he went into private practice, subsequently becoming what many considered the greatest architect of his time. He created the philosophy of organic architecture, in which buildings "grow" out of their natural surroundings. He used new structural materials, as well as natural colors and textures, and designed spacious interiors, in which rooms seemed to flow one to another. Among the buildings that he designed was the Imperial Hotel in Tokyo (built 1916-22). Due to its construction, it was the only large building to withstand the severe earthquake of 1923—a circumstance which brought Wright much fame. Other buildings which he designed were the Roby House in Chicago, the Millard House in Pasadena, California, and the Solomon Guggenheim Memorial Mausoleum Building in New York City. His most creative period began in about 1936, and among the buildings he designed at this time were his own winter quarters and workshop at Taliesin West, near Phoenix, Arizona.

On April 6 1959 while just two months away from his 90th birthday, he was at his drawing board working on a design for a group of houses in a desert landscape, when he gasped and twisted with extreme pain. He was rushed to St. Joseph's Hospital in Phoenix, where he was operated on the following day for an intestinal obstruction. He was on the road to recovery when, on April 9, he suddenly turned over in his bed and died.

His body was sent to his home town of Spring Green, Wisconsin, where on April 12 it lay in state in his Taliesin East living room. Residents of the small community filed past his casket. He was dressed in a light tan suit, and had a white shirt, and a loosely knotted tie. The coffin was draped in red.

Shortly after 5:00 p.m., the funeral procession left Taliesin, with his casket being borne on a grain wagon pulled by two sturdy farm horses. This type of procession, customary in rural areas in Europe, was requested by Mrs. Wright, a native of the small European state of Montenegro. The cortege arrived at the Taliesin Chapel at about 6:00 p.m. A clergyman from Madison's First Unitarian Church officiated at the simple service. He quoted from the works of John Donne, Stephen Spender and Ralph Waldo Emerson (*q.v.*), as well as from the Bible. Tall candles burned near the casket, and a wood burning stove provided the only heat. At the committal at the Jones Family Cemetery, the clergyman quoted from the book of Job. The architect's secretary, Eugene Masselink, read Wright's "Work Song," from his autobiography. The Jones Family Cemetery on County Trunk T, three miles south of Spring Green on Wisconsin Highway 23, Spring Green, Wisconsin 53588.

# *Wright, Orville and Wilbur*

Orville and Wilbur Wright, aviation pioneers, were the first men to achieve sustained, powered, and controlled airplane flight, which they did at Kittyhawk, North Carolina, in 1903.

Orville, the younger, was born on August 19, 1871, in Dayton, Ohio. Wilbur was born April 16, 1867, near Millville, Indiana. The brothers opened a bicycle repair shop in Dayton in 1892, and in their spare time began experimenting with aerodynamics and gliders. After building kites and other machines, and making some unsuccessful attempts to achieve sustained flight, Orville, on December 17, 1903, piloted a four-cylinder engine-controlled biplane on a 12-second 120-foot flight on the beach at Kittyhawk, North Carolina. They built more airplanes, and by 1905 had developed a usable powered plane. In 1908, a year in which Wilbur made some exhibition flights in France, while Orville made flights in the United States, the brothers gained a contract in Europe to produce airplanes. In 1909 they contracted with the U.S. Army to produce the world's first military airplane.

In May, 1912, Wilbur was stricken with typhoid fever, at his home in Dayton. On May 19 it was reported that his condition was serious and that he had a fever of 105°. His family was called to his bedside. On May 29 his temperature rose from 104° to 106°. He began to have chills, but his condition improved around midnight. He died

*The graves of the Wright brothers: Dayton, Ohio.*    (Photos: Kramer Photography)

a few hours later, however, at 8:15 a.m. on May 30. His brother Orville said: "The death of my brother has been an irreparable blow to all of us. Although I have given no thought to business affairs, the work started by him will be carried on. His death came as a fearful shock right when we were in the midst of plans for a bright future."

Wilbur's body lay in state in Dayton, and was viewed by 25,000 people. A simple funeral service was held at the First Presbyterian Church on June 1. Burial took place at Woodland Cemetery, Dayton.

After the death of his brother, Orville retired from business to carry on his own private research. During World War I he was a consultant to the U.S. Army. In the years that followed he engaged in research.

He died at 10:40 p.m. on January 30, 1948 in Miami Valley Hospital, Dayton. He had been in and out of the hospital since October 1947, suffering from lung diseases, pneumonia, and arteriosclerosis.

A funeral service was held at the First Baptist Church at Dayton, on February 2. Flags in Dayton were flown at half-mast, and schools in Dayton were dismissed early. Burial was in Woodland Cemetery, Dayton. At the time of burial a formation of five P-80 planes flew over the cemetery. Woodland Cemetery, 118 Woodland Avenue, Dayton, Ohio 45409.

# *Young, Brigham*

Brigham Young, leader of the Church of Jesus Christ of Latter Day Saints, (also known as the Mormon Church), and colonizer of Utah, was born on June 1, 1801 in Whitingham, Vermont. After working as a farmer, carpenter, and painter, he settled in Mendon, New York, where, in 1832, he converted to the Mormon religion. In

1835 when Joseph Smith, founder of Mormonism, organized a council of Twelve Apostles, Young was named one of them. From 1839-1841 he worked with the Mormon mission in Liverpool, England. After the lynching of Joseph Smith in 1844, Young was elected president, and leader, of the Mormon Church.

In the face of anti-Mormon sentiment, he led his followers out of Illinois in 1846. He then led the Mormons across the Great Plains and Rocky Mountains until, on July 24, 1847, he arrived at the site of what is now Salt Lake City, Utah. Upon arrival, he uttered the words: "This is it!"—thereby giving a new phrase to the language. There the Mormons constructed farms, businesses and cooperative stores. The area was established as the territory of Utah in 1850 and Young became its territorial governor. He held this position until 1857, when President James Buchanan (q.v.), who sent federal troops to establish the primacy of federal rule, had him replaced. Young at first resisted, but in 1858 gave way. He continued as president of the Mormon Church until his death. In August 1852 Young had publicly endorsed polygamy, and in 1871 he was indicted on a polygamy charge, although he was not convicted. He was married at least 27 times, and at the time of his death he was survived by 17 wives and 47 children.

*(ABOVE): Brigham Young's grave in Salt Lake City, Utah.*

*(RIGHT): A statue of Brigham Young, which stands in the vicinity of his grave.*

(Photos: Church of Jesus Christ of Latter Day Saints)

On August 23, 1877, aged 76, he suffered an attack of cholera morbus which was said to have been brought on by eating green corn and peaches. Doctors were consulted but his condition grew worse. Morphine was administered. He fell into a coma on August 26. Meanwhile he was attended by four physicians and elders of the church. On August 28 he remained unconscious, and those at his bedside thought that he had died. Artificial respiration was administered for more than nine hours. Shortly before 4:00 p.m. on the afternoon of August 29 he murmured: "Joseph,

Joseph, Joseph," and said: "I feel better." He then died.

His body was taken to the tabernacle of the Mormon Church in Salt Lake City where 25,000 Mormons passed his bier. Four years previously he had written: "When I breathe my last, I wish my friends to put my body in as clean and wholesome a state as can conveniently be done... dressed in Temple clothing, and laid nicely into my coffin."

The funeral service was held on September 2 at 11:30 a.m. The great tabernacle organ played "The Dead March" from Saul and Mendelssohn's "Funeral March." Following the ceremonies, 4,000 people marched eight abreast to his grave in Salt Lake City. The Brigham Young Gravesite, 140 East First Avenue, Salt Lake City, Utah 84103.

# Ziegfeld, Florenz

Florenz Ziegfeld, the theatrical producer whose revue shows became famous with his slogan "Glorifying the American Girl," was born on March 21, 1869 in Chicago, Illinois. After producing a number of musical revues, he formed a musical comedy production called the Ziegfeld Follies, which were staged on Broadway in New York almost every year from 1907 onwards, until the Depression brought the series to an end in 1931. He personally selected all of the girls for his revues, and approved all costuming and other effects. Many well-known composers wrote scores for the Follies, and many stars were associated with them, such as Eddie Cantor, Fanny Brice, W.C. Fields, and Will Rogers (q.q.v.).

In July 1932 it was reported that he was a patient in an undisclosed Mexican sanatorium, and was under constant medical care as a result of a breakdown which was "traceable to an attack of pneumonia" that he had suffered the previous year. On July 18 it was reported that he had been moved to a Hollywood, California, hospital and that both his lungs were affected by pleurisy. It was said that he was in "very serious but not critical condition."

He died on July 22 at 10:31 p.m. Only his attending physician and a nurse were in the room at the time of death. A simple Episcopal funeral service was held on July 24 in the chapel of Pierce Brothers Mortuary in Los Angeles, attended by such notables as Eddie Cantor, Will Rogers, and William Randolph Hearst(q.v.). His body lay in a silver coffin covered by red and white roses. Burial was at Forest Lawn Cemetery, Memorial Park, Glendale, California. On June 8, 1974. His body was, however, later re-buried in Valhalla, New York. Kensico Cemetery, Valhalla, New York 10595.

---

# Note:

The author welcomes information and pictures about other notable Americans for possible inclusion in the next edition of this book.

# Index